NARRATIVES
OF CIVIC DUTY

Studies of the Weatherhead East Asian Institute, Columbia University

The Studies of the Weatherhead East Asian Institute of Columbia University were inaugurated in 1962 to bring to a wider public the results of significant new research on modern and contemporary East Asia.

NARRATIVES OF CIVIC DUTY

How National Stories Shape
Democracy in Asia

Aram Hur

CORNELL UNIVERSITY PRESS   ITHACA AND LONDON

First published 2022 by Cornell University Press

Library of Congress Cataloging-in-Publication Data

Names: Hur, Aram, 1984- author.
Title: Narratives of civic duty : how national stories shape democracy in Asia / Aram Hur.
Description: Ithaca [New York] : Cornell University Press, 2022. | Series: Studies of the Weatherhead East Asian Institute, Columbia University | Includes bibliographical references and index.
Identifiers: LCCN 2022005308 (print) | LCCN 2022005309 (ebook) | ISBN 9781501765476 (hardcover) | ISBN 9781501766213 (paperback) | ISBN 9781501766183 (pdf) | ISBN 9781501766190 (epub)
Subjects: LCSH: Citizenship—Moral and ethical aspects—Korea (South) | Citizenship—Moral and ethical aspects—Taiwan. | Citizenship—Moral and ethical aspects—Germany. | Nationalism—Moral and ethical aspects—Korea (South) | Nationalism—Moral and ethical aspects—Taiwan. | Nationalism—Moral and ethical aspects—Germany. | Democracy—Moral and ethical aspects—Korea (South) | Democracy—Moral and ethical aspects—Taiwan. | Democracy—Moral and ethical aspects—Germany. | National characteristics, Korean. | National characteristics, Taiwan. | National characteristics, German.
Classification: LCC JF801 .H866 2022 (print) | LCC JF801 (ebook) | DDC 323.6—dc23/eng/20220607
LC record available at https://lccn.loc.gov/2022005308
LC ebook record available at https://lccn.loc.gov/2022005309

For my parents,
whose duty sustains me

Contents

Illustrations

FIGURES

TABLES

Acknowledgments

They say the dots always connect backwards. Looking back, it was only natural that I would write a book about duty and belonging. As the daughter of a South Korean civil servant, I grew up moving between Korea and the United States every several years, splitting my life between two countries and cultures. Belonging was never a given. Yet this constant taught me a great deal about the power of belonging. Belonging, when felt deeply and wholly, motivated a sense of duty that went beyond what was expected or needed. Belonging and duty were two sides of the same coin: one cannot exist without the other.

When I first began to think about the book in graduate school at Princeton, belonging and duty were words that were seen to be at odds with the rational democratic citizen. The atrocities of World War II had left a ghastly wound in the study of nationalism and shown that too much belonging led to blinding duty, which led to bad things. Yet I had grown up seeing a different side of belonging and duty. I watched as my father worked tirelessly for the betterment of his country. I watched as my mother did everything she could in a foreign place for the betterment of her children. And I watched a nation come together during the worst financial crisis in its modern history, sacrificing wedding rings and family heirlooms, to give its young democracy a fighting chance. It seemed too simplistic to label such exceptions of constructive nationalism as particularities of Confucian "culture." There was something else—a brighter side to national belonging, duty, and democracy that needed to be better understood.

This book is the culmination of a near decade-long pursuit of trying to understand that puzzle. Developing, vetting, and ultimately convincing others of the argument that the moral pull of the nation can help democracies—at a time when a nationalist resurgence is seemingly fueling democratic backsliding in a handful of prominent cases—has been an uphill battle. I could not have done it if not for those who helped push me along the way.

At Princeton, where the core ideas of the book began as a dissertation, I benefited from the encouragement and wisdom of so many. This book simply would not exist in its current form if not for my advisor, Christopher Achen. I learned many lessons from Chris, but perhaps the most important one is that good scholarship begins with knowing who you are. There is an unspoken connection among Chris's students—a shared understanding of how lucky we were and continue to be for his unfailing mentorship. Mark Beissinger and Evan Lieberman both treated my early ideas with an intellectual seriousness that motivated me to refine them until they were deserving of it. Robert Wuthnow, around the corner in the sociology department, was always a source of good common sense and incredibly expansive knowledge. Along with official graduate advisors, I spent too many hours in Andreas Wimmer's office, who was always generous with both his time and encouragement. Carles Boix, Rafaela Dancygier, Grigo Pop-Eleches, Amaney Jamal, Markus Prior, Tali Mendelberg, and Marty Gilens offered helpful comments and critiques that made the project better. Michele Epstein at the Center for the Study of Democratic Politics was a safe haven from the very first day.

I also want to thank two former advisors. Matthew Baum at the Harvard Kennedy School helped me see that my ultimate passion was in political science, while Ted Glasser, my undergraduate advisor in communication at Stanford, invited me to take a doctoral seminar as a sophomore and sparked my love of research. I may not have ended up in political science or in academia had I not met either of them.

Fieldwork takes a village, and I was fortunate to have found a strong village wherever I went. In South Korea, Won-ho Park at Seoul National University made it possible to collect original survey data on civic duty. At the National Election Commission, Jisun Oh and Sungwon Hwang ate many lunches with me, meticulously going over the questionnaire and logistics for the turnout field experiment. I am forever indebted to the folks at the Election Study Center at National Chengchi University in Taiwan. Sufeng Cheng made Taiwan feel like a second home in a way only she can, and she was critical to getting the interview wording just right. The internet survey got off the ground thanks to Eric Yu and Jiasin Yu. Chi Huang was always there for a dose of gumption whenever I needed it—and to open the office doors on the weekends when I thought no one else would be working. The students and staff at the Election Study Center—too many to name individually—were my family away from home. I miss working side by side in the cubicles, our many meals together, and the night market, where they hilariously urged me to try the "thing" on a stick covered in peanuts. Dachi Liao and Alex Tan went out of their way to help me during my stints down in Kaohsiung.

Data collection and writing would not have been possible without generous funding from the Mamdouha Bobst Center for Peace and Justice, the Princeton Institute of International and Regional Studies, and the East Asian Studies department at Princeton University. Parts of chapters 4 and 5 have been adapted from previous work published as a journal article, "Citizen Duty and the Ethical Power of Communities: Mixed-method Evidence from East Asia" in the *British Journal of Political Science*, and chapter 6 builds on a prior journal article, "Is There an Intrinsic Duty to Vote? Comparative Evidence from East and West Germans," published in *Electoral Studies*.

I have shamelessly subjected every new friend, colleague, and mentor since graduate school to the ideas and writings in this book. At New York University's Wagner School of Public Service, where I spent three years as a postdoctoral fellow, I thank Mona Vakilifathi, John Gershman, Jacob Faber, Tatiana Homonoff, and Salo Coslovsky for their friendship and feedback. Dean Sherry Glied and Vice Provost Cybele Raver, who oversaw the provost postdoctoral program, gave their support when it mattered most. My biggest debt at NYU is to Tony Bertelli, who turned out to be exactly the mentor that I needed in that transitional period. In the politics department, Amy Catalinac, Hye Young Yoo, and the singular Gwyneth McClendon offered steadfast encouragement and, as women do, practical and actionable advice.

The book came to final fruition at the University of Missouri, where I began as an assistant professor in the seat fittingly once held by Doh Chull Shin, one of the pioneers of comparative political behavior in East Asia. In a short time Sheena Greitens has become a source of support in too many ways to count. I also thank Lael Keiser, my department chair, who made the transition to faculty life and Missouri as smooth as possible, Vanya Krieckhaus, Jay Dow, Mary Stegmaier, Seungkwon You for their comments on the project, and the lively junior faculty crew, including Heather Ba and Weijie Wang, for laughs and support just when I needed them. Gidong Kim went above and beyond as a research assistant in the final phase of the manuscript, and Yuan-Yuan Hsu sourced data that were hard to find. I was also fortunate to meet wonderful friends in Columbia as I juggled writing the book with being a mostly single mom during the academic year. Sarah and Sang, Dr. Cho, Leah, Susanna and James, Songyi and Jaewon, Eunjoo teacher, Mansoo Yu and family, Lucy and Annalin—thank you for lifting me.

A book workshop held at the University of Missouri in the fall of 2019, in which Prerna Singh, Cara Wong, Ian Chong, and T. Y. Wang graciously read and commented on the entirety of the manuscript and Chris Achen chaired, proved to be a pivotal turn for the manuscript. In the final years of writing, I have also benefited from the example and advice of many academic friends and mentors. From our days back in Princeton, Bryn Rosenfeld continues to inspire me as we have grown as scholars and mothers. I also thank Michael Barber, my fishbowl partner, as well as Nick Carnes, Emilee Chapman, Lauren Davenport, Sarah El-Kazaz, Song Ha Joo, Adam Liff, Erin Lin, Dinsha Mistree, Baxter Oliphant, and Carlos Velasco. Joan Cho, Pattie Kim, and Ju Yeon Julia Park have been my steadfast Korean academic sisters. Thanks also to Allison Anoll, Celeste Arrington, Victor Cha, Paul Chang, Erin Aeran Chung, Diana Fu, Sara Wallace Goodman, Stephan Haggard, Joseph Juhn, Dave Kang, Tom Le, Taeku Lee, Gerry Munck, Gi-wook Shin, Dan Slater, Kharis Templeman, Maya Tudor, Dennis Weng, and Andrew Yeo for helpful conversations and camaraderie along the way. I had the honor of giving the Korea Society's 2021 Sherman Emerging Scholar lecture based on the book, for which I thank Tom Byrne, Stephen Noerper, and Jonathan Corrado. I also thank Yang-Yang Zhou and Alan Jacobs for featuring the book project on one of the early episodes of the *Scope Conditions* podcast.

I was lucky enough to catch Roger Haydon just before his retirement from Cornell University Press. Roger shepherded the manuscript up to the review process, and even in that brief window together, I got a taste for why he is widely regarded bar none in academic publishing. Sarah Grossman took up the baton and has not missed a beat. Her honesty, support, and ability to see the author as a whole human has meant so much to me as a first-time author. Two anonymous reviewers generously provided feedback that sharpened and deepened the manuscript. Thanks also to the editors of Columbia University's Weatherhead East Asia Institute for including the book in their series.

Finally, my family. My sister, Beauram, has singularly sustained my spirits through this process, even though there is a good chance she may never read the whole book. I thank Calvin for sustaining her. Mrs. Hong, Neema, and King, who keep everything afloat. My in-laws, Dr. Byung and Jung Lee, as well as Youn Unni, John, Will, and Nadia, have been nothing but supportive of my academic career, even when it meant that I missed some family gatherings and took many travels away from their son, which brings me to my husband.

Phillip Lee has felt each failure and triumph in this process alongside me, as if they were his own. He also never let the wine supply run dry. His unwavering duty to me, to "us," has given me the sense of belonging I so yearned to find in adulthood and the courage to embark on our greatest adventures, our children Leo and Aria. Both of you light up my soul and teach me that certain kinds of duty know no limits.

Perhaps the biggest lesson that having children has taught me, however, is how I am myself the product of such unconditional duty. My father's unfailing love for his country is what initially inspired me down this path, but his unfailing faith in me is what kept me on it. As for my mother, it is hard to put into words all that she has done throughout my life so that I would one day be sitting here, writing the acknowledgments to my first book. All I can say is that I realize more and more the depth of her duty with each passing day that I am a mom. I dedicate this book to them.

Note on Transliteration

Korean-language names and terms have been romanized following the Revised Romanization of Korean. Chinese-language names and terms have been romanized following the pinyin system. Following custom in Korea and Taiwan, surnames typically precede given names.

Exceptions were made for names, places, and terms with different official or English spellings that are widely known and accepted in academic and policy writings (for example, Park Chung-hee, Kaohsiung, Chiang Kai-shek) and for authors who have previously published in English under alternate transliterations.

Part I

DUTY, AGAINST THE ODDS

Han Sook-ja gently runs her fingers over her now wrinkly hands, lingering for a moment on the empty ring finger. She remembers vividly the day that her husband got fired, and the day that Kia Motors, where her husband had spent most of his engineering career, officially filed for bankruptcy. Like many other Asian countries at the time, South Korea saw its foreign debt soar as the credit bubble burst, causing its currency value to plummet. As the big conglomerates eventually crippled under pressure, unemployment rates spiked to unprecedented levels in what would become known as the 1997 Asian financial crisis—the worst economic recession in East Asia's modern history to date.

In response, South Korean citizens did something little short of remarkable. The idea for a national gold drive was originally hatched by a women's church group. The plan was simple: citizens could sell their personal gold, much of it sitting around in their closets, to the national banks for cheap. Then the state could resell that gold on the international market and use the profits to pay off the foreign debt. It was essentially a donation drive to save the struggling country. Mrs. Han looks down again at her ring finger: "When the gold drives began, I knew what I had to do. I sent the kids off, grabbed my wedding ring, my husband's ring, and the gold bar we had received as a wedding gift from his parents and went to the bank."[1]

Mrs. Han would join approximately 3.5 million South Koreans—roughly one in four households—who contributed to the gold drives. By the end, the drives had raised 225 tons of gold, worth about $2 billion.[2] International media expressed awe at the sight of citizens lined up in the bitter January cold, ready to give away their wedding rings, milestone gifts, and family heirlooms.[3] I ask Mrs. Han if she ever regrets giving away her rings. Her answer is quick, as if it were obvious: "Of course, I don't. It was the only right thing to do. What use is keeping that for ourselves when our country is dying? This is what we do. It's what we have always done for Korea."

In strictly economic terms, the gold drives were a drop in the bucket of the more than $100 billion in foreign debt that South Korea owed. The movement's real value, however, lay in how it reaffirmed the national spirit and sparked a collective sense of duty among South Koreans to do their part in the crisis. In a national survey by the Korea Development Institute two decades later, 54 percent of citizens answered that a strong national spirit, exemplified by the gold drives, was the driving force behind South Korea's recovery.[4]

Why did so many South Koreans participate in the gold drives? The standard answer in political science is incentives, but this argument quickly falls apart when faced with the realities of the fiscal crisis. Materially, selling gold for below market price is a definitional loss. Social incentives may have pushed some individuals, but it was just as easy to freeride. Perhaps others had wildly optimistic assumptions about South Korea's prospects for economic recovery and future benefits. But still, why so many citizens—many of them personally hurt by the crisis—would willingly sacrifice their irreplaceable possessions for the sake of their young and struggling democracy is hard to explain. The more intuitive answer seems to be exactly what Mrs. Han said: "It was the only right thing to do." For many South Koreans, the gold drives were first and foremost about fulfilling a moral obligation—a matter of civic duty.

Civic duty is the sense of obligation to be a good citizen, even when it is costly to do so. The term usually conjures images of exceptional sacrifice during moments of crisis, from citizens like Mrs. Han to soldiers who risk their lives. But, in fact, much of democratic life is made up of less extraordinary, more everyday forms of civic duty that are no less important. Take, for instance, the civic duty to vote. Voting is an essential citizen act that sustains democracies. But because it is voluntary in most democracies, voting is typically a losing proposition: it incurs real costs in time and effort, but the probability of payoff, which hinges on being the pivotal voter in an election, is usually close to nil. The authors of a seminal article on the calculus of voting therefore concluded that actual turnout rates in most advanced democracies could not be explained without the "D-term"— a sense of civic duty.[5] Civic duty also sustains "quasi-voluntary" citizen roles in a democracy, such as paying taxes or obeying the law. Noncompliance with such roles is punishable, but because monitoring is never universal, democracies implicitly rely on citizens to comply voluntarily.[6] Thus, both in periods of crisis and in the everyday, democracies rely a great deal on widespread civic duty.

For these reasons, scholars of democracy have long recognized something like civic duty to be integral to democratic success. Alexis de Tocqueville, in his quest to understand what made democracy possible in nineteenth-century America, noted that "each person is as involved in the affairs of his township, canton, and the whole state as he is in his own business."[7] That sense of personal obligation to state affairs also features in Albert Hirschman's theory of democratic performance. Loyalty, that "special attachment" to an institution that "holds exit at bay and activates voice" when the firm's quality deteriorates, is what saves democratic states from breakdown.[8] Scholars of democratic stability also hone in on a similar concept of diffuse system support: "Outputs and beneficial performance may rise and fall while this support, in the form of a generalized attachment, continues."[9] These classic works converge on a similar conclusion: strong and stable democracies depend on a special kind of attachment between citizens and the state.

What motivates a sense of civic duty in democracies? Why do some people feel such duty to engage, contribute, and even sacrifice for their democracies while others do not? Why do some democracies have more of such citizens than others? These are not simply interesting behavioral puzzles. They are questions that cut to the heart of what makes democracies work.

Civic duty has always been seen as something that is nice to have in democracies. Yet its critical importance to democratic resilience has manifested in recent cases of democratic backsliding.[10] Many Third Wave democracies have fallen prey to demagogues capitalizing on populist backlash to rapidly growing income inequality in places like Venezuela and Hungary.[11] Even in advanced democracies like the United States, festering social divisions have metastasized into full-blown political tribalism, stoking widespread incivility and threatening what some have dubbed the next civil war.[12] A raging global pandemic that spreads through contagion has only deepened existing fissures between "us" and "them" in many democratic societies.

Contemporary forms of democratic erosion have sent a clear signal to scholars of democracy that formal institutions, such as checks and balances, are not enough to ensure democratic longevity.[13] When liberal democracy was first gaining traction as the dominant regime type in the latter half of the twentieth century, an emphasis on institutional design made good sense. The priority was successfully replicating the blueprint. Democratic consolidation from authoritarian or postcolonial states was the end goal.

Yet the twenty-first century has shown that democratic consolidation is not a destination but an ongoing process. As partisan leaders and would-be autocrats exploit popular support to subvert the very institutions meant to protect democracies, the importance of informal norms—the moral commitments of leaders and citizens to their democracy—has been laid bare. Scholars of democracy generally agree that the last bastion against democratic breakdown lies with the moral compass of the people: the willingness of leaders to respect and forbear toward the opposition and the willingness of ordinary citizens to resist acting as "partisans first, democrats second," even if that means forgoing immediate payoffs.[14]

What can democracies do to foster more civic duty in the face of growing divisions and increasingly opposed interests? Can civic duty be grown? Political science has surprisingly little to say on such questions because, for all that we know about the democratic benefits of civic duty, we know relatively little about its cause. The rest of the book sets out to uncover the motivational roots of civic duty.

East Asia as a Lens

East Asia may appear to be a curious place to start an inquiry into what motivates civic duty in democracies. After all, the region was hardly seen as fertile soil for vibrant civic life. In fact, much of what was written about East Asia during the Third Wave of democratization cautioned against the region's weak civic and democratic potential.

For one, East Asia's Confucian culture was seen as distinct or even antithetical to the liberal values championed in Western democracies.[15] Confucian principles of deference to authority and hierarchy were seen as clashing with a voluntarist and pluralist civic life and better fit with strong-man rule. As Lee Kuan Yew, former prime minister and founding father of Singapore, bluntly put it, "But Asian societies are unlike Western ones. The fundamental difference between Western concepts of society and government and East Asian concepts . . . is that Eastern societies believe that the individual exists in the context of his family. He is not pristine and separate."[16] For similar reasons, Samuel Huntington, a leading scholar on Third Wave democratization, went as far as to say that "'Confucian democracy' is clearly a contradiction in terms" and that only sustained economic development could hold the contradiction together before it fell apart.[17]

East Asia's strongly racialized identities were also seen as a democratic impediment. Ethnic nationalisms of the developing world were increasingly seen as the illiberal mirror of civic nationalisms of Western democracies.[18] More often than not, history seemed to suggest that strong ethnic identities led to exclusion, violence, and bloodshed—the antithesis of vibrant civic life.[19] Such assumptions appeared to be borne out in East Asia, where Japan's ethnonationalist ambition exerted a devastating toll in terms of racial violence and genocide during World War II.

Based on earlier scholarship on democratization, then, East Asia should be hostile ground for something like civic duty to take root. Yet East Asia has spectacularly defied such expectations. Strong displays of civic duty were visible even when the region's democracies were very young, from the 1997 gold drives in South Korea's only decade-old democracy to the impressively high turnout rate in Japan's first ever democratic election in 1946.[20] A quarter century later, South Korea has once again made global headlines with its swift response to the COVID-19 pandemic. Much of that success was attributed to high levels of civic duty among citizens to comply with the state's zero-tolerance quarantine measures and masking policy, even as many other democracies struggled with voluntary compliance.[21]

How was civic duty able to flourish in a region apparently burdened by Confucian traditions and strong ethnic legacies? The reason why vibrant examples of civic duty in East Asia are so puzzling is that civic duty has long been seen as part of the unique domain of democratic culture. In *The Civic Culture*, the seminal book that animated a generation of interest in civic attitudes, the authors sought to identify the elements of a political culture that were most compatible with stable democracies.[22] In it, they dedicated an entire chapter to "the obligation to participate." Civic duty thus became largely synonymous with having the right kind of democratic culture. This cultural approach still pervades contemporary studies of democracy, where phrases such as "cultural change" or "culture transformed" are used to describe changes in civic attitudes.[23] It is also no mistake that most studies of civic duty focus on its quintessentially democratic manifestation, the civic duty to vote. The pervasive belief that civic duty is uniquely democratic has led to a near-exclusive focus on strengthening democratic culture as the means to foster more civic duty. More civic education, where youth are acculturated into democratic values at an early age, is typically prescribed as the remedy for societies with thinning civic duty.[24]

Yet vibrant civic duty in East Asia—a region seen as sorely lacking in the foundations for a democratic culture—suggests that culture alone does not suffice as an explanation. Displays of civic duty in very young democracies just transitioning out of authoritarianism, or signs of weakening civic duty in advanced democracies, also fly in the face of the assumption that civic duty is the product of having a mature democratic culture. Civic duty does not appear to grow naturally with democratic age. Something important remains missing from our understanding of what motivates civic duty.

The Argument in Brief

My approach to civic duty focuses less on the "civic" and more on the "duty." I take seriously Mrs. Han's answer to why she participated in the gold drives: "It was the only right thing to do. . . . It's what we have always done for Korea." I contend that civic duty is less a product of culture or character—or even a commitment to democratic values per se—than is often thought. Rather, I show that it is most immediately grounded in a sense of obligation to the special community of people that constitute that democracy: "my" nation.

The claim that civic duty has national roots is bound to strike many scholars of democracy as surprising, given that nationalism has earned quite an uncivic reputation for tearing democracies apart. How can nationalism have such contradicting effects on democracy? The conceptual heart of the book is clarifying why nationalisms behave differently in different contexts. The national theory of civic duty I propose is neither a universal one about the blinding powers of nationalist loyalty nor a particularistic one about the special properties of Korean or East Asian nationalisms. It is one about the historicized identity politics between nation and state that calls attention to nationalisms as narratives of duty.

Early scholars of nationalism were fascinated with the different bases of modern national identities. The ethnic versus civic distinction that quickly emerged fell into a "good" versus "bad" Manichean dichotomy after the atrocities of World War II and other genocides in the late twentieth century, all committed in the name of the ethnic nation.[25] The prevailing wisdom was that nationalism, especially of the ethnic kind, led to bad things for democracy. Subsequent scholarship on nationalism therefore moved on to other aspects, such as the nation's psychological or affective effects.[26]

Yet there is so much more to the content of nationalism than its ethnic or civic basis. If nations are "imagined communities," as Benedict Anderson famously said, then it matters how they are imagined.[27] For many, the abstract idea of the nation is made real through national stories. National stories are the folklore of the national people: stories passed down through generations about national successes and failures, about who stood with us or against us in those moments, and how we survived as a national people.[28] Such stories are based on nationalist history, but they are much more than a chronicle of historical events. They are *relationship* stories. Like parables, they define "good" versus "bad" ties between the national people and other groups and entities, offering moral guidance on what one owes to each of them as a member of a particular nation. National stories define the boundaries of national obligation.

One of the key relationships embedded in national stories is the historicized link between the national people and the state. National stories provide intuitive answers to profound questions of representation. For instance, does the state in which I live stand for the best interests of "my" national people or those of a national "other"? Depending on the answer, national stories signal whether the state should be seen as inclusive or exclusive to the boundaries of national obligation. I find that this powerfully shapes whether a person feels a sense of civic duty to her democracy. When the democratic state in which one lives is seen as standing for "my" nation, the sense of obligation felt toward the national people extends to the state, motivating a sense of civic duty to engage, contribute, and even sacrifice on that state's behalf. In contrast, when national stories frame the democratic state as belonging to a national "other," or worse, as threatening to the livelihood of one's national people, then a sense of obligation to "my" nation motivates a kind of anti-civic duty against that state—a political duty to abstain, resist, and even rebel against the demands of that democracy.

I show that Mrs. Han's impressive exemplar of civic duty is actually part of a larger, predictable pattern among citizens who have internalized national stories that closely link the national people and their democratic state as if one. To understand variations in civic duty, both across individuals and democracies, the book therefore suggests that we need to turn our attention to the historicized national identity politics within a given state and the kinds of national stories it produced. The moral boundaries drawn by these stories powerfully explain why citizens are willing to make sacrifices, big and small, for the sake of their democracies.

Seeing civic duty as a nationalist phenomenon unmoors the long-standing assumption that nationalism is detrimental to liberal democracy. Nationalism is often linked with xenophobia, wars, and separatist movements—forces that typically tear democracies apart. As philosopher John Dunn once remarked, "Nationalism is . . . the deepest, most intractable and yet most unanticipated blot on the political history of the world since the year 1900."[29] By the close of the twentieth century, nationalism had gained a reputation as something to be "contained" if liberal democracy were to flourish.[30]

Like any other political resource, nationalism put in the wrong hands can harm democracies. Nothing in this book refutes that. But my findings also suggest that it would be a big mistake for liberal democracies to do away with nationalism for this reason.[31] What gives nationalism its emotive and political power are the stories that buttress it. Destructive manifestations of nationalism are often products of specific kinds of national stories, where a national people has long seen itself as excluded from or victimized by its democratic state. Other kinds of national stories closely link a national people with its democratic state, as if they were one. Nationalism based on such stories manifests in ways that instrumentally benefit democracies, through greater civic duty and responsible citizenship, even through hard times. These differences have less to do with having a better kind of nationalism or cultural fit with liberal democracy and more to do with the moral relationships embedded in national stories.

As global leaders increasingly call for a revival of democratic civility around the world, many have explicitly condemned the resurgence of nationalist sentiments.

At the centennial remembrance of World War I, French president Emmanuel Macron took thinly veiled aim at Donald Trump, condemning the America First nationalist mentality and stating that "patriotism is the exact opposite of nationalism."[32] Macron is certainly not alone in seeing the "old demons" of nationalism as a threat to today's democracies and the liberal order.

Yet the answer that this book offers about how to strengthen civic duty and build more resilient democracies is not less nationalism but more nationalism of a certain kind. It calls for renewed attention to national stories and the moral relationships that connect a national people to its state. National stories are significantly shaped by the critical junctures in the nation-state formation process, particularly through democratization. But as with any kind of story, its value lies in how people choose to tell and remember the narrative.[33] National stories are therefore living beliefs, concurrently shaping and being shaped by a national people's lived experience.

Perhaps the most optimistic implication from this book, then, is that civic duty is something that can be renewed and grown. A national people's fractured relationship to the democratic state can be repaired through conscious nation-building efforts based on inclusive public policies, political leadership, and national service programs. There is more that democratic states can do to proactively foster their own resilience than a purely democratic culture explanation would suggest. For democracies in East Asia and elsewhere that have long been seen as burdened by their cultural or ethnic legacies, or for democracies currently struggling with weakened civic ties due to internal divisions and strife, it is a heartening story. The rest of the book builds the empirical case that it is also likely true.

Plan of the Book

How does one trace the national roots of something like civic duty—an intrinsic sense of obligation that cannot be directly manipulated, that internalizes through slow socialization, and is easily confounded by structural factors such as pathways to democratization? The empirical task at hand is neither easy nor neat, especially given the ever stringent standards for causal inference in the social sciences.

Political scientist Theda Skocpol made the following statement in a recent interview that reflects the methodological principle taken in this book: "Recognize that a good enough answer to an important question, important both substantively in the field and in the real world, has more value than a definite answer to a trivial question."[34] To show that national stories and the specific nation-state relationships they embed explain variations in civic duty, I strategically combine macro- and micro-level tools to paint a holistic picture. No single case or analysis in the book is meant to be taken as definitive evidence on its own. Rather, like individual instruments in a symphony, each contributes to uncovering a remarkably consistent pattern that, taken together, supports national stories as a powerful motivator of civic duty in democracies.

The book is divided into three parts. Part I, opened by this chapter, introduces the puzzle of civic duty and the theoretical argument of the book. Chapter 2 takes a deep dive into the national theory of civic duty and the concept of "national stories"—where they come from, who tells them, and why there is good reason to suspect that they matter for civic duty. Drawing on works in political theory and nationalism studies, I explain why nations have come to exert a special moral pull on many of their members. I then introduce a predictive model of how national stories moderate the civic effects of nationalism. Depending on the nation-state relationship they embed, national stories can channel the nation's moral pull in support of or against the democratic state that houses it. Chapter 2 concludes with an overview of the empirical strategy used in the rest of the book to systematically test the theory.

Part II is the book's empirical backbone: an in-depth comparison of what motivates civic duty in South Korea versus Taiwan. The two East Asian democracies make a compelling "most similar" pairing for this study. Both were Japanese colonies during the twentieth century, experienced authoritarian rule before democratization from below, developed rapidly during the 1980s, and bore similarly strong ethnic nationalisms in the process. But the two democracies differ in a critical way—the nation-state relationship embedded in their national stories.

Chapter 3 details the historicized national identity politics in each country that led to such divergent national stories. In South Korea the "racialization" of Korean national identity as a survival response to Japanese colonialism powerfully unified the people and the eventually independent state as if one body through democratization. In contrast, Taiwan's independence from Japan was marked by aggressive efforts by the Kuomintang (KMT), who came over to rule from the Chinese mainland, to "re-Sinicize" the islanders. Such efforts seriously backfired and instead birthed an oppositional Taiwanese nationalism—a contentious relationship that has persisted even after democratization due to enduring legacies of KMT ownership over the state.

The latter half of chapter 3 illustrates how such contrasting nation-state relationships manifest in national stories and come to shape people's sense of civic duty. I analyze the personal narratives of young citizens facing military service in the two democracies. Personal narratives are stories that individuals tell about their own lives. The storytelling agency reveals a great deal about a person's worldview and how she understands her relationships, including that between "my" nation and the state. I find that national stories embed specific behavioral scripts for how a "real" Korean or a "good" Taiwanese should act toward the state. These contrasting moral blueprints explain the divergent youth responses to similar military demands from the state: the surprisingly strong civic duty among overseas Koreans who choose to fulfill military service, even when they can be legally exempt, versus the generally weak civic duty among Taiwanese youth to serve in the All-Volunteer Force (AVF).

Chapters 4 and 5 further examine the contrasting basis of civic duty in South Korea and Taiwan. I employ survey and experimental methods in both democracies to test whether the contrasting national effect found in military duty extends to other common forms of civic duty as well. Chapter 4 uses nationally representative surveys in South Korea to show that many citizens feel a civic duty to vote and pay taxes out of an obligation to the nation. This "thick" civic duty exhibits the valuable properties of an intrinsic commitment: a South Korean's sense of civic duty to contribute to her democracy depends less on the expected payoffs from compliance as her national identification strengthens. In a turnout field experiment around a mobile election, I find that priming national obligation as the reason to vote yields substantial gains in the sense of duty to vote and actual turnout in one of the largest treatment effects documented in the experimental turnout literature.

Taiwan exhibits similarly high levels of civic duty to South Korea in surveys. Yet chapter 5 uncovers very different underpinnings to this civic duty, with implications for its nature and durability. For the majority of citizens who identify as Taiwanese and have internalized an oppositional national story against the KMT-legacy state, I find essentially no national effect on their civic duty to vote or pay taxes. Instead, political interest and income are the strongest predictors of civic duty—factors that correlate with how much one stands to gain back from contributing to the state. "Thin" civic duty of this kind, which is conditional rather than intrinsic, is unlikely to endure when payoffs begin to run low. Even in a survey experiment on the willingness to help state efforts on earthquake prevention—a recurring natural disaster that affects everyone on the island— priming national obligation did little to increase a sense of civic duty to contribute among Taiwanese identifiers. The only group in Taiwan for whom I find significant national effects is the shrinking minority of China identifiers, whose national story upholds a strong identity linkage to the KMT-legacy state.

The paired evidence from South Korea and Taiwan in part II builds a rigorous case for the internal validity of the national theory of civic duty. Yet the reader will undoubtedly be curious about the bigger picture. How do the findings from South Korea and Taiwan travel to patterns of civic duty in other democracies?

Is the import of national stories generalizable enough to change the way that we think about nationalism and the civic foundations of democracies at large?

Part III takes up these questions of external validity. Chapter 6 begins with an application of the theory to Germany, a democracy with entirely different cultural and historical legacies from both South Korea and Taiwan. The theory is used to explain a curious phenomenon in German democracy: despite more than three decades since reunification, a stable turnout gap between the East and West persists. Unlike existing explanations, which focus on the economic and democratic deficits in the East, I approach the puzzle from the lens of stunted civic duty. Pairing historical analysis with contemporary survey data, I trace the East's weaker civic duty to vote to legacies of regionally distinct national stories during Germany's division. For many East Germans, an abrupt and one-sided reunification led by the West suddenly left them under the newly expanded state of "the other" Germany, fracturing beliefs of nation-state linkage. Weaker civic duty among former Easterners manifests in lower turnout but also in more troubling ways, as right-wing extremist movements feed off the feelings of nation-state disconnect in the East.

Chapter 7 expands to a cross-national test of the theory based on the broadest sample of democratic citizens for whom reliable survey data on civic duty exist. Across more than 27,000 individuals in twenty-seven democracies in the sixth wave of the World Values Survey, I find that stronger national identification is associated with greater civic duty to vote, pay taxes, and defend one's country in the event of war. Combining these data with the Ethnic Power Relations dataset, I further show that the national pull on civic duty varies predictably with a group's inclusion status in the state, an institutional proxy for historicized beliefs of nation-state linkage.

Chapter 8 brings us back to the opening discussion on nationalism, civic duty, and democratic resilience. Given what the book has shown about the national roots of civic duty, what kinds of contemporary pressures will most durably shape democratic trajectories going forward? The chapter uses East Asia as a window for exploring this big question. The political stakes of democratic survival are exceptionally high in East Asia heading into the twenty-first century. China has obliterated any doubt about its rise as the next global superpower to rival the United States. As the gravitational center of world politics pulls eastward, the question is what form that new regional axis will take.[35] Will an undaunted China and a nuclear North Korea gradually unravel the liberal order in Asia, or will the East Asian democracies survive as pivotal checks?

Threats to democracy are typically seen as coming from the outside, from authoritarian neighbors. This book turns the gaze inward, to the identity threats rising from within democracies themselves. An unprecedented demographic crisis alongside rising inequality is uprooting the national stories on which civic duty has long been based in South Korea and Taiwan. Their democratic futures will depend significantly on how they reimagine their national stories at this critical juncture. Through the two democracies, the chapter illuminates the kinds of nationalist and civic challenges faced by other contemporary democracies also struggling with intensifying sociodemographic pressures. I leave the reader with a discussion on what democratic states can do to actively foster civic duty and cultivate their own resilience through such periods of change.

A NATIONAL THEORY OF CIVIC DUTY

Why do some people feel a sense of civic duty to engage, contribute, and even sacrifice for their democracies while others do not? Why do some democracies have more of such citizens than others? This book takes seriously what citizens like Mrs. Han say. When asked why she donated her wedding rings to the national gold drives to help South Korea during the Asian financial crisis, Mrs. Han answered: "It was the only right thing to do. . . . It's what we have always done for Korea."

For Mrs. Han, participating in the gold drives was first and foremost about doing right by her nation. My approach to why people feel a sense of civic duty to their democracies focuses on the role of national belonging. The theory builds on a central tenet of communitarianism: that certain special communities, by virtue of being an integral part of people's self-identities, come to exert a powerful moral pull on their members. I argue that for many modern individuals the way that national membership is socialized makes the nation one such special community.

Yet the theory is not about the blinding power of nationalism but rather about national identity *politics*. Based on the lived political experience of a national people under the state, different kinds of national stories gel. Some stories paint the state as if one with the nation, extending the powerful duty felt among the national people in support of the state and its needs. Other stories frame the state as exploitative and a threat to the national people. Depending on how national stories define the boundaries of national obligation vis-à-vis the state, nationalism can pull in support of civic duty or against it in different democratic contexts.

A national theory of civic duty offers novel answers to long-standing questions about the relationship between nationalism and democracy. It suggests that the civic strength of democracies has less to do with having an ethnic or civic nationalism, or the right cultural "fit" with liberalism, and more to do with the state's historicized relationship to the national people it represents. The national identity politics of a democracy, and the kinds of national stories it produces, serve as an important measure of a democracy's strength, beyond what formal institutions or easily observable metrics of democratic quality suggest. The chapter closes with an overview of the two-level research design employed in the rest of the book to empirically test the theory.

The Moral Pull of Special Communities

Civic duty—the sense of moral obligation to be a good citizen—is a form of political loyalty to one's state. Max Weber, in his study of political legitimacy, theorized two different bases for such loyalty. The first is procedural rationality (*Zweckrationalität*), where citizens commit to a political authority because it offers them the "'conditions' or 'means' for the successful attainment of the actor's own rationally chosen ends."[1] Such contractual loyalty, which Margaret Levi calls "contingent consent," lies at the heart of liberalism: good governments make good citizens. Scholarship in this tradition has therefore emphasized factors such as procedural fairness, transparency, and political trust as the primary drivers of good citizenship.[2]

Civic duty, however, appears to tap into something other than procedural rationality. When researchers asked habitual voters in Canada why they religiously come out to vote, no matter the harsh weather or long lines, a common line of response was that it is "something I owe to society."[3] References to community—about who "we" are—were also made by Americans displaced by Hurricane Sandy who traveled all the way back to their wrecked home districts in order to vote: "They didn't want to deliver voting booths down here. They wanted us to go across the bridge because they didn't think there was going to be enough people here to vote. I just said, 'No, no, no.' This is us. This is our home."[4]

Civic duty therefore bears closer resemblance to Weber's second basis for political legitimacy: value rationality (*Wertrationalität*). In this framework citizen commitment to a political authority stems from a "conscious belief in the absolute value of some ethical, aesthetic, or other form of behavior, entirely for its own sake and independently of any prospect of external success."[5] Anecdotal accounts of civic duty seem to suggest that for many democratic citizens, this "absolute value" lies in a special kind of attachment to one's community.

Communitarianism, a rich tradition in political theory, sees certain communal memberships as the source of moral obligations, including political ones. Individuals are citizens of a democracy, but they are also members of various communities. Some of these memberships are special in that individuals come to see them as an integral part of their self-identity. For some, these may be communities of birth, such as family, hometown, or ethnic group. For others, they may be communities of choice, such as an alma mater, religious group, or professional organization. Which communities come to hold this special status is inherently subjective and personal: it depends on a given person's life trajectory. But almost all individuals have at least a few special communities that help define them as persons—as a daughter, a Christian, a Detroiter, or French.

Communitarian political theorists argue that such special communities, by virtue of the intrinsic value that they hold to a person's identity, exert powerful moral pull on their members. As Michael Sandel explains:[6]

> Can we view ourselves as independent selves, independent in the sense that our identity is never tied to our aims and attachments? I do not think we can, at least not without cost to those loyalties and convictions whose moral force consists partly in the fact that living by them is inseparable from understanding ourselves as the particular persons we are—as members of this family or community or nation or people, as bearers of that history, as citizens of this republic. Allegiances such as these are more than values I happen to have, and to hold, at a certain distance. . . . They allow that to some I owe more than justice requires or even permits, not by reason of agreements I have made but instead in virtue of those more or less enduring attachments and commitments that, taken together, partly define the person I am.[6]

An earlier generation of social scientists saw such moral pull to be limited to communities that Clifford Geertz called "the givens": "Congruities of blood, speech, custom, and so on, are seen to have an ineffable, and at times overpowering coerciveness in and of themselves."[7] Primordialism, as it was called, fell out of favor as subsequent identity scholarship demonstrated the highly flexible nature of groupness. People's identities were better understood as *identifications* that varied with social and political contexts.[8] In particular, social identity theorists demonstrated through a series of experiments that group loyalties were quite malleable to different "us" versus "them" categorizations, directly challenging the idea of fixed or innate ties.[9]

Taking seriously the socially constructed nature of groups, however, need not negate the entirety of the primordialist contribution. In fact, the two traditions have more in common than often thought. Contemporary identity scholarship certainly refutes the idea that individuals are uniquely bound by the "givens." But the key insight from primordialism was not necessarily that all identities are fixed, but that certain kinds of groups exerted "overpowering coerciveness in and of themselves"—an intrinsic pull on their members. Primordialists saw such ties as based on something ineffable—literally indescribable—about communities of birth. Constructivist theories of identity locate the source of such pull in a person's psychological identification with a group as "mine," rather than any essentialist characteristic of a group. Constructivism therefore expands the scope of special communities that individuals can experience *as if* they were "givens."

Nation as Special Community

I argue that for many modern individuals the nation is a special community. To follow Benedict Anderson's definition, the nation is an "imagined community," reified by a shared understanding among its members, who see themselves as belonging to the same political collective.[10] It is a community defined not by physical territory, but by the "desire to live together, the will to perpetuate the value of the heritage one has received in an undivided form."[11]

The actual origins of contemporary nations belie such ethereal descriptions. Many nations that exist today were created by political elites for the instrumental purposes of standardizing labor, expanding markets, or modernizing warfare.[12] But for most ordinary individuals, the day-to-day lived experience of nationhood conceals such pragmatic origins. As Katherine Verdery notes, often the very point of nationalist socialization by states is to create the illusion of nativity, true to the root meaning of the word nation, which is "to be born."[13] Established nation-states construct this aura of naturality through what Michael Billig calls "banal" nationalist rituals, such as singing the national anthem before major sporting events and the quiet ubiquity of national symbols in state buildings: "In established nations, there is continual 'flagging,' or reminding, of nationhood. . . . In so many little ways, the citizenry are daily reminded of their national place in a world of nations. However, this reminding is so familiar, so continual, that it is not consciously registered as reminding."[14]

But beyond such ritualistic flagging, another aspect of nationalist socialization—the kind that takes place within the intimacy of the home—makes national memberships feel *as if* they were "givens" for many individuals. The nation has many ways of seeping into the personal realm of "home." The national language is not just what is used in public schools and official documents; it is often one's mother tongue—how a person first learns to call her mother and father. The national culture is not just an abstract list of foods or traditions; it is the comfort foods that one grew up eating in the kitchen and the childhood songs one knows by heart and will one day sing to one's own children. The national history is not just what is commemorated on official holidays or written in textbooks; it is the parables of heroes and villains that grandparents would tell at family gatherings to their wide-eyed grandchildren. Such rituals are not explicitly nationalistic. But over time, they build an almost instinctual boundary around the national "us."

Such intimate processes of socialization integrate the nation as part of an individual's sense of place and origin in a world of nations. This sentiment is powerfully captured in *Noli Me Tángere,* a Filipino nationalist novel. The main character, Ibarra, upon returning to the Philippines after his studies in Europe, has the following exchange with a native general:

> "How long have you been away from the country?" Laruja asked Ibarra.
> "Almost seven years."
> "Then you have probably forgotten all about it."
> "Quite the contrary. Even if my country does seem to have forgotten me, I have always thought about it."[15]

The nation as home is what gives it its moral pull over so many and allows it to demand "special duties" from its members.[16] As Anderson notes: "For most ordinary people of whatever class, the whole point of the nation is that it is interestless. Just for that reason, it can ask for sacrifices."[17] Many communities are selectable, but "home" carries a sense of fatality and permanence.

It is important to clarify, however, that the nation's pull will not be the same for everyone, even among members of the same national community. The nation's status as a special community depends on the extent to which a person identifies with it as "mine." Strength of national identification can be shaped by the intensity of nationalist socialization, formative experiences, or pathway to national membership. All such factors yield variation in a person's strength of national identification, and consequently, the extent to which she feels and responds to the moral pull of her nation. Cara Wong illustrates this variability:

> In the case of a nation, it is very likely that a Jew residing in a West Bank settlement does not have the same image of or feelings about her nation as does a Jew residing on the Upper West Side of Manhattan, even if both were born in Israel. . . . And individuals who hold the very same image of their nation may have vastly different feelings of communion with other members: some would die to protect their nation, while others would fail to see why it is worth defending.[18]

Thus, national obligation as discussed here is a far cry from the popular image that the words "nationalism" and "obligation" typically conjure together—of lemmings blindly marching off a cliff. The nation's moral pull is not an irrational loyalty rooted in something ineffable but a rational psychological attachment rooted in a person's "internalized sense of belonging to the nation."[19]

Yet the lemmings metaphor brings up a common concern about the nation's moral pull. Throughout history, people have committed heinous acts in the name of duty to the nation, from discrimination and xenophobic violence to full-blown genocide. Such negative examples of nationalism have long dominated public discourse. It is only recently that scholars have begun to document the positive capacities of nationalism, as a driving force behind better public-goods provision and progressive welfare, higher turnout, and pro-social behaviors toward ethnic others.[20] Given this duality in nationalism's effects, some researchers have sought to distinguish the good kind of patriotism from bad variants of nationalism. They conceptualize the former as a positive love for the in-group and the latter as chauvinistic contempt for the out-group.[21] The claim is that the two variants lead to different outcomes: patriotism as civic versus nationalism as uncivic.

I intentionally use the term "nationalism" here without differentiating between patriotic versus chauvinist variants. Like any form of moral parochialism, identifying with the nation entails both positive bias for the national in-group and negative bias against the national out-group. One aspect might outweigh the other depending on the context, but they are two sides of the same coin. As Rogers Brubaker notes, "Attempts to distinguish good patriotism from bad nationalism neglect the intrinsic ambivalence and polymorphism of both. Patriotism and nationalism are not things with fixed natures; they are highly flexible political languages, ways of framing political arguments by appealing to the patria, the fatherland, the country, the nation."[22] Acknowledging the common roots of patriotic and chauvinist expressions of nationalism forces us to face the hard questions. What explains the Janus-faced manifestations of nationalism? Under what conditions does the nation's moral pull take civic versus uncivic forms in democracies?

I argue that the democratic manifestations of nationalism have less to do with having a good or bad variant and more to do with how different nationalisms are embedded vis-à-vis the state. National stories—the folk histories told and shared by the national people—play an important role in clarifying that relationship. How national stories delineate the moral boundary between a national people and the democratic state in which they live powerfully shapes whether the nation's pull manifests in support of civic duty to that democracy or against it.

What exactly are national stories? Who writes them, how are they learned, and how do they come to shape citizen behavior? The next section turns to these questions.

National Stories and Beliefs of Nation-State Linkage

Communities of many kinds are sustained by stories. Such stories include the officially documented history of a group but, more importantly, the everyday oral histories that are shared informally and intimately among members. Storytelling of the latter kind is powerful because it deconstructs communal membership down to a personal level. It reflects the history of the group as seen through the eyes of everyday members. As such stories are shared across networks and generations, they become an integral part of the emotional attachments that make an imagined community real. For instance, stories about the trials and tribulations of the family, as told by grandfathers to fathers to sons, sustain felt commitments to the family lineage in a way that no official ancestry record ever could.

National communities are also sustained by national stories. National stories, as I conceptualize them in this book, are distinct from what is commonly known as the constitutive narrative or origin story of the nation.[23] These are typically officialized in time immemorial and constructed top-down by political elites. Gérard Bouchard describes these near-canonized narratives about the nation's founding as the national "master myth," which is based on "relatively stable symbolic configurations."[24] National stories, on the other hand, are closer to Bouchard's concept of "derivative myths," which are applications and adaptations of the master myth to current political or social situations. Beneath the officialized narrative about who we are, national stories do the work of explaining how we ought to live.

National stories are the folklore of the national people. They are stories, passed down through generations, about what happened to us, who stood by us versus who wronged us in moments of need, and how we survived. National stories are based on real historical events in the life cycle of the nation, such as wars, natural disasters, regime change, and other crises. But they are much more than a neutral catalogue of the nation's history. Told through a personal lens—what it was like to actually live through those times—they add a dimension of parable: collective lessons learned and guidelines for the future.

As an example, the Korean War was a major historical event in South Korea's nation-state formation process. National stories include the near idiom-ized personal stories that most South Korean fathers who came of age during the 1940s and '50s have told their children about what it was like during the war—stories about how the family was unintentionally split when the North suddenly attacked, how the Northern Communist soldiers confiscated the family's land and possessions, how a South Korean father carried his starving toddler nephew on his back for days to escape. Such stories are not explicitly nationalistic or pedagogical. But they embed important cues about which groups to trust and which to be wary of as a member of a particular nation. Many South Korean children who grew up on such national stories about the Korean War have internalized a deep wariness against the North.

National stories are relationship stories. By delineating between national friends and foes, national stories lay out a collective blueprint for how we ought to live as a national people. Foes can be a national "other," as in the case of a colonizer or foreign enemy, but they can also be events that threaten the nation, such as a famine, natural disaster, or economic crisis. Even the most pacifist nations inevitably experience periods of national exigency, when the national people collectively face a challenge. Such crucibles yield national stories that reflect the people's learnings on how to best endure, survive, and triumph. National stories are therefore part of what Peter Hall and Michèle Lamont broadly refer to as the "collective imaginaries" of nations—a set of stories that connect a nation's past to its future by defining the "strategies of action" for continued development:

> If nations are "imagined communities," as Benedict Anderson has suggested, it matters how they imagine themselves. Collective imaginaries are sets of representations composed of symbols, myths, and narratives that people use to portray their community or nation and their own relationship as well as that of others to it. . . . By presenting a community's past in a particular way, collective narratives influence the expectations of its members about the future, suggesting paths of collective development available to the community and "strategies of action" feasible for individuals within it.[25]

I argue that this relational aspect of national stories pivotally shapes nationalism's civic or uncivic manifestations in democracies. Rogers Brubaker has noted how the nation is "produced—or better, it is induced—by *political fields* of particular kinds."[26] A key aspect of that field is the role of the state in moments of national exigency.

Nation and state are often conflated in everyday discourse, but they are two distinct concepts. The nation is the imagined community of people who see themselves as belonging to the same political collective. The state, on the other hand, is the political infrastructure or system of institutions that governs over a defined physical territory. The "nation-state" is thus a particular configuration, where the territorial lines of a state overlap with a singularly imagined national community. Other configurations include multinational states, where multiple national communities existing within a single state, or divided nations, where an imagined national community stretches across multiple states.

The state is an important protagonist in national stories. Implicitly or explicitly, national stories define the state as a champion, a failure, or even a betrayer of the national people through critical junctures. Whether the state has historically stood as a protector or persecutor of the national people gels into a certain understanding of the supportive or oppositional nature of the state—what I call belief of nation-state linkage.

Nation-state linkage builds on the idea of contextual nationalisms from Rogers Brubaker. Responding to what he describes as the Manichean myth of "good" civic nationalisms versus "bad" ethnic nationalisms, Brubaker proposes "state-framed" versus "counter-state" nationalisms as a more useful analytical framework: "In the former, 'nation' is conceived as congruent with the state, and as institutionally and territorially framed by it. In the latter, 'nation' is imagined as distinct from, and often in opposition to, the territorial and institutional frame of an existing state or states."[27] Brubaker's framework shifts the focus from what nationalism *is* to what nationalism *does*. It is the nation's relationship with the state, rather than the content of national identity, that shapes whether nationalism barks, bites, or runs loyally alongside the democracy that houses it.[28] National stories are the vehicle through which critical know-how about this linkage is learned and passed on through generations.

Nation-state linkage will be seen as strong when national stories portray the state to represent the best interests of "my" nation. Stories will emphasize the interdependent, linked fate relationship between the national people and the state as if one. Strong linkage is more than a tit-for-tat evaluation of how well the state is serving me now. It is a deeper belief about the state's intent toward the national people, learned over the collective lived history under that state.[29] Such national stories will tend to be common in democracies made up of a singular national community, where national consciousness grew hand-in-hand with democratic consolidation.[30] But even with the structural advantage that nation-states have, strong linkage is not a given. Because linkage is a living and breathing belief, even nation-states must show a consistent commitment to the best interests of the national people through critical moments.[31]

In contrast, nation-state linkage will be seen as fractured or even opposed when national stories frame the best interests of "my" nation as something to be protected from, rather than by, the state. Such national stories can be produced through a variety of pathways. Structural factors, such as arbitrarily drawn borders or sudden reunifications or divisions, can result in states with multiple national communities, where at least part of the citizenry comes to see the state as representing the best interests of a national "other." Such is the case for many ethnic Russians in Ukraine or Catalans in Spain, for example. Fractured or opposed linkage will also be common in places where a national consciousness was forged out of state persecution, or where democratization excluded—either formally or informally—certain national groups from equal ownership over the state. These scenarios describe nationalist tensions in Taiwan, India, or the United States at different points in history. In such cases the national stories of nondominant groups will tend to focus on experiences of exclusion or even predation by the state, internalizing an oppositional relationship between a national people and the state in which they live. Thus, in a given polity, national stories can range from largely homogeneous, bifurcated, or largely heterogeneous across the citizen population.

An illustrative example of how distinct beliefs of nation-state linkage are seeded, and the different political responses they invoke, can be found in Walker Connor's account of early modern China. Connor wrote the following at a time when the Chinese state was actively, and often brutally, consolidating a multiethnic population under a Han nationalist identity: "The Han Chinese are apt to view the state of China as the state of their particular nation, and are therefore susceptible either in the name of China or in the name of the Han Chinese people. But the notion of *China* evokes quite different associations, and therefore different responses, from Tibetans, Mongols, Uighurs, and other non-Han people."[32]

Who writes the role of the state in national stories? National storytelling evolves through an interactive process between the state and the national people. Although national stories are told by members of the nation, the state holds significant top-down agency in providing the raw material for national stories. For instance, the state can instigate or quell conflicts, respond to crises through good or bad public policies, decide which groups to privilege at the expense of others, and craft how it communicates all of this to the people it governs through political rhetoric and public education. National stories will ultimately reflect how people perceive such state actions based on their own lived experiences, which may or may not accord with the state's original intent. Yet the state remains an active participant in the writing and rewriting of national stories. National stories exist at that interactive nexus, in stable equilibrium rather than permanent fixture.

National stories are a powerful lens through which individuals make sense of their political worlds. They guide national members toward safe and good behaviors and away from dangerous or bad ones by providing relational context to the political choices they face. One of those choices is how to respond to the expectations and demands of the democracy in which one lives, which brings us to civic duty.

Toward a National Theory of Civic Duty

National stories and the beliefs of nation-state linkage they embed define the boundaries of national obligation. They dictate to which groups or entities one owes something as a member of a particular nation. I argue that whether a person feels a sense of civic duty to her democracy is significantly shaped by whether the democratic state in which she lives is seen as inclusive or exclusive to that moral boundary.

When national stories paint the democratic state as an extension of the nation—when belief of nation-state linkage is strong—the democratic state is seen as falling within the boundary of national obligation. Then, for individuals who identify with the nation, the intrinsic obligation they feel to care for and contribute to "my" national people motivates a parallel, political duty to the state—a sense of civic duty. When Brubaker noted that "patriotic identification with one's country—the feeling that this is *my* country, and *my* government—can help ground a sense of responsibility for . . . actions taken by the national government,"[33] he was describing the particular case of strong nation-state linkage.

Alternatively, when national stories paint the democratic state as standing for a national "other"—when belief of nation-state linkage is fractured—the state is seen as falling outside the boundaries of national obligation. For such individuals, national obligation will have little to do with a sense of civic duty to their democracy. They may still feel a civic duty to vote or pay taxes for other reasons, but an intrinsic obligation to contribute to the democracy of "my" nation is likely not one of them.

In still other cases, national stories paint the democratic state as not only exclusive of, but also threatening to, the best interests of "my" nation, seeding opposed beliefs of nation-state linkage. Such beliefs frame an obligation to care for "my" nation as contradictory to any actions that support the state. For such individuals, national obligation is likely to drive a kind of anti–civic duty to abstain, resist, or even outright reject the political demands of that democracy.

The theoretical logic is shown in figure 2.1. Two factors simultaneously shape how national obligation motivates both whether and how strongly a person feels a sense of civic duty to her democracy. The first individual-level factor is her strength of national identification—the extent to which she sees her nation as a special community and feels its moral pull. Even individuals who belong to the same objective national community will differ here, as psychological attachment to the nation is inherently subjective.

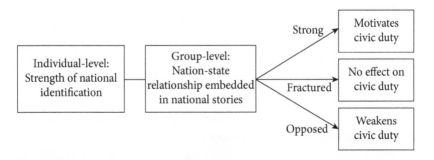

FIGURE 2.1. A national theory of civic duty.

The second group-level factor is the belief of nation-state linkage socialized from national stories. This linkage is the pivotal lever that determines the civic or uncivic direction of the nation's moral pull. Depending on the nature of that linkage—strong, fractured, or opposed—national obligation can either motivate a sense of civic duty to one's democracy, have no relation to it, or even weaken it. Belief of linkage can vary across individuals within the same national group based on different formative experiences as members of the nation. But the contours of linkage will tend to vary most significantly across different national groups, each with its own relationships to the state. Thus, the theory accounts for why some individuals feel a sense of civic duty while others do not within a given democracy, and also why some democracies tend to have more of such individuals than others.

The National Roots of Civic Duty

The theory reimagines civic duty in democracies as a product of national identity politics, rather than something rooted in culture or character. The political experiences of inclusion, exclusion, or oppression of a national people by their democratic states are gelled into national stories that clarify the moral linkage between nation and state. That linkage shapes how the intrinsic obligation that many individuals feel to "my" nation manifests in their lives as democratic citizens. More so than having a particular kind of culture or nationalism that is fit for democracy, my claim is that beliefs about the boundaries of national obligation, and whether it includes the state in which one lives, most immediately shape a person's sense of civic duty to contribute to her democracy.

At this point one may ask, however, to what extent is this a theory about democracy? The theory seeks to explain what motivates civic duty in democracies, but as vigilant readers will have noticed, there is nothing uniquely democratic about the argument developed in this chapter. My claim is that a national people's moral linkage to the democratic state, not necessarily to democracy as a value or principle, drives their sense of civic duty. What matters is the historicized relationship to the state, rather than the regime type. The same logic could be applied to explain why many rational citizens feel a sense of civic duty to an authoritarian state.

This duality to the theory is likely normatively upsetting to some because civic duty has long been seen as the unique domain of democracies—a political virtue that only democratic citizens possess. Not only is this assumption empirically false, as many citizens of autocracies express feeling a sense of civic duty,[34] but it also impedes us from asking important questions about change and growth in civic duty. If civic duty is a natural product of democratic maturity, then how do we explain impressive displays of civic duty in very young democracies and civic decline in mature democracies, as recent episodes of democratic backsliding have shown? By decoupling civic duty from democracy and recognizing that civic duty is ultimately about a special loyalty between citizens and their state, democratic or not, the theory moves beyond democratic essentialism in seeking an answer to the question of how to foster civic duty.

Nevertheless, a national theory of civic duty carries unique import for democracies. As others have found, factors such as social pressure or psychic benefits also motivate a sense of civic duty through the expectation of payoffs. But not all civic duty is alike. It is worth emphasizing that the outcome in figure 2.1 is not the level of civic duty, but its basis. Incentive-based obligation to the state that is based on give and take, or thin civic duty, will wax and wane based on fluctuations in state performance or status. Identity-based civic duty is also not immutable. But once internalized, it tends to be quite sticky: it takes a lot more to shift someone's ties to her special community than to modify her payoff calculation from an underperforming state. Civic duty rooted in national obligation should therefore exhibit the rare properties of moral commitment: for someone who feels it, payoff considerations that typically motivate compliance should no longer matter. This kind of thick civic duty is principled.

The intrinsic nature of nationally motivated civic duty is why it merits special attention in democracies. During hard times, authoritarian states can always fall back on the threat of force to coerce citizen sacrifice. Liberal democracies are founded on political principles that preclude such options. Instead, when the usual incentives for participation run low, they need to reach deep into the reserves of thick civic duty. For all of liberalism's emphasis on individual freedom and autonomy, democracies need strong and particularistic attachments to the state in order to stay resilient—what Anna Stilz calls the paradox of "liberal loyalty."[35] The theory suggests that the nation's moral pull can be a powerful foundation for such loyalty.

Taking seriously the national roots of civic duty challenges the long-standing negative bias against nationalism in democracy studies. Given the tempestuous relationship between nationalism and liberalism that defined the late twentieth century, the assumption that nationalism is detrimental, and perhaps even antithetical, to liberal democracy is hardly surprising. Nothing in the theory denies the potential dark side of nationalism for democratic life. But the theory identifies the danger not as nationalism per se, but nationalisms that are turned against the state by scheming demagogues. In response to growing signs of democratic regress around the world, the theory calls on democratic leaders to exert more, not less, effort on nationalism. The effort that is needed is not symbolic flag-waving, but conscious and careful policy making to seed the kinds of national stories that can repair linkages between a national people and the state over time.

That nationalism is an important part of democracy's civic foundation also urges democracy scholars to rethink how strong versus weak democracies are conceptualized and measured. Research on democratic quality has tended to focus on formal institutions and standardized metrics of political stability. For instance, the most commonly used democracy indexes are based on factors such as an independent judiciary, frequency of party turnovers, and protection of freedom of speech and civil rights. The theory highlights a less obvious, but no less important, dimension to democratic quality. Truly strong democracies not only do well in good times but also persevere through bad times. For the latter, the theory suggests that the national identity politics that underlie formal democratic institutions matter powerfully. Even democracies that appear similarly successful on the outside can stand on very different civic foundations on the inside.

Perhaps the most important implication from the theory, however, is that civic duty is something that can be grown. National stories are told through a personal lens, but they are responses to real political events and actions taken by the state. Democratic leaders and policymakers therefore hold a lot more agency than previously thought possible—beyond what is determined by culture, character, or age of a democracy—to cultivate their democracy's civic potential.

The Empirical Approach

How would we know if individuals really feel a sense of civic duty to their democracies out of a moral obligation to their nations? Intrinsic motivations are difficult to study empirically because, unlike extrinsic motivations, they cannot be directly observed or manipulated. How does one measure "some unaccountable absolute import attributed to the very tie itself," as Geertz once described?[36]

Testing the theory in figure 2.1 faces two distinct empirical challenges. The first challenge is the presence of various macrolevel confounders that can plausibly lead to a spurious relationship between nationalism and civic duty. For instance, collectivist cultural values can simultaneously foster both a stronger sense of obligation to the national group and a greater duty to the state. On the other hand, the past experience of colonialism can seriously dampen both strength of national identification and loyalty to any kind of political authority. Macrolevel confounders such as culture, colonialism, or pathways to democracy are problematic for inference because they are either entrenched at the societal level or represent critical junctures that already happened in the past. Given the deep, formative ways that these factors can shape the variables of interest in this study, simply controlling for them in a regression setup is insufficient.

The second challenge, this time at the microlevel, is what David Broockman calls "observational equivalence."[37] The issue is that intrinsic and extrinsic motivations often produce the same observable outcomes. For instance, say that I observed a positive association between stronger national identification and the civic duty to vote in survey data. This could be because national identification motivates an intrinsic obligation to contribute to the democracy of "my" nation. Or it could be because national identification produces greater expectation of extrinsic payoffs, such as social praise from co-nationals. This might seem like a matter of semantics, but parsing out whether national identification functions as an intrinsic or extrinsic motivation is important in this study as it leads to very different implications about the nature of the civic duty that is produced. The challenge is to find creative ways to convince the reader that the moral pull of the nation matters.

The two-level research design in the book aims to address both kinds of empirical challenges simultaneously. The first level uses "most similar" comparative case selection to address the issue of macrolevel confounders. South Korea and Taiwan, which make up the empirical backbone of the book, make an excellent pairing for this purpose. The two democracies are nearly identical on the macrolevel variables that could most likely confound the relationship between nationalism and civic duty. Only about 1,500 kilometers apart, both democracies sit at entry points into the Asia continent, have strong Confucian legacies, are racially homogeneous, and hold primarily ethnic conceptions of nation. Both were Japanese colonies in the early twentieth century, and after independence each experienced a period of military authoritarianism followed by bottom-up democratization and fast economic development through the 1980s. It is difficult to find a more naturally controlled pairing for this study.

Despite such similarities, however, the two democracies have very different kinds of national stories. Nationalist movements prior to democratization panned out in divergent ways in the two democracies, embedding sharply contrasting nation-state linkages into their national stories. Whereas a bloodline-based, racial reimagination of the Korean nation strongly tied the national people and the state as one body through democratization in South Korea, in Taiwan a Taiwanese nationalism born out of opposition to the ruling pro-China elites and their efforts to re-Sinicize the island produced national stories with fractured linkage, with many citizens seeing the democratic state as standing for a national "other."

As I will elaborate in chapter 3, the distinct nation-state linkages born out of these nationalist movements set up contrasting theoretical predictions. South Korea is a "positive case," where I expect civic duty to have a strong national basis for most citizens, whereas Taiwan is a "negative case," where I expect the nation's pull to have a negligible or even negative effect on civic duty for a substantial portion of the citizenry. The inferential logic behind this pairing is that the exceptional degree of structural and historical parallels between the two democracies effectively rules out most alternative explanations, such that whatever differences I observe in the national effect on civic duty between the two democracies is unlikely to be due to a macrolevel confounder.[38]

The second level of the research design employs a multimethod identification strategy to test the contrasting microlevel predictions set up by the South Korea and Taiwan pairing. To address the issue of observational equivalence that bedevils empirical studies of intrinsic motivations, I triangulate across three different methods to identify the presence (or for many individuals in Taiwan, the predicted absence) of the nation's moral pull toward civic duty in each democracy. Each method used—personal narrative interviews, statistical survey analysis, and experiments—relies on a distinct identification strategy to tease out moral intent in a way that complements the limitations of the other two methods. Taken alone, each would be insufficient to fully convince both researcher and reader of the nation's moral pull toward civic duty. But taken together, a consistent pattern of evidence that emerges across all three methods should build a strong case even to the most skeptical reader.

Table 1 lays out the two-level design. The strength of the design lies in how it simultaneously leverages macro- and microlevel strategies. The design allows for both cross-case comparisons within a single method (A-B, C-D, E-F), as well as within-case comparisons across methods (A-C-E, B-D-F). This setup allows the researcher to answer the following kinds of questions: For most citizens in South Korea, is there consistent evidence across different methods that national

TABLE 1 Two-level research design

		MICRO-LEVEL MIXED-METHOD IDENTIFICATION		
		PERSONAL NARRATIVES	STATISTICAL ANALYSIS OF SURVEYS	EXPERIMENTS
MACRO-LEVEL	**South Korea** *strong linkage case*	A	C	E
"MOST SIMILAR" CASE PAIRING	**Taiwan** *weak linkage case*	B	D	F

obligation motivates civic duty? Does the predicted contrast in the national effect between South Korea and Taiwan hold up consistently within each method? The design bakes in both internal and external validity checks on the theory, setting an unusually high bar for comparative inference. The rest of the book now turns to how well the empirical evidence meets that test.

Groups have always been important to the study of democratic citizenship, but in a liberal framework they have been a powerful mediator at best. For instance, scholars have shown that group identifications significantly shape people's desires for relative status, understandings of self-interest, and willingness to cooperate with each other in contexts of redistribution, public goods provision, and collective action.[39] In such works, groups matter because of how they shape the expected payoffs of political action—that is, through the pursuit of interests.

What is distinct about the theory of civic duty advanced here is that special group identifications matter in themselves, through a moral capacity that is distinct from the motivational power of payoffs. My claim is that, once internalized as part of a person's self-identity, national identifications and the national stories that sustain them take on a powerful moral force of their own. They shape not only a person's definition of self-interest but also the boundary of her moral obligations. When one's national obligation is seen as inclusive of the democratic state, it can motivate the kind of civic duty that sometimes defies even the most costly calculations of self-interest.

In a discussion about interests and ethics in democratic citizenship, Laura Stoker described the citizen as "an individual with her own unique hopes and desires who is at the same time joined with others, part of and continually giving shape to a common social political life." An accurate account of democratic citizenship therefore requires an approach that "neither denies the real concerns of individuals nor disregards the exigencies of a society and the requirements of communal life."[40] So far, our understanding of civic duty has emphasized the former set of motivations, leaving citizens like Mrs. Han—who described her decision to donate to the South Korean gold drives as "the only right thing to do" for Korea—as exceptions to the rule. This chapter offers a theory of civic duty that takes seriously the moral pull of special groups, specifically the nation. How common are citizens like Mrs. Han, who approach the roles of democratic citizenship through a distinctly national lens? The next three chapters turn to the empirical evidence from South Korea and Taiwan.

Part II

NATIONAL STORIES IN SOUTH KOREA AND TAIWAN

In a small lunch shop in Muzha, Taiwan, over a bowl of cold noodles, two college friends discuss their upcoming military service. To incoming conscripts, the government is offering the option to stay on as a full-time, paid professional soldier in the All-Volunteer Force (AVF) after completing mandatory service.

Neither of the young men wishes to join. They both shake their heads vehemently at the idea. But their reasons are very different. One friend sees nothing to gain from being a professional soldier:

> When I graduate, I will be able to get a better job. Higher pay. But in the military, I could get hurt and have to listen to orders. And if China attacks, we cannot win. Impossible. So why would I give up my freedom, my life, for that?

At this point, the other friend interrupts.

> I will still fight if that happens. I don't want to die, but all of my family is here. Taiwan, this island, is my home. If I don't protect it, who will? But serving in the military is different. I don't know who the military fights for. Who does it really protect, us Taiwanese?

National stories embed important cues about the historical relationship between a national people and the state in which they live. By delineating the boundaries of national obligation, and whether they are inclusive or exclusive of the state, these cues can powerfully shape who feels a sense of civic duty to their democracy. What do national stories actually look like? How is something like nation-state linkage learned? The second part of the book begins by illustrating how national stories work in South Korea and Taiwan, taking a deep dive into this illuminating comparison.

I begin by tracing the divergent nationalist histories of South Korea and Taiwan during the early nation-building period. Despite their similarities in culture, geopolitics, and colonial rule by Japan, the two democracies experienced very different nationalist movements after independence in the mid-twentieth century. In South Korea a racial reimagination of the Korean nation quickly emerged as dominant, homogenizing all Koreans across different backgrounds, but also binding the nation and state as if one body through democratization. In Taiwan a Taiwanese nationalism born out of repression and resistance against the ruling mainlander elite from China pitted nation and state against each other for many islanders.

Objective nationalist history—the actors, events, and outcomes—serves as the raw material for the contrasting flavors of national stories that developed in South Korea versus Taiwan. It sets the discursive frame on which "folk" national stories of the everyday people are based. But as the national people reinterpret the historical events through subjective storytelling, they imbue history with normative meaning. For instance, was the Korean War a good or bad thing for the national "us"? What did it teach us about our friends and foes? National stories fill in these meaning gaps.

To really understand how national stories work, then, one has to look at them through the eyes of the national people. The latter half of the chapter turns to this task by examining how national stories shape civic duty toward military service in the two democracies. I analyze almost two hundred personal narratives—153 written narratives from South Korea and 41 oral narratives from Taiwan—of young adult citizens in both places. Personal narratives are the life stories of individuals as told by themselves. The story-telling agency reveals a great deal about the subjects' worldviews: their beliefs of right and wrong, cause and effect, and relationships. I apply process tracing, a method used in comparative historical analysis to identify critical junctures, to these life histories to identify what role, if any, national stories play in shaping a sense of civic duty (or lack thereof) toward military service.

On the surface the national stories that emerge are not explicitly nationalistic. They are stories about the father's own military experience or family parables of what life was like during the Korean War or under military rule. Yet these stories embed clear cues about the nature of nation-state linkage that are learned as "national scripts": specific rules of conduct on how one should behave toward the state as a member of the nation. Like other manners and norms learned within the home, national scripts dictate how a "real" Korean or "good" Taiwanese should respond to his state's needs. Even before they come of age for military service, young men in the two democracies are socialized into very different national scripts: a real Korean man is defined by state-supportive citizenship, whereas a good Taiwanese is always wary of the state.

The personal narratives illustrate how the different nationalist movements in South Korea and Taiwan forged distinct national stories. The contrasting beliefs of nation-state linkage embedded in these stories explain the surprising civic duty among overseas Koreans who return to serve in the military, even when they can be legally exempt, versus the relatively weak civic duty among Taiwanese youth who refuse to serve in the All-Volunteer Force (AVF).

South Korea: Strong Linkage in a Nationally Unified Democracy

Today, South Korea is widely seen as a prototypical example of an ethnic nation-state. Korean national identity is still primarily defined in ethno-racial terms, based on descent or blood lineage.[1] South Korea routinely ranks as one of the most ethnically homogeneous polities in the world.[2] Yet however taken for granted an ethnic Korean identity may be, especially to those who identify as such, this section looks at the nationalist history of Korea that made it so. I trace the pervasive belief of an ethnic Korean nation and the strong, *as if* natural linkage between the national people and the state to strategic decisions made by political elites to secure the nation's survival through critical moments in modern history.

The "racialization" of Korean identity—the reimagination of Korea as a blood-based, ethnic community—was largely a survival response to Japanese colonialism in the early twentieth century. Initially, as modernization brought a rising threat from the West, nationalist leaders sought to position Korea within a broader pan-Asian cultural identity.[3] Japan's imperial conquest into Asia and eventual colonization of the Korean peninsula threw such efforts violently off course. The Japanese, ignited by their own nationalist mission, legitimized their rule based on racial supremacy over Koreans.[4] This imposed racial hierarchy forced Korean nationalist discourse away from claiming cultural affinity with the rest of Asia. Recognizing the colonizer as the primary threat, Korean nationalist leaders turned to distinguish the Korean race from the Japanese.

The ethnic pivot proved to be crucial in keeping the belief of a Korean nation alive through Japanese rule. At the heart of the reimagined Korean nation was the idea of *danil minjok*—a community descended from a singular bloodline.[5] To popularize this belief, nationalist leaders revived folklore like the myth of *Dangun* as the origin story of the Korean bloodline, dating it back to 2333 BC. Such efforts shifted the locus of national history from specific dynasties and monarchs to family lineages of the everyday Korean people. Shin Chae-ho, a prominent nationalist leader and historian, wrote in *A New Reading of History* (*Doksasillon*), "A country's history is the record of a minjok's life narrative. Without the minjok, there would be no history, and without history, a minjok would have little understanding of its country, such that the responsibility of history weighs heavy."[6]

This minjok-based reimagination of Korea gave the nation a new lifeline under colonialism. Even if not politically autonomous under the Japanese, the Korean nation would continue through the minjok's pure bloodline. The *as if* nativity of Koreanness, and critically, its imperviousness to foreign influence, is evident in the account of another prominent nationalist Yi Kwangsu, who wrote in *A Theory of the Korean Nation* (*Joseonminjongnon*): "Koreans cannot but be Koreans ... even when they use the language of a foreign nation, wear its clothes and follow its customs in order to become non-Korean."[7]

From the perspective of nation-state linkage, the significance of the racialization of Korean identity was its powerful homogenizing capacity. Minjok served as "a category inclusive of every Korean without regard to age, gender, or status distinctions."[8] What used to be semipermanent categories of class that vertically divided Korean society gave way to an inclusive basis for national unity. The horizontal reimagination of Korea as a singular, blood-related collective also left little room for competing identity claims. To do so would be, in a sense, to betray one's own family, which violated one of the fundamental pillars of South Korea's Confucian society.

The principle of a singular ethnic Korean nation continued as the dominant discursive frame through critical junctures in Korea's nation-building process. After independence from Japan, Korean elites were bitterly divided over Cold War ideologies on how to best lead the nation. The pro-Communist northern faction aligned with the Soviet Union and the anti-Communist southern faction supported by the United States eventually fought each other in the Korean War, ending in an unresolved armistice between North and South Korea.

Yet even through civil war and division, the basis for strong nation-state linkage was preserved within each Korean state. Political leaders on each side espoused radically different ideologies, but they framed their mission as one of the same: to protect the best interests of the Korean minjok. The division was not about "who we are," but in which direction "we" should go. Thus, even as the two Koreas remain de facto separate states today—one a dictatorship and the other a democracy—a "strong, almost mythical vision of homogeneity permeates both parts of Korea."[9] The principle of one ethnic nation is officially upheld in political rhetoric and education on both sides and is invoked by each state to legitimize authority over the entirety of the Korean people and the peninsula.[10] The two

Koreas therefore represent a case of divided states within a singular nation, rather than a divided nation, preserving strong nation-state linkage within each.

As different factions competed for power in postwar South Korea, protecting the best interests of the Korean minjok remained the shared justification. Following the war, the anti-Communist faction in South Korea ruled with a strong hand, brutally repressing any remaining pro-Communist forces in the name of national survival. As authoritarian control peaked with Park Chung-hee's *Yusin* Constitution, however, a growing number of students, intellectuals, and laborers mobilized in dissent. This antiregime opposition gained political momentum through the late 1970s, blossoming into what would become known as the *minjung* movement and the driving force behind South Korea's eventual democratization in 1987.

Yet the way that the minjung movement framed its demand for democracy— as a restoration of the nation-state, rather than a rejection of it—is testament to the binding power of Korea's minjok-based national reimagination. The minjung movement united different oppressed segments of South Korean society under the principle of "three mins": minjung [people], minjok [nation], and minju [democracy].[11] At the heart of minjung was a call to revive the original, anticolonial conception of minjok nationhood, where power lay in the hands of the everyday people:[12] "In taking to the streets to protest dictatorship, labor exploitation, gender violence, and police abuse, South Korean citizens were symbolically designating themselves—the people—as the rightful subjects of their country's history."[13] The movement repurposed the familiar frame of protecting the autonomy of the Korean minjok from foreign powers but this time aimed it against the United States, which it saw to be propping up South Korea's military dictatorship for its own security interests.[14] In these ways, anticolonial discourse of minjok nationhood was recontextualized for postcolonial movements toward democratization. As historian Namhee Lee writes: "The rise of the *minjung* movement in South Korea was intimately tied to the critical reevaluation of modern Korean history; giving alternative and new meanings to past events was key to developing the notion of *minjung* in the *minjung* movement."[15]

Regime change typically results in abrupt disruptions to nation-state linkage. But Korea's national basis for democratization reified, rather than challenged, the strong nation-state linkage laid by the Korean minjok narrative nearly a century prior. The minjung movement was not primarily a liberal endeavor nor an opposition to the ancien régime. Rather, its mission was the restoration of the original minjok ideal that the rightful state is one that belongs to the national people. Charles Kim characterizes the "wholesome modernization" discourse that dominated student and youth dissident movements during this era as essentially one of recovering nation-state linkage: "It was premised on the idealistic belief that the unity of the Korean ethnos, or 'the people'—and, by extension, that of eth-nos and state—was actually realizable."[16] Thus, South Korea's democratic state today represents, in a deep sense, the successful self-determination of the Korean national people.

South Korea's nationally unified democracy today was not for lack of inter-nal conflict. Nor was it a structural given for having an ethnically homogeneous population. Rather, the inclusive appeal of a minjok-based national narrative, and strategic decisions by both incumbents and opposition to appeal to the nar-rative even as they competed for power, effectively constrained political discourse to remain within a singular national boundary.[17] National stories in South Korea should therefore embed strong beliefs of nation-state linkage for most citizens who are ethnically Korean. There should be little doubt that the democratic state represents the best interests of "my" nation, as opposed to any other nation. South Korea is thus a compelling positive case for the theory, where for most citizens I expect civic duty to be strongly rooted in a moral obligation to the Korean nation.

Taiwan: Weak Linkage in a Nationally Divided Democracy

The island democracy of Taiwan sits just southwest of the Korean peninsula and exhibits many parallels to South Korea. Among Third Wave democracies, "outside of Europe, few countries have consolidated democracy—and established a relatively liberal form of it—more quickly and successfully than South Korea . . . and Tai-wan."[18] Indeed, the two democracies followed nearly identical pathways to democ-ratization. Both were Japanese colonies in the early twentieth century, and after independence each endured a period of military authoritarianism until bottom-up pressures from domestic opposition catalyzed eventual democratization. Much like South Korea, Taiwan is also a democracy where there has been no shortage of nationalist fervor. Whether one identifies as Taiwanese determines most aspects of its democratic politics, from vote choice to partisanship to policy evaluations.[19]

Yet a very different nation-state landscape lies underneath in Taiwan, which John Hsieh describes as a "divided society."[20] To understand why, we must travel a bit further back than Japan's colonization. In the premodern period the island was gradually inhabited over centuries by native aborigines and various settlers who had migrated from the southern coast of modern-day China. Before the Japanese took over, the island was for a long time a peripheral territory of the Qing dynasty. Physical distance from the mainland meant that the island was haphazardly ruled. The Qing rulers made little effort to inculcate a centralized identity among the islanders: "If people thought about [identity] at all, most would probably have identified themselves as Chinese. They would also identify with their family or local village, with their ethnic group (Fukienese or Hakka), and among Fukienese, with place of origin in Fukien."[21]

Against such a backdrop, Japanese colonialism left a very different identity imprint in Taiwan than it did in Korea. The Japanese imposed a methodically centralized governing system and invested in the formal education of islanders through public education, rapidly transforming the island from a miscellany of merchants to a major rice producer with a landed middle class.[22] Such investments were for the benefit of the colonizers, who needed a strong food supply chain as Japan continued her imperial expansion into the Asia continent. Japanese colonialism was far from benevolent in Taiwan. Multiple islander uprisings were brutally put down, including systematic purges of islander elites. But in terms of its legacy on identity politics, the shared experience of colonialism under the Japanese forged a newfound sense of solidarity among the inhabitants as "the islanders."

Such developments set the stage for the relative disdain that many islanders felt toward the mainlander newcomers when the island was returned to Chinese rule after World War II. The Chinese Kuomintang (KMT) military that came over under the leadership of Chiang Kai-shek had less interest in ruling the island and more interest in winning back the mainland in the ongoing Chinese civil war. As China did not have a centralized military system at the time, many KMT soldiers were ruffians or of lower class, naturally clashing with the Japanese-educated islander elites. Tensions grew as the KMT treated islanders as second-class citizens and confiscated their land and resources to fund war efforts on the mainland. Many islanders who traced their origins back to mainland China felt deeply betrayed at the hands of what were supposed to be their own people. The return to Chinese rule under the KMT proved to be a "recolonization rather than decolonization."[23]

Brewing hostility between the islanders versus the Chinese KMT finally peaked in what is known as the 2–28 Incident. On February 28, 1947, a mass islander protest against the KMT regime was brutally put down through a massacre of civilians and a targeted purge of islander elites. Although the exact death toll is unknown, George Kerr—an American official who reportedly observed the incident firsthand—estimates that anywhere between ten thousand to twenty thousand islanders were killed. In one of the few surviving works of antigovernment historiography, Su Bing provides graphic details:

> As soon as [the KMT soldiers] landed in Keelung, they shouted, "The Taiwanese are not Chinese! Kill them! Kill them!" They fired and rushed

into the city. . . . Cutting off ears and noses of the arrested, amputating arm and legs, or pushing their victims off roofs, the Chinese soldiers went through a catalogue of massacres. Some people, bound together with several other people by wires piercing through their palms and ankles, were tied in a row, and were thrown into the Keelung Harbor.[24]

The identity rift between the mainlanders and islanders only grew deeper once the KMT migrated en masse to the island in 1949 after losing the Chinese civil war. Formally establishing the island state as the semipermanent base for the Republic of China, with the ultimate goal of recapturing the mainland, the KMT launched an aggressive re-Sinicization effort across the island. This nationalization campaign included prohibiting the use of all local islander dialects and customs. Textbooks were rewritten to include only the history of the Chinese mainland, and the National Palace Museum showcased only the Chinese cultural relics that the KMT had raided from the mainland.[25] There was an urgent sense among the KMT elite that the success of re-Sinicization was directly linked to their potential return to the mainland. Embodiment of Chinese nationalist culture was seen as "a kind of *totalizing* force" for the island state, "in so far as its fate was perceived to be synonymous with the national destiny itself."[26]

Yet the KMT's nationalization efforts backfired. The aggressive and often violent imposition of a Chinese national identity that had all but grown distant to most islanders over generations of physical separation "ended up emphasizing, rather than muting, the differences between [the mainland Chinese] view of culture and the Taiwanese."[27] The KMT had underestimated the depth of antagonism that many islanders already harbored toward the mainlanders—one that was ironically rooted in the belief of coethnicity that many islanders saw to be betrayed.

The KMT's re-Sinicization efforts therefore resulted in exactly the opposite of the intended effect: they stirred the beginnings of a Taiwanese national identity, as separate from a Chinese identity. The KMT's re-Sinicization campaign laid bare the linguistic and cultural divides that had grown over time between the once coethnic groups. Even though many islanders recognized their shared Han Chinese origins with the mainlanders, generations of distinct historical experiences—from Dutch imperialism in the seventeenth century to tensions with native aborigines to Japanese colonialism in the twentieth century—had forged a unique political consciousness among islanders. Unlike the mainlanders, who were tellingly referred to as *waishengren*—literally "out of province people"—and who saw return to the mainland as fulfilling their national destiny, the Taiwanese were already in their national home.

The Taiwanese nationalist movement gained political momentum through the 1970s, organizing in opposition to the KMT as *dangwai* or "outside the party."

The dangwai movement united grievances against the KMT regime under the banner of Taiwanese nationalism and pushed for democratization.[28] Unlike in South Korea, however, democratization in Taiwan was framed not as a restoration of nation-state linkage that had been lost. Rather, democratization was a means to achieve nation-state linkage for the first time, something that had never existed for Taiwanese living under a KMT-controlled state. The struggle for democratization was fundamentally a competition between two competing factions over which nationalist vision the state would represent.[29]

Growing bottom-up pressures, along with then-KMT leader Chiang Ching-kuo's personal commitments to liberalism, pushed the KMT state to gradually democratize, leading to the first direct presidential election in 1996. Yet democratization failed to be the blanket victory that Taiwan nationalists had imagined. The pro-Taiwan opposition formalized as the Democratic Progressive Party (DPP) but found itself significantly disadvantaged against the well-resourced and well-entrenched KMT party. The DPP lost the first democratic election, and while it took over the presidency from 2000 to 2008, Chen Shui-bian's turbulent incumbency meant that the DPP did not gain solid footing until its recent return under Tsai Ing-wen.[30] Thus, democratization failed to mark the beginning of a new nation-state unequivocally centered on Taiwanese national identity. Instead, democratization simply refashioned the preexisting nationalist conflict into competing political parties based on fundamentally different visions for Taiwan.[31] Thus, unlike in South Korea, where restoring nation-state linkage served as the impetus behind democratization, Taiwanese democracy was born into a bifurcated nationalist landscape.

National identity remains divided on the island today. Most citizens of islander descent identify as "Taiwanese only" in surveys and see Taiwan as a separate nation from China, both culturally and politically. In this book I refer to them as "Taiwan nationalists." Meanwhile, many in the younger generation have moved past the ethnic tensions that once defined islander versus mainlander conflict. Part of this shift has been the natural result of generational turnover, in addition to the fruits of a bipartisan effort led by former president Lee Teng-hui to create a new, civic Taiwanese identity.[32] These individuals identify as Taiwanese in the political sense of seeing Taiwan as a democratic nation independent from China. I label this group as "New Taiwanese" (*xin Taiwanren*). Finally, a minority of citizens who descended from the mainlander KMT and still see Taiwan to be part of a larger Chinese nation identify as "both Taiwanese and Chinese" in surveys. An even smaller subset of this group used to identify as "Chinese only," but that segment has all but disappeared in recent years as Taiwan's de facto independence has solidified. Thus, under a single state, national imaginations remain divided and contested. What "Taiwan" means to a particular citizen comes down to "a question of personal history"[33]—of when one's family migrated to the island and their experiences under KMT rule.

What about the national identity of the state? In an electoral sense the KMT has held the presidency for a cumulatively longer period since democratization and was the incumbent party at the time that most of the data for this book were collected in 2013.[34] But in a deeper sense the power legacies of what used to be an exclusively KMT-controlled state still cast a long shadow over how most ordinary citizens view national ownership of the democratic state. During military rule the KMT embedded its China nationalist vision into the very infrastructure of the state, from appointing mainlanders to leadership positions of key bureaus to establishing a surveillance system that reached deep into Taiwanese society to monitor political dissidents.[35] And even though Taiwan's democratization owed a great deal to bottom-up pressures by the opposition, its timing was a prime example of what Dan Slater and Joseph Wong call democratization by the "strength to concede."[36] The KMT was well aware of its electoral advantage in terms of political resources, connections, and party institutionalization.[37] It also maintained control over the political narrative through regime change, framing liberalization as the final step of fulfilling the "Three Principles of the People" of Sun Yat-sen—none other than the Chinese revolutionary and founding father of the KMT—rather than as a concession to the DPP. Thus, from an institutional perspective, both in terms of who currently holds more power and the historical pattern of state ownership, the democratic state still largely reflects the KMT's nationalist vision.

At the societal level, persistent norms that date back to the days of KMT rule also shape the public's beliefs about the pro-KMT identity of the state. For instance, most civil servants are still of mainlander descent. Civil service, especially within the military, is seen as a kind of family profession within this group, a legacy from the days when state leadership positions were almost exclusively restricted to mainlanders. That one of the first reforms enacted by Chen Shui-bian, the first DPP president, was to diversify the ethnic backgrounds of senior military officers is telling. Former Defense Minister Andrew Yang explains the reason for such overhaul regarding the military, the oldest branch of the state: "This is a national armed forces. It doesn't serve any political party. But ordinary citizens still get this idea that the armed forces is in favor of [the KMT], because you have a long history of the military, party, and country being unified as one entity. So they still have this impression."[38]

Indeed, if one visits Taiwan without any knowledge of its political history, every "national" monument or institution—from the Chiang Kai-shek Memorial to the Chinese cultural relics in the National Palace Museum to National Sun Yat-sen University—pays homage to the KMT's China nationalist vision for the island. And while the island democracy is colloquially referred to as Taiwan, its official name still reflects its national identity as it was established by the KMT: the Republic of China. Thus, most ordinary citizens still perceive the democratic state to be biased in favor of the KMT's China nationalist vision—and particularly so under a KMT incumbent president.

Thus, unlike in South Korea, beliefs of nation-state linkage should be fractured for many citizens in Taiwan. For self-identified Taiwan nationalists, what many still see as a KMT legacy state cannot represent the best interests of "my" nation. Linkage will be similarly fractured for New Taiwanese. If Taiwan is a nation defined by its democratic values, then it should be independent from authoritarian China. But as long as democratic Taiwan remains within the power hold of Beijing, it cannot fully represent this civic nationalist vision. The only group for whom nation-state linkage should be strong is the minority of China nationalists. Taiwan therefore serves as an illuminating comparison to South Korea. Despite similarly fervent nationalisms and successful democratization, it is a negative case for the theory, where a sense of obligation to "my" nation should fail to exert any significant pull toward civic duty for most citizens.

How do these contrasting beliefs of nation-state linkage in South Korea versus Taiwan manifest? How are they learned and internalized? The next section breathes life into the idea of national stories by examining how they work in the context of civic duty toward military service in both democracies. I find that nation-state linkage is learned primarily in the home through specific national scripts embedded in national stories. These scripts dictate how one ought to behave toward other groups as a member of a particular nation, including the state. They serve as a moral guide for what a real Korean or good Taiwanese owes to the state as it makes demands on the lives of the national people.

National Stories and Military Duty in South Korea and Taiwan

To see how national stories come to shape a sense of civic duty toward military service in South Korea versus Taiwan, I apply a process tracing method to the written and oral personal narratives of volunteer soldiers in the two democracies. Process tracing is conventionally used in comparative historical analysis, where the sequencing of critical events is used to determine cause and effect. I apply this method to the analysis of an individual's personal history. By identifying the critical junctures of a person's life from childhood to adulthood, I trace how national membership is seeded, how nation-state linkage is learned through national stories, and how it grows into a durable lens through which one sees the various demands and expectations of one's democracy, including military service.

South Korea and Taiwan both have compulsory military service, but there are pockets for whom service is essentially voluntary, where it makes sense to examine a sense of civic duty to serve beyond what is mandated by law.[39] I compare the surprising civic duty among overseas Koreans who return to serve in the military despite having the option to become legally exempt versus the generally weak civic duty among Taiwanese youth to sign up for the all-volunteer force (AVF). Both democracies face real security threats from unresolved and escalating disputes with authoritarian brother-sister regimes of North Korea and China. Yet the ways in which South Korean and Taiwanese youth have responded to the military needs of their states have been strikingly different, not just in the number of volunteer soldiers, but more importantly, in their justifications for why they choose or refuse to serve. This chapter uncovers the national stories behind these differences.

South Korea: Overseas Koreans as Volunteer Soldiers

"Overseas Korean" refers to a South Korean citizen who is also a permanent resident or citizen of another country.[40] Overseas Korean men are still required to serve in the military, but a commonly exercised pathway to legal exemption exists: one can maintain permanent residence in a foreign country and delay military service until the age of thirty-six, at which time the obligation expires. Because of this option, military service is typically seen as a matter of choice for overseas Koreans.

Exercising that choice usually proved to be a catch-22, however. Forgoing military service meant having to reside outside South Korea until age thirty-six, which effectively closed the door on having a career or basis for permanent return to South Korea. On the other hand, serving in the military often jeopardized permanent residency status in most foreign countries, which requires continuous, full-time residency. A two-year absence for military service violates that condition.

In 2004 the South Korean government instituted a new policy for overseas Koreans. For those willing to fulfill their military service, the government now pays for round-trip flights to the country of foreign residence during scheduled military breaks and for the return flight back after completion of service. The scheduled returns break up the two-year service period so that it no longer jeopardizes permanent residency status and greatly eases the financial burden.

Still, choosing military service is hardly an alluring proposition for overseas Koreans. Service takes two years away from what is usually a pivotal time in a young man's career trajectory, and the opportunity costs are almost always higher than the nominal government salary. Overseas Koreans also face significant cultural costs. Many grew up in a foreign country for most or all their lives, in societies with typically less stringent hierarchies than in South Korea. Entering the Korean military is therefore a daunting prospect.

Yet, as figure 3.1 shows, the number of overseas Korean soldiers has grown exponentially since the policy was enacted. As of 2016, a total of 3,379 men have chosen to serve. The South Korean government often points to these numbers as exemplary displays of patriotism. This interpretation is not wrong, but my analysis of over 150 personal narrative essays from overseas Korean soldiers suggests that the truth is more nuanced. It is not necessarily that a love for Korea runs so deep that it blinds these men to the costs of military service. Rather, for many of them, military service is about enacting an internalized national script—learned from national stories told by their fathers and grandfathers—that dictates that a real Korean man sacrifices for the state. For overseas Koreans who choose to identify as Korean, military service is therefore seen as a matter of duty, rather than a matter of choice.

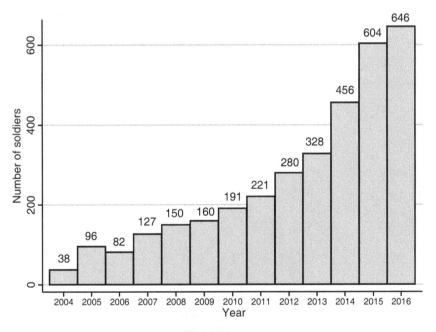

FIGURE 3.1.   Trend in number of overseas Korean soldiers. Statistics are from South Korea's Military Manpower Administration.

Taiwan: Transition to an All-Volunteer Force (AVF)

A different kind of shift in military policy has been unfolding in neighboring Taiwan. In efforts to modernize defense, the government has been transitioning away from conscription and toward an AVF model, where most of the military would be made up of full-time, professional soldiers.[41] The initial goal was to complete the transition by 2014, where 176,000 soldiers or about 80 percent of military manpower would consist of AVF recruits. But that deadline was quickly pushed back as recruitment fell dismally short of the government quota in the initial years of the program, as figure 3.2 shows. Recruitment appears improved since 2014, but the gain is superficial: it is the result of "a downward revision of the annual benchmark to an easily achievable number."[42] Even with the government offering increasingly attractive benefits packages, the number of recruits has capped at a barely sustainable rate to keep AVF afloat. At the time of writing, the future of AVF still remains unclear.

The poor recruitment rate is surprising when one looks at the incentives offered for AVF. In 2014 the Executive Yuan increased the monthly salary for AVF soldiers, bringing up the base to NT $33,625, or a little over $1,100.[43] That makes AVF competitive with other entry-level jobs, as the Ministry of Labor estimated the average monthly salary for a recent college graduate to be NT $25,175 in 2013. In fact, the national average salary for all jobs is NT $37,771, just slightly higher than AVF's starting base. Financially, AVF is a sensible and even attractive option.

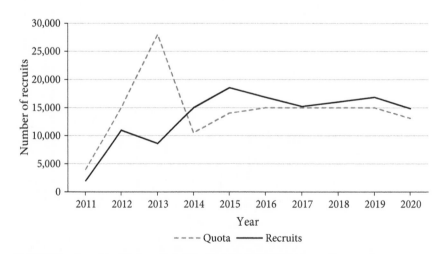

FIGURE 3.2. Recruitment for Taiwan's All-Volunteer Force (AVF). Statistics are from the Republic of China's Ministry of National Defense.

So why are not more Taiwanese youth choosing to serve in AVF? Defense scholars in Taiwan generally point to two reasons. The first is that a military profession carries a negative cultural stigma. "Good iron does not make nails; good men do not make soldiers" is a well-known Confucian proverb that has particular salience in Taiwanese society because of the hostilities that many islanders suffered at the hands of the KMT military.[44] As Arthur Ding, a prominent military scholar in Taiwan, notes: "There was no so-called military institution or a well-established conscription system in China at the time, so soldiers were mostly peasants from the countryside."[45] For many islanders, the KMT soldiers affirmed the low social and moral status of soldiers such that even today Sydney Chu, a professor at the Military Academy, notes that "joining the army or taking arms is not the mainstream of our Confucianism."[46]

A second reason is corruption in the military. A generalized distrust of the military dates back to the days of KMT martial rule, but recent events have exacerbated such perceptions. On July 4, 2013, a conscript named Hung Chung-chiu died during routine training, leading to widespread speculation of physical abuse by his superiors. The lack of transparency in the KMT government's initial response sparked a series of student protests, with more than 100,000 youth taking to the streets.[47] While the protests successfully instigated a public investigation that indicted thirty-seven military officers for the death, the incident confirmed long-held suspicions of corruption and abuse in the military—a "fatal blow" to the state's recruitment efforts for AVF.[48]

Cultural stigma and low trust in the military certainly deter some potential recruits. Yet in personal narrative interviews with Taiwanese youth, I uncover another powerful reason that is missing from public discourse about AVF: fractured or even opposed beliefs of nation-state linkage. Many Taiwanese youth see AVF through a national lens, rather than assessing costs and benefits. Taiwanese national stories ingrain a deep belief among many Taiwanese youth that serving "my" nation and serving the state are two different things. In fact, they are opposed: serving in AVF is seen as a betrayal of Taiwanese national identity. Thus, unlike many overseas Koreans, for whom military service is seen as a natural duty of a Korean man, serving in AVF invokes little sense of national duty for most Taiwanese youth. The next section turns to the personal narratives of both youth groups to show how national stories come to be such a powerful frame.

Personal Narrative Analysis

I collected nearly two hundred written and oral personal narratives from current and potential military recruits in South Korea and Taiwan. Personal narratives are stories that individuals tell about their own lives, in their own words. Unlike a standard question-and-answer format interview, personal narrative interviews are open-ended and grant story-telling agency to the individual. The subject is free to choose the significant characters and events in his life and connect them in ways that are meaningful to him. Personal narratives are therefore richly informative about a person's worldview—his sense of right and wrong, agency and blame, and cause and effect.[49] As sociologist Robert Wuthnow explains: "Narratives are the cultural frameworks in which individuals interpret their social situations, imagine themselves in other situations, and make choices about who they want to be and how to behave."[50] For these reasons, personal narratives are a powerful tool for understanding "why certain actions are taken or not taken."[51]

In South Korea, I collected 153 personal narrative essays written by overseas Korean soldiers between 2007 and 2013. The Military Manpower Administration (MMA) publishes an annual collection of essays, titled *Daehansaram Daehaneuro*,[52] written by overseas Korean soldiers about their decision to serve and their military experience. There are obvious trade-offs in relying on personal narratives selected by the MMA. On the one hand, the MMA narratives are high quality and drawn from exactly the sample that this study aims to understand. On the other hand, the MMA collection excludes the narratives of overseas Koreans who chose not to serve. Research on emigration suggests that most "new wave" overseas Koreans—those who left in the 1960s and onwards—were pulled by better economic opportunities and therefore maintain positive national ties to South Korea.[53] But some families could have left Korea due to political persecution during the authoritarian period and likely harbor very different kinds of national stories. The MMA sample excludes such cases.

For the analytical purpose of this chapter, I weigh more heavily the benefits of using the MMA sample. The bias from excluding the narratives of nonserving overseas Koreans is problematic if the goal is to estimate the population effect of a set of variables on the civic duty to serve among overseas Koreans. The goal of this chapter, however, is illustrative rather than predictive. The aim is to process trace *how* a sense of civic duty develops among those overseas Koreans who do choose to serve, seemingly despite the odds. For that purpose, sampling on the unlikely outcome is a sensible strategy.

For Taiwan, I conducted forty-one personal narrative interviews with current and potential AVF recruits. Since low recruitment despite attractive incentives is the puzzle to be explained in Taiwan, most individuals in the sample are men who have chosen not to serve in AVF. Most interviews were conducted face-to-face over several months in 2013, with a supplementary round conducted virtually. I snowball-sampled college students from two universities—National Chengchi University near Taipei and Sun Yat-sen University in Kaohsiung.[54] In Taiwan, where national identity is fragmented, this geographic sampling maximizes the potential range of national stories captured through the interviews. Historically, Taipei and the northern part of the island tend to lean pro-KMT, whereas Kaohsiung in the south is the birthplace of the Taiwanese opposition. Mirroring the essay prompt in South Korea, the interview protocol in Taiwan asked subjects to share stories from their life that led to their decision on AVF. The interviews were open-ended with occasional steering questions to ensure that I collected enough stories from each life period to identify the critical junctures.

All personal narratives were analyzed using within- and cross-case methods recommended for qualitative causal analysis.[55] Within-case analysis focuses on identifying the causal arc that drives a specific personal narrative. Each subject's narrative was process traced into a "data map" that identifies the critical juncture(s): a visual mapping of the distinct periods that emerge from a person's life story and the corresponding rhetorical schema that appear in each. Cross-case analysis then examines whether certain causal arcs constitute a more general pattern across groups. This is done through a matrix display, where each data map is refashioned linearly as a single row in a matrix. Each row displays the top-level schema codes for distinct life periods, such that it is possible to visually group together personal narratives with similar causal arcs. The cross-case step is particularly useful for analyzing personal narratives in Taiwan, where nationalist history suggests that distinct national stories should emerge across different national identity groups.

Personal narrative analysis grants a fascinating look into how nation-state linkage is learned through national stories. National stories are typically shared within the home, from stories that grandparents tell of the "olden times" during family gatherings to more intimate stories shared from father to son about their childhoods. When told across generations, national stories gain a dimension of parable. Lessons learned are crystalized in national scripts. These are specific behavioral prescriptions on how a real Korean or a good Taiwanese should behave, including how they should interact with the state—whether to support, avoid, or oppose it. Such scripts are part of what sociologist Ann Swidler calls a "tool kit" of "symbols, stories, rituals, and world-views, which people may use in varying configurations to solve different kinds of problems."[56] The nature of nation-state linkage is reflected in these "strategies of action" that national members use to navigate their political actions and decisions.

Long before they face the choice of military service, overseas Koreans and Taiwanese youth have been socialized into distinct national scripts. They access different moral blueprints on how to respond to the state's demand. Many overseas Koreans, even if they have spent limited time in Korea, grew up on national stories from their fathers and grandfathers that painted military service as a natural part of becoming a real Korean man. In contrast, many Taiwanese youth have learned from their parents and grandparents that a good Taiwanese is one who is always wary of the state—a national script hardened over decades of islander repression and persecution during KMT rule. As the second friend in the opening dialogue of this chapter asks: "Who does [the military] really protect, us Taiwanese?" Thus, for most Taiwanese youth, military service is a subject of doubt, rather than duty.

Overseas Korean Soldiers and Becoming a "Real" Korean

At first blush the personal narratives of overseas Korean soldiers suggest zealous patriots. References to claiming one's "Koreanness" abound. Yet this characterization belies the more nuanced way that nation, state, and military duty are interlinked. What frames military service as a matter of civic duty for many in this sample is a deeply ingrained Korean national script that a real Korean man is one who sacrifices for the state. Most overseas Koreans receive little to no Korean public education and thus little exposure to state-led efforts to inculcate military service as a constitutional duty.[57] Rather, this script is learned within the home, from the national stories that fathers tell their sons.

On the surface the national stories appear to be personal anecdotes from the fathers' early life in South Korea. But the national people's historicized relationship to the South Korean state is seamlessly woven through these personal memories, especially in the fathers' stories about their own military service: stories about how serving in the military changed them for the better; how it taught them to be "true sons of the nation"; how they made lifelong friends with those in their military cohorts. Often, the fathers' stories reference national stories, as told to them by the grandfathers, of the hardships of living through the Korean War and how the state military became an integral part of national survival after the division.

Strong nation-state linkage is embedded in the seeming inseparability between Korean manhood and fulfilling military service to the state. The statement that "to become a real Korean man, you have to serve in the military"[58] is common to the point of being a national idiom. Subjects frequently connect military service with the notion of continuing the Korean and family bloodline. The excerpts below show that phrases such as "Korean blood coursing through his veins," "invisible tie," and "my father and grandfather before that" are used to explain or justify why military service is seen as "a given," "my duty," or "no longer a choice":

> I am embarrassed when people call me a patriot. I just really love this young and vibrant country called Korea. . . . As someone who was born in Korea, speaks Korean, and has Korean blood coursing through his veins, serving in the military is a given.[59]

Probably my most honest answer is "because I felt like I should." I think that all men who are born in Korea are connected with an invisible tie called the military. Whether you lived abroad for a long time or have permanent residency elsewhere, this is the way it is for Korean men.[60]

This is not something that should be, or that I want to be, praised for doing. I am simply serving right now because it is my duty, as it was for my father and grandfather.[61]

Why did I have to be given the choice? It tormented me. Then I began to think of my grandfather who passed away in 2002. He strictly forbade me from speaking English or acting American in the house. "You are Korean, so do not be afraid and proudly face the world head on," he would say. At that moment, I realized that [serving in the military] was no longer a choice.[62]

The critical juncture that activates this national script is usually a catalyst that brings a festering identity struggle to a head. Many overseas Koreans wrote about being torn between dual national identities. An acute experience of "othering" in their country of residence would typically force an identity choice, and for those who choose to identify as Korean, returning for military service is seen as a natural rite of passage. The following excerpt illustrates this common narrative arc:

"Where are you from?" When a foreign friend would ask me, I would give a long explanation of how I was an ethnic Korean who was born, raised, and calls Indonesia home. Then I came to Korea for university. I'm not mixed race and I'm fluent in Korean, unlike most overseas Koreans. But because of this, it was harder. On the outside and by how I speak, I was 100% Korean, but culturally, I was totally different. I became more and more stressed about having to behave like a natural Korean. . . . Perhaps there were many reasons for deciding to go to the military, but I think the biggest reason was that I felt like I was getting lost in the ambiguity of who I am—where I'm from and what Korea means to me.[63]

The centrality of military duty to national survival is due to South Korea's precarious situation after the Korean War, where protecting the country from a potential Communist infiltration from the North was seen as the top security priority. Military conscription was seen as a national necessity. Such history is intricately woven into the national stories told within the home. The repertoire of sacrificial citizenship passed down from Korean father to son explains why, despite real financial and cultural costs, many overseas Koreans feel a sense of civic duty to return for military service—and do so in the name of the nation.

Fighting for Whom?
Taiwanese Youth's Reluctance toward AVF

Personal narrative interviews with forty-one Taiwanese youth about their stance on AVF reveal very different kinds of national stories that associate being a good Taiwanese with counterstate citizenship. To be Taiwanese is to always be wary of the state's intent. This national script embodies the fractured or opposed beliefs of nation-state linkage that can be traced back to the history of islander abuse and exploitation by the ruling KMT state. Such history is largely excluded from the public curriculum, but it is nevertheless kept alive through the national stories that Taiwanese grandparents and parents tell about life under martial law. Thus, while many Taiwanese youth express deep love for their nation and are willing to fight for it, serving in AVF is seen as contrary to "who I am" and evokes little sense of national duty or honor.

Figure 3.3 shows a particularly illuminating data map of Subject #5, organized by the critical junctures that emerged from his personal narrative. The top left quadrant shows that a Taiwanese identity is seeded early within the home through national stories that draw a boundary between a Taiwanese "us" versus a Chinese "them." Recalling significant memories from his childhood, the subject shares that at every family gathering, his grandfather would rally the children and tell stories about the days of KMT rule and brutality against the Taiwanese as if they were "ghost stories." Mentioning his first family trip to Beijing, he remembers how his parents would comment that "we" do not spit on the street or talk loudly. His parents never explicitly discussed elections or politics with him growing up, but he notes that they only watch "green" television at home.[64]

Moving to the top right, we see that a counterstate national script gels as the national stories the subject grew up with color his interactions with the state. A critical juncture for the subject occurs in high school when he is dismayed at the discrepancy between the textbooks versus what he had learned from his grandparents: "Chiang Kai-shek is not a hero. He killed a lot of Taiwanese!"[65] This sense of betrayal by the state intensifies during university years as he follows Taiwan's trade deals with China: "[The government] failed to protect ordinary Taiwanese. It only cares about the *waisheng* businessmen who give a lot of money to the government." When the Hung Chung-chiu incident came to light, the subject joined the protests that summer for a public investigation of the military. Such experiences affirm a political instinct that has been fostered early in the home: "A good citizen should supervise the state. Make sure that it is protecting the people."

The bottom rows illustrate how this counterstate national script frames the subject's views of the military and ultimately shapes his decision not to serve in

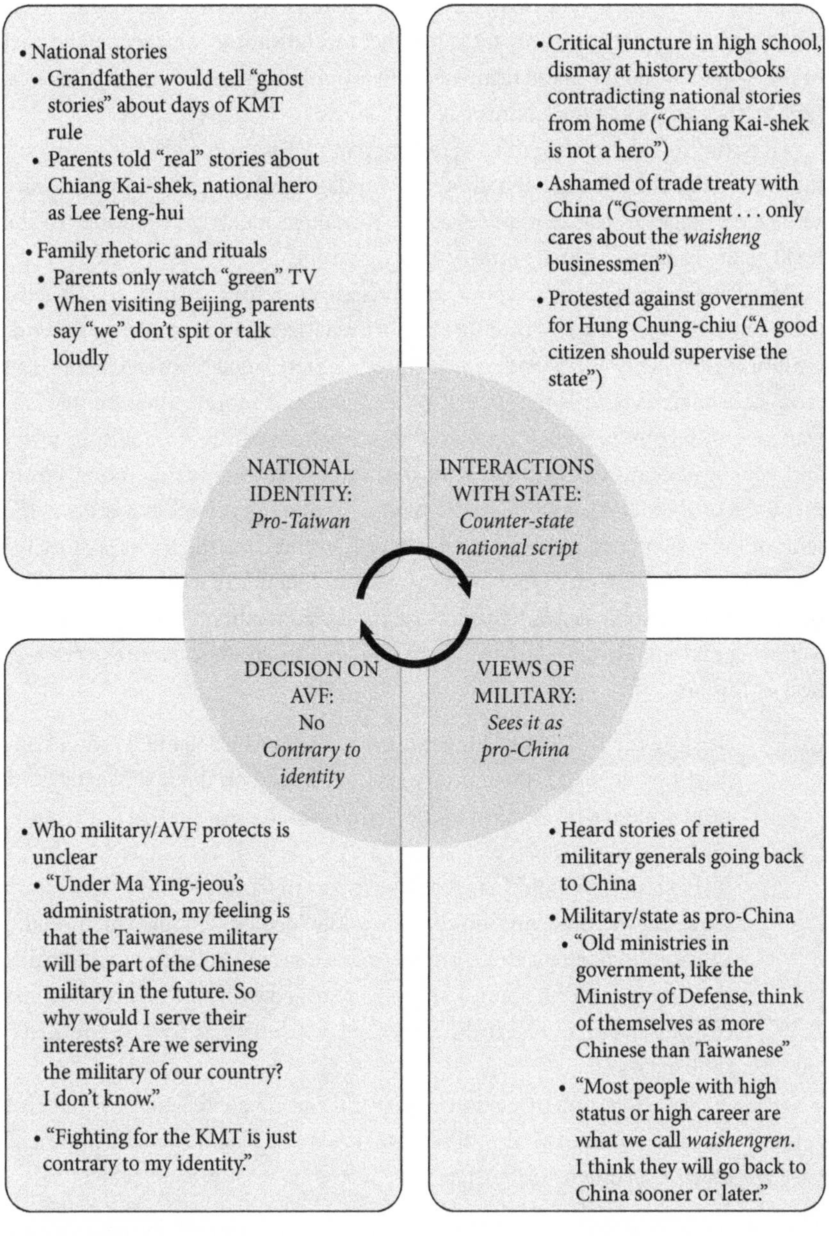

- National stories
  - Grandfather would tell "ghost stories" about days of KMT rule
  - Parents told "real" stories about Chiang Kai-shek, national hero as Lee Teng-hui

- Family rhetoric and rituals
  - Parents only watch "green" TV
  - When visiting Beijing, parents say "we" don't spit or talk loudly

- Critical juncture in high school, dismay at history textbooks contradicting national stories from home ("Chiang Kai-shek is not a hero")
- Ashamed of trade treaty with China ("Government . . . only cares about the *waisheng* businessmen")
- Protested against government for Hung Chung-chiu ("A good citizen should supervise the state")

NATIONAL IDENTITY:
Pro-Taiwan

INTERACTIONS WITH STATE:
Counter-state national script

DECISION ON AVF:
No
Contrary to identity

VIEWS OF MILITARY:
Sees it as pro-China

- Who military/AVF protects is unclear
- "Under Ma Ying-jeou's administration, my feeling is that the Taiwanese military will be part of the Chinese military in the future. So why would I serve their interests? Are we serving the military of our country? I don't know."

- "Fighting for the KMT is just contrary to my identity."

- Heard stories of retired military generals going back to China
- Military/state as pro-China
  - "Old ministries in government, like the Ministry of Defense, think of themselves as more Chinese than Taiwanese"

- "Most people with high status or high career are what we call *waishengren*. I think they will go back to China sooner or later."

FIGURE 3.3. Data map of a Taiwanese personal narrative.

AVF. Almost every statement about the military is focused on the perception that, deep down, it is not committed to protecting Taiwanese people. Specifically, "on the table, the enemy is very clear. But under the table, we don't know. Under Ma Ying-jeou's administration, my feeling is that the Taiwanese military will be part of the Chinese military in the future. So why would I serve their interests? Are we serving the military of our country? I don't know."

Thus, for the subject in figure 3.3, rejection of AVF is ultimately not about cultural stigma or risks. Rather, it is about the fundamental dissonance that military service on behalf of the state poses to his Taiwanese identity: "Fighting for the KMT [state military] is just contrary to my identity."

The Taiwanese national script of counterstate citizenship, which starkly contrasts with the Korean script of state-supportive citizenship, is rooted in the contentious history between islanders and the KMT state ruled by mainlanders. But cross-case analysis reveals that it is also sustained by a more contemporary Taiwanese group consciousness fixated on enduring inequalities in political power and economic status. Group consciousness is "a self-awareness among group members of their status as a deprived group,"[66] where deprivation is seen as the fault of the system, not the individual. Many Taiwanese see the legacies of exclusive KMT rule as the root of that unfair system and therefore see the best interests of the national people as something to be protected from, not by, the state. The following excerpts from the narratives of pro-Taiwan youth show the pervasiveness of this lens:

> Because the KMT has a longer history, and because the ROC was established by the KMT, the military system is based on the KMT system. So, most military officers or soldiers are favorable to the KMT direction. (Subject #6)
>
> In class, they would say that we are part of China. I was in elementary school at the time, and I didn't know the ideology behind the thought, so I had no feelings. But a professor at university delivered a totally different way to think about it. I was so stunned by how we have the same education but think so differently. It was brainwashing by the KMT. (Subject #17)
>
> The government is almost all *waisheng*. Their thinking is different and life standard is also different. Taiwanese are poorer, and *waisheng* have government support, so they have a better life. (Subject #4)

The Taiwanese national script decouples the idea of a good Taiwanese from a good citizen and antagonizes them, whereas the Korean national script fuses them together. A good Taiwanese is not someone who sacrifices for the state, but one who monitors, questions, and keeps his distance from it. As Subject #9, whose father had been punished during the authoritarian period for speaking Taiwanese in public, chillingly said: "Most parents in Taiwan would tell their children not to be involved in political affairs, because that's how they are alive now."

Of all the state branches, the military is most susceptible to this Taiwanese national script, as the Republic of China was officially established by the KMT military: "During the martial law period from 1949–87 the military was loyal not to the state but to the ruling party, the Kuomintang (KMT). The ruling party and military were effectively one and the same."[67] Thus, for many Taiwanese youth, serving in AVF violates a basic national ethos and inspires little sense of civic duty in the name of nation.

Of course, the island is home to different strains of national stories, and an important counterpoint is the national script learned in pro-China identifying families. Such individuals are rare in the younger generation, but I was able to identify one such individual in my sample. Subject #12 comes from a two-generation family of civil servants and calls his home Taipei, not Taiwan, since "other people won't think Taiwan is a country." The way that he approaches military service is fundamentally different from that of pro-Taiwan youth. Talking about AVF as a form of civil service, he describes the importance of continuing the family tradition: "After university, I plan to work for the government just like my father and grandfather did before me. I can make more money doing other things, I'm sure, but to me, it's the most honorable thing to do." Yet he is resistant to sign up for AVF, not for reasons of national identity but due to concerns about the current military's effectiveness. "Because now we only have to do military for one year, rather than two years, my father says that the military [during his time] was stronger than the military now. He said that is not a military—that is just for fun, like a club, getting together for one year." If the military were to reform back to a serious defense system for the state, he would serve: "If the military gave us a better impression, that it is honorable and good for our country, then I would volunteer."

So who are the volunteers currently serving in AVF? I have only three such individuals in my sample, but a common thread across their personal narratives is a lack of strong nationalist socialization. All three individuals came from households that, for one reason or another, prioritized social mobility of the nuclear family over national loyalties. With no clear national story outlining a moral linkage to the state, these individuals approach AVF from a predominantly cost-benefit point of view. For instance, a woman in an administrative position for AVF explains that "the pay is really good," and that she doesn't think of it as a matter of national allegiance: "Green or blue, I think that's something that belongs to the last generation. As long as it's good for Taiwan, and for my family,

I don't care what happens." Similarly, a man in AVF said he joined because his father, who runs a small restaurant in Kaohsiung, saw it as an opportunity to climb the social ladder: "Unlike him, I graduated from university. So he thought I could rise very quickly up the ranks in the military."

The narrative analysis reveals the centrality of national stories to AVF's recruitment problem. A direct implication is that the government needs to shift its recruitment strategy, which has been focused on increasing benefits to attract soldiers. Such efforts are likely to fall on deaf ears for many Taiwanese youth whose reluctance to serve in AVF is a matter of identity. Chingpu Chen, a defense scholar in Taiwan, explains the limits of an incentive-based recruitment strategy:

> Right now, the government is portraying [AVF] as a good benefit to attract young people to come. And they come, find out it's not the case, and they leave. That's a very short-sighted policy. Because the message that you send out to people is that this is a job, a temporary job. . . . But I think human nature is, if you want me to sacrifice, you have to tell me my sacrifice is worth something. That something can be your family or your country. You have to instill this kind of value.[68]

That intrinsic value, which tells youth that "my sacrifice is worth something," lies not in increasing a salary but in repairing the historically damaged linkage between the Taiwanese people and the state. As Andrew Yang, former minister of national defense from 2013, points out: "A lot of young people identify themselves as 'we are Taiwan and Taiwanese.' . . . That certainly has some impact in terms of attracting the young people to join the armed forces, because they don't consider the ROC armed forces as the honorable, respectable institution that can really shoulder the responsibility to protect the Taiwanese people. It is not a symbol of the nation."[69]

Divergent nationalist histories in South Korea and Taiwan produced distinct flavors of national stories. Despite a great number of historical, political, and demographic similarities, different strategic decisions by nationalist leaders resulted in contrasting national linkages to the state, making the two democracies a compelling pair through which to examine a national theory of civic duty.

Using the case of civic duty toward military service, I illustrated what national stories look like at the level of family vernaculars. The collective know-how of a national people, which reflect lessons learned from historical experiences with the state, are codified into specific national scripts that dictate how a member of the nation should behave toward the state. Such scripts are learned through the national stories that parents and grandparents tell their children about the generations that came before them. None of the personal narratives mentioned anything like "nation-state linkage." But the analysis shows how that relational linkage is crystalized into national scripts that become second nature. A Korean script that associates state-supportive citizenship with being a real Korean frames military service as a natural duty for overseas Koreans who choose to identify as Korean. In contrast, for many Taiwanese youth, a script that ties being a good Taiwanese with counterstate citizenship frames serving in AVF as something that is opposed to, and even a betrayal of, one's national identity.

It is not that Taiwanese youth are any less committed to protecting their nation than overseas Koreans.[70] Speaking to almost any young Taiwanese will dispel such notion in an instant. Rather, that deep sense of national obligation remains disconnected from the state and military service. As Subject #6 put it bluntly, "If somebody attacked us, I will protect the island. Even if I die, I will protect my family, my people. But not my government."

By tracing how national stories come to elicit such differing moral attachments to the state, the chapter brings to life the contrasting predictions about the national basis of civic duty in South Korea versus Taiwan. We should expect to see a strong national effect on civic duty across most South Koreans, whereas for the majority of citizens in Taiwan the national effect on civic duty should be negligible or even negative. In the next two chapters I expand the empirical analysis to nationally representative surveys and experiments to rigorously test these predictions, looking at other forms of civic duty beyond military service that all democracies share and need.

STRONG CIVIC DUTY IN THE NAME OF NATION IN SOUTH KOREA

When asked why she donated her wedding rings to the national gold drives during the Asian financial crisis in South Korea, Mrs. Han's answer was simple: "It was the only right thing to do. . . . It's what we have always done for Korea." I traced the root of this answer to South Korea's minjok-based nationalist history and the unifying national stories it produced. Widespread beliefs of nation-state linkage in South Korea should harness the moral pull of the nation in support of the democratic state for most citizens, motivating a sense of civic duty to contribute to it. To what extent does the touching sentiment expressed by Mrs. Han describe the broader South Korean citizenry?

I turn to two empirical studies in South Korea to systematically test the power of a national pull toward civic duty.[1] Both studies are replicated in Taiwan in chapter 5, where the theory yields contrasting predictions. Here, I begin with a nationally representative survey of South Korean citizens to examine the national effect on two common manifestations of civic duty in democracies: the civic duty to vote and the civic duty to pay taxes. I find that stronger national identification not only predicts greater civic duty in South Korea, but it also reduces the explanatory power of payoff-based motivations. For strong national identifiers, how much they care about who wins the election or how much they trust the government do not matter to their sense of civic duty to vote or pay taxes, respectively. Such patterns are consistent with citizens who are morally motivated by a sense of obligation to their nation. In short, they describe citizens who see acts of civic duty as "the only right thing to do."

The second empirical study complements the survey findings with a turnout field experiment, which leverages randomization to better identify the causal effect of national obligation on civic duty. The experiment, designed around a mobile election, tests whether priming national obligation as the reason to participate in the election increases the sense of civic duty to vote and, importantly, actual turnout. The treatment significantly increases the civic duty to vote and yields one of the largest turnout effects so far documented in the field experiment literature.

The findings in this chapter suggest that high levels of civic duty in South Korea are, for the most part, a national phenomenon. Both survey and experimental evidence paint a picture of the South Korean citizen that is largely consistent with Mrs. Han's testimony. The empirical patterns also echo the personal narratives of overseas Koreans in chapter 3, where strong beliefs of nation-state linkage manifested in national stories associating state-supportive citizenship with being a real Korean. For many South Koreans national identification exerts a powerful moral pull toward civic duty and, in turn, to their democracy.

Survey Evidence

Given South Korea's nationalist history and the unifying national stories it produced, I predict that most citizens should feel a civic duty to contribute to their democracy out of national obligation. I begin by examining a nationally representative survey of South Koreans to see whether the data support that prediction. The obvious starting point is to see whether stronger national identification is associated with greater civic duty to vote and pay taxes among South Koreans. But this observation alone will surely not satisfy some readers, as it does not tell us anything about what is driving that relationship. The association could be driven by an intrinsic obligation to the nation, as the theory suggests. But it could also be driven by extrinsic payoffs attached to national membership, such as the desire for national status or praise from conationals, both of which have little to do with the moral pull of the nation. This ambiguity is what David Broockman calls the challenge of "observational equivalence": both intrinsic and extrinsic motivations often yield the same observed outcome.[2]

Parsing out the motivation matters because it has differing implications for the kind of civic duty that is produced. Unlike a moral obligation to the nation, extrinsic payoffs attached to national membership will cease to be pull factors toward civic duty when national status declines. Such thin civic duty based on payoffs is much more vulnerable to crises or performance failures—precisely when democracies most need to reach into their civic reserves. It certainly does not describe individuals like Mrs. Han, who sacrificed her personal possessions for the country precisely when Korea's national reputation was suffering. To isolate that kind of thick civic duty, I need to differentiate individuals in the survey who are morally motivated from those pursuing expected payoffs. The next section describes my method of applying insights from political theory to statistical modeling.

Modeling Moral Motivations

Intrinsic motivations are not directly observable, but they can yield observable effects. A rich tradition in political theory, known as duty-based or deontological ethics, argues that moral obligation has special properties that distinguish it from other kinds of human motivations. An implication from this literature is that morally motivated people behave differently from those motivated by extrinsic payoffs. I apply this insight to how I model the national pull toward civic duty in South Korea.

Immanuel Kant, widely regarded as the father of deontological ethics, is most forthright about the special nature of duty. For Kant, the defining feature of duty is that it "rejects kinship with inclinations."[3] That is, it follows the principle of what is right versus wrong, as opposed to an inclination for what is desirable: "A good will is good not because of what it accomplishes or effects, not by its aptness for the attainment of some proposed end, but simply by virtue of volition; that is, it is good in itself, and considered by itself is to be esteemed much higher than all that can be brought about by it in favor of any inclination, nay even of the sum total of all inclinations."[4] For a Kantian, duty is a nonconsequentialist motivation: its value does not depend on the consequences or outcomes of the action. For a person who feels a sense of duty to act, then, the expected payoffs from that action, however beneficial or costly, should have no bearing. Kant explained, "Even if it should happen that, owing to special disfavor or fortune . . . this will should wholly lack power to accomplish its purpose, if with its greatest efforts it should yet achieve nothing, and there should remain only the good will . . . then like a jewel, it would still shine by its own light, as a thing which has its whole value in itself. Its usefulness or fruitfulness can neither add nor take away anything from its value."[5]

Applying this Kantian framework to the national theory of civic duty yields the following description: for a person who sees contributing to her democracy as an obligation to her nation, the expected payoffs from doing so should not matter to her sense of civic duty. This statement can be expressed mathematically as follows:

$$Pr(Y_i = 1) = Pr(d_i = 1) + Pr(d_i = 0 \ \& \ p_i \geq 0) \tag{1}$$

Equation (1) states that individual i feels a sense of civic duty to contribute to her democracy ($Y_i = 1$) in one of two scenarios: either she feels a moral obligation to her nation ($d_i = 1$), or despite no such moral pull ($d_i = 0$), she expects positive payoffs from doing so ($p_i \geq 0$). True to Kantian principle, payoffs only matter once the moral motivation—national obligation—is absent.

For simplicity's sake, equation (1) assumes that the moral pull of the nation is binary: either one feels it or does not. But constructivist theories of identity suggest that this moral pull is grounded in a person's strength of psychological identification with the nation. Thus, it makes more sense to model the moral pull as a continuum, ranging from weak to strong, rather than black or white. I therefore rewrite equation (1) in continuous probabilities:

$$Pr(Y_i) = Pr(d_i) + [1 - Pr(d_i)] * Pr(p_i \geq 0) \tag{2}$$

The true probabilities in equation (2) are estimated using the survey data. The moral pull of the nation, $Pr(d_i)$, is estimated with $\hat{d}_i$, the observed strength of national identification;[6] payoffs, $Pr(p_i \geq 0)$, are estimated with $\hat{p}_i$, the expected payoffs from voting or paying taxes as measured in the survey. I can then rewrite the components of equation (2) in their linear approximations as follows: $Pr(d_i) = Pr(d_i | \hat{d}_i) \ \alpha + \beta \hat{d}_i$ and $Pr(p_i \geq 0) = Pr(p_i \geq 0 | \hat{p}_i) = \alpha + \beta \hat{p}_i$. Multiplying out and reorganizing by variable gives the following:

$$Pr(Y_i | \hat{d}, \hat{p}) = \alpha + \beta \hat{d}_i + \gamma p - \delta \hat{d}_i \hat{p}_i \tag{3}$$

Equation (4) substitutes the key variables from the theory into equation (3):

$$civic \ duty_i = \beta_0 + \beta_1 (national \ identification)_i + \beta_2 (payoffs)_i$$
$$+ \beta_3 (national \ identification \times payoffs)_i + \beta_4 (controls)_i + \varepsilon \tag{4}$$

Equation (4) models a person's sense of civic duty to contribute to her democracy as a function of three things: her strength of national identification, expected payoffs, and the negative interaction between them ($-\delta \hat{d}_i \hat{p}_i$). In statistical terms, an interaction relationship means that the effect of one variable depends on the value of the other. The negative interaction in equation (4) predicts a kind of trade-off: as strength of national identification increases, the estimated effect that payoffs have on a person's sense of civic duty decreases.

The resulting model with the interaction is the unique product of taking seriously what political theory says about the special nature of moral motivations. Equation (4) serves as the base estimation model for predicting civic duty in the survey analysis portions of the book. Whether an interaction emerges from the data serves as the observable test for a morally motivated citizen.[7] In cases like

South Korea, where the theory predicts national identification to exert a moral pull toward civic duty for most citizens, we should observe a significant negative interaction between national identification and payoffs. In cases like Taiwan, however, where the theory predicts that Taiwanese national identification should fail to exert any moral pull toward civic duty for many citizens, we should observe no significant interaction with payoff motivations.

I focus on two manifestations of civic duty that all democracies share and need: the civic duty to vote and the civic duty to pay honest taxes. In South Korea, where beliefs of nation-state linkage should be strong and widespread, the first prediction from equation (4) is a positive national effect across both kinds of civic duty ($\beta_1 > 0$). The second prediction is a negative interaction between national identification and the estimated effect of payoffs on civic duty ($\beta_3 < 0$).

Data and Measures

I use two different surveys to analyze what motivates civic duty in South Korea. The first is the Korean National Participation Study (KNPS) run by Seoul National University, where I was able to include a question on the civic duty to vote. The survey draws on a nationally representative, face-to-face sample of 2,047 South Korean citizens and was conducted a few weeks before the national parliamentary elections in 2012, making the duty-to-vote question especially timely. For civic duty to pay honest taxes, I use the sixth wave (2010–2014) of the World Values Survey (WVS). Of all the cross-national surveys that include South Korea, this is the only survey that concurrently asks about both national identification and the civic duty to pay taxes.

The civic duty to vote is typically measured by asking individuals how strongly they agree or disagree with the statement that voting is a citizen's duty in a democracy. This wording suffers from significant over-report, however, as most established democracies have strong injunctive norms in support of political participation.[8] To minimize this bias as much as possible, I use a validated wording developed by André Blais and Christopher Achen that has quickly become the gold standard for measuring the duty to vote:

> Different people think differently about voting. Some people think that voting is a responsibility, and you should vote even if you don't like any of the candidates or parties. Other people think that it is all right to vote or not vote, and the decision depends on how you feel about the candidates or parties. Do you think voting is a responsibility or that it is all right to either vote or not vote?[9]

There are two advantages to the wording of this question. First, it offers respondents an alternative to voting as a duty that is just as acceptable in liberal democracies— voting as a matter of personal choice. This greatly reduces social desirability bias, which is the main reason for over-report. Second, the question spells out behaviorally what it means to see voting as a duty—that one votes even when one has no preference for a candidate or party. Respondents who said "voting is a responsibility" were coded as feeling a civic duty to vote (=1), while those who said it is "all right to either vote or not vote" were coded as not (=0). In the KNPS sample, 65 percent of respondents said they see voting more as a matter of responsibility than a choice.

For the civic duty to pay taxes, I use a question battery in the WVS that asks respondents about a list of morally ambiguous actions, of which "cheating on taxes when you have the chance" is one. Respondents were asked to rank each action on a 1-to-10 scale of justifiability. I coded respondents who said cheating was "never justifiable"—who exhibited a principled commitment to paying honest taxes—as feeling a civic duty to pay taxes (=1), those who said it was "always justifiable" as feeling no duty (=0), and all other gradations of justifiability as a continuous range in between. In the WVS sample 67 percent of South Koreans said that cheating on taxes was "never justifiable." Only 2 percent said cheating was "always justifiable," and the remaining 31 percent fell in between.

The main independent variable in the analysis is strength of national identification. Typically, this is measured by asking respondents how strongly they identify with being French, American, and so on. The effectiveness of this wording varies with context, however. For instance, in places with multiple national groups, it will only capture identification with the most dominant group, potentially missing important identifications with nondominant national groups. In other places, where national identity is primarily understood in ethnoracial terms, asking subjects how much they identify with something that is seen as "a given" may not be very sensible.

South Korea is an example of the latter case. In focus groups with Seoul National University students, the standard national-identification wording proved to be very awkward in a national context where being Korean is primarily seen as a matter of birth lineage. Almost everyone replied that "of course" they strongly identify as Korean, and the wording yielded very little variation. Instead, a better measure for capturing variation in strength of psychological attachment to one's Korean identity turned out to be national pride: "How proud are you to be Korean?"[10] Unlike the identification wording, the pride wording takes being Korean as a given and then asks about positive attachment to that identity. The national-pride measure generates a good deal of variation: 28 percent of the sample said they are "very proud," 58 percent said "somewhat proud," while the remaining 14 percent expressed no pride.

The payoff motivation for civic duty used in the analysis varies by the type of citizen action. For the duty to vote, I use a standard payoff variable in turnout studies: how much a person cares about who wins the election.[11] Those with stronger preference in the election outcome stand to gain more psychic, expressive, or even material benefits from voting than those without. For the duty to pay taxes, I use the level of trust in the national government, a key payoff variable from the contractual literature on tax compliance. The logic is that "vertical trust" between citizens and the state incentivizes tax compliance by increasing the certainty of future returns from the state: "Compliance involves a similar risky relationship; citizens undertake some immediately costly effort like paying taxes, and face some risk that future collective benefits expected in return for compliance may not materialize.... Any citizen who does not 'trust' the government and other citizens to meet expectations would be foolish to comply with a law unless otherwise motivated by fear or duty to obey."[12] The measure comes from a question battery in the WVS that asks about confidence in a list of public institutions, of which "the government (in your nation's capital)" is one.

The statistical models also control for attitudinal and demographic predictors of civic duty. For the duty to vote, I control for collective values—how much a person believes the individual should always sacrifice for the group—to account for arguments about Confucian collectivist culture or obedient personalities; interpersonal trust to account for arguments based on social capital; and known predictors of turnout from prior studies: political interest, education, age, and partisanship.[13] Since the duty to vote was measured dichotomously, estimates are from logistic regression. For the duty to pay taxes, I control for support for big government to account for general ideological disposition toward taxation; interpersonal trust to account for social capital; female to account for the gendered nature of fiscal responsibility in Korean households; income class to account for variations in tax burden and age for tax experience. Estimates are from ordinary least squares (OLS) regression predicting the strength of duty to pay taxes honestly. Variables have been rescaled to range from 0 to 1 so that the size of the coefficients can be easily compared.

Findings

Estimates of the national effect on civic duty in South Korea are shown in table 2. Starting with the duty to vote, for a person who has no preference in the election outcome, feeling strong versus weak national identification is associated with 5.5 times higher odds of seeing voting as a matter of civic duty rather than

TABLE 2   Estimates of national effect on civic duty in South Korea

	DUTY TO VOTE	DUTY TO PAY TAXES
	LOGISTIC	*OLS*
National identification	1.70***	0.11**
	(0.84)	(0.03)
Payoffs	1.43***	
Strength of preference in outcome	(0.57)	
Trust in national government		0.06*
		(0.03)
Interaction		
National identification x payoff	−1.81**	−0.06
	(0.92)	(0.04)
Controls		
Collective values	0.27	
	(0.23)	
Political interest	2.13***	
	(0.25)	
Interpersonal trust	0.56**	0.009
	(0.27)	(0.01)
Support big government		0.11***
		(0.02)
Demographic controls	yes	yes
Constant	−2.93***	0.76***
	(0.60)	(0.03)
Pseudo R-squared	0.07	0.05
N	1567	1172
Data source	KNPS	WVS

Estimates for duty to vote based on logistic regression, those for duty to pay taxes based on ordinary least squares regression. All variables rescaled 0 to 1 in both models.

*** p < .01

 ** p < .05

   * p < .10

personal choice. Importantly, the interaction between national identification and preference in the election outcome is also robustly negative: as strength of national identification increases, the extent to which a person cares about who wins the election matters significantly less to her sense of civic duty to vote.[14] A similar pattern emerges with the civic duty to pay taxes. Stronger national identification is associated with an 11 percent greater sense of duty to pay taxes, and that is the marginal effect for a person who has no trust in the national government. The interaction is also directionally negative, although the coefficient is shy of statistical significance.

Interaction relationships are best assessed visually, so figure 4.1 plots the predictions from both models.[15] Starting with the duty to vote, we see in the top left quadrant that stronger national identification takes the predicted probability of

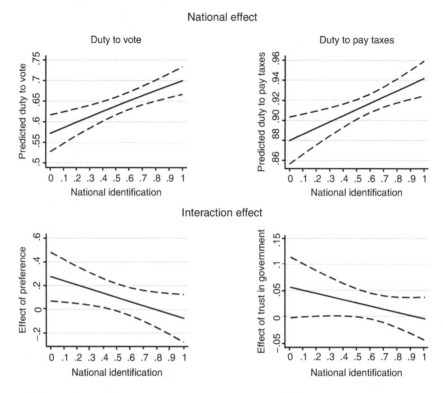

FIGURE 4.1. Predicted civic duty by national identification in South Korea. Predicted values are based on estimates from table 2, holding covariates at their actual values versus their means. Dashed lines mark the 95 percent confidence intervals.

seeing voting as a civic duty from 0.56—a little better than a coin toss—to 0.70, a more certain bet. The bottom left quadrant shows the interaction with strength of preference in the election outcome. As national identification strengthens, the estimated effect of preference on the duty to vote steadily decreases until it reaches zero. That is, for a South Korean who strongly identifies with her nation, the extent to which she cares about which party wins no longer matters to her sense of civic duty to vote. Such a pattern is uniquely indicative of the moral pull that comes from national identification.

Patterns for the civic duty to pay taxes largely mirror those from the duty to vote. The top right quadrant shows that stronger national identification takes the predicted duty to pay taxes from 0.88, which is already high, to almost 0.95. In other words, in South Korea strong national identification goes hand in hand with the belief that cheating on one's taxes is "never justifiable." The bottom right quadrant suggests that national identification has this effect through its moral pull, as it does with the duty to vote. The effect of trust in government on the civic duty to pay taxes gradually decreases as national identification strengthens, until it no longer matters for a South Korean who strongly identifies with the nation.

This section presented the first quantitative test of the national theory of civic duty in South Korea. Where a minjok-based reimagination of the nation sustained strong linkage between the national people and the state through democratization, I predicted that national obligation should drive a sense of civic duty for most citizens. Indeed, I found strong national effects across both the civic duty to vote and the civic duty to pay taxes. Payoffs also mattered a good deal, as contractual theories of citizenship would predict. However, they mattered most for South Koreans with weak national identification. For those with strong national identification, which describes about seven of every ten South Koreans, preference in the election or trust in the government no longer mattered to their sense of civic duty to vote or to pay taxes.

Civic duty in South Korea appears to have strong national foundations. But to what extent are South Koreans actually moved by this nation-based civic duty? When acting upon civic duty imposes costs, as it almost always does in real political life, do South Koreans still follow through on their national obligation? To further validate the survey findings, I turn to an experimental study.

A Turnout Field Experiment

If the power of moral obligation is its principled nature, then the most convincing way to test for its pull is to see whether individuals follow through even at a cost to themselves. To see whether this is the case for South Koreans, I conducted a field experiment around a mobile election hosted by the country's National Election Commission (NEC).

Expending time and effort to vote in a mobile election is certainly not the same as donating one's wedding ring during a financial crisis. But as extraordinary as the latter is, democratic citizenship is mostly comprised of smaller, more ordinary acts of sacrifice like the former. While there are clear differences in scale between the two events, the mobile election presents a parallel incentive structure to the national gold drives: participation is voluntary and immediately costly while the effectiveness on the outcome is uncertain. The mobile election experiment should therefore be taken as a microcosm of how national obligation and civic duty shape everyday citizen sacrifices in South Korea.

Design

The mobile election was hosted by the NEC as a pilot test for a new mobile voting application that enables voting by SMS text message. A total of 2,097 valid participants were recruited among NEC employees, who were then randomly assigned to vote on one of the two days over which the election was held on August 13 and 14, 2013.

The ballot was designed to mimic the mixed personal and public stakes of a real election. Some of the items were directly relevant to the quality of NEC life, such as how to improve engagement between senior and junior employees, and the NEC announced prior to the election that it would incorporate the poll results to make improvements to the bureau. Other items were of public importance, such as which celebrity should be the face of the NEC's upcoming clean-election campaign. This mix of items ensured that even though the election was a pilot, NEC participants saw both private and public incentives to vote, as they would in a real election.

Two potential concerns arise from using NEC employees, most of whom are career civil servants, as an experimental sample. The first is an ethical one: priming civil servants can have unintended downstream effects on their performance and incur public costs. In this case, however, I expect any residual effect from priming national obligation to improve the quality of the NEC's mobile-voting application, such that the likelihood of negative externalities to the public are minimal to none.

The second concern has to do with the representativeness of the treatment effect. Civil servants are unlike the average South Korean citizen. On the one hand, given their professional socialization, NEC employees may be more responsive to cues about national obligation, yielding an overestimate of the national effect. On the other hand, civil servants may already feel higher-than-average levels of national obligation, resulting in a ceiling effect that underestimates the power of national pull. These are empirical questions for which the nationally representative survey data in the previous section offer a useful benchmark.

The experiment was conducted as follows. One day before their assigned election day, all participants received an email titled "Directions for the Mobile Election." The treatment message was embedded in the email. For the control group ($N = 1073$), assigned to the first day, the email contained purely informational instructions on how to use the mobile application to cast a vote. For the treatment group ($N = 1024$), assigned to the second day, the email contained the same instructions with an additional message that primed national obligation as the reason to vote: "You are the face of Korea. Our forefathers' sacrifices helped make our nation the democracy it is today. It is our duty to the Korean nation to vote and do our part."

The treatment is tailored to Korea's national context to maximize its effectiveness. Fulfilling national obligation is described as a natural part of being ethnically Korean ("you are the face of Korea"), and the historical linkage between the national people and South Korea's democracy today is highlighted by mentioning "our forefathers' sacrifices."

To be clear, the aim is not to create a sense of national obligation where it does not exist or even to boost it among people who only feel it weakly. Such moral ties are products of long socialization that, like other deeply ingrained aspects of self-identity such as gender or religion, cannot be manipulated in an experimental context. Instead, the aim is to increase the salience of a preexisting sense of national obligation. John Zaller shows that individuals' survey responses are strongly affected by "top of the head" considerations when they are answering questions.[16] Similarly, the experimental treatment is intended to bring national obligation to front of mind for individuals in the treatment group as they decide whether or not to vote the next day.

There are two outcomes of interest in the experiment. The first is the sense of civic duty to vote, which was measured by a preelection survey. The link to the survey was included in the bottom of the "directions" email that everyone received before the election. The survey asked about a variety of political and social attitudes, including a question on the civic duty to vote, using the same wording as in the survey analysis from the previous section.[17] The preelection survey was optional. I have measures of the duty to vote for the 244 participants from the control group and 113 from the treatment group who opted in. Selection bias is a concern, a point to which I return shortly.

The second outcome from the experiment is actual turnout in the mobile election. This book is focused on explaining civic duty, the duty-based lens that precedes citizen action. But civic duty would be quite meaningless if it did not produce real and tangible benefits to democracy. The turnout experiment provides an opportunity to test the full causal chain. To track actual turnout, all participants were assigned a unique random-digit ID that was linked to their mobile phone numbers. Once participants had cast their votes via text message, I matched the mobile number with the corresponding unique ID to validate turnout status for each participant.

The main prediction is that priming national obligation should increase both the civic duty to vote and actual turnout in the treatment group compared to the control group. Increased salience of national obligation should frame the decision to vote in moral rather than payoff terms for participants in the treatment group, making it more likely that they vote despite the costs in time and effort that voting entails. In a nationally unified democracy like South Korea, any such priming effects should be harnessed in support of turnout.

Two points are worth discussing for the more technically inclined readers. A common worry about mailer experiments such as this one is whether participants actually received the intended treatment. Qualtrics, the firm I used to send out the preelection survey, unfortunately does not keep track of which individual emails were opened. But the issue of noncompliance is most likely minimal in this experiment. Because the mobile election was a pilot for a new voting technology, none of the participants had used the application before. As the email was titled "Directions for the Mobile Election," it is very likely that the participants who voted opened the email for instructions on how to use the application, such that the intent-to-treat effect on turnout closely approximates the true complier effect.

The second technical issue is selection bias in the optional preelection survey. The duty to vote is only measured among voluntary survey takers from the control and treatment groups. Because the survey takers from each group are no longer randomly selected, simply comparing the measured duty to vote between the control and treatment groups is like comparing apples to oranges. To best address this issue, I calculate the matched treatment effect for the duty to vote, where I compare only among control-treatment pairs that are matched on age category, education, gender, and years spent at the NEC. Matching does not fix selection bias, but it weights the survey takers in the control versus treatment groups such that they are conditionally comparable on all observable characteristics, except for their exposure to the treatment message.

Figure 4.2 shows the experimental results. Priming national obligation increases the civic duty to vote by 13 percentage points among matched control-treatment pairs, taking the average duty to vote from 0.43 in the control group to 0.56 in the treatment group. This treatment effect is unique to the duty to vote. I also included several placebo questions in the preelection survey. These asked about interest in mobile voting or voting efficacy—attitudes that were related to the election experience but unrelated to support for the democratic state, such that there was no theoretical reason to expect a treatment effect. The treatment had no significant effect on these placebo attitudes.

Actual turnout also increased by 6 percentage points, from 75 percent in the control group to 81 percent in the treatment group, as shown in figure 4.2. How small or large is this effect? In the context of turnout field experiments, it is substantial. It exceeds most estimates found in get-out-the-vote studies using mailers, phone calls, and even some face-to-face canvassing efforts.[18] To my knowledge, the treatment effect from priming national obligation falls short of only two other estimates in this literature: that from a massive face-to-face canvassing effort in New Haven, Connecticut, and another from a social-pressure study where nonvoters would be publicized on a neighborhood list.[19] Both strategies are either too expensive or too controversial to implement on a broad scale.

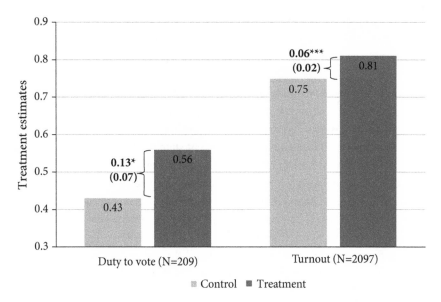

FIGURE 4.2.   Treatment effects in South Korea's turnout field experiment.
*** p < .01, ** p < .05, * p < .10. The treatment effect on the duty to vote,
which was measured through an optional preelection survey, is estimated
only on matched control-treatment pairs among survey takers, which reduces
the total sample size to 209. The estimate is based on the nearest neighbor
method with bootstrapped standard errors. The intent-to-treat effect on turnout
is estimated using the entire experimental sample.

Interestingly, the effect of priming national obligation is significantly larger
than the civic-duty treatment from the neighborhood list study. In that prior
study simply telling citizens that voting is their civic duty increased turnout by
only 1.8 percentage points.[20] This experiment shows that targeting the identity-
based source of such civic duty—a sense of obligation to the nation—can yield a
turnout gain three times larger in places like South Korea.

Even though the experimental sample consists of NEC employees, nationally
representative survey data from the previous section suggest that the size of the
treatment effect likely approximates the population effect. In figure 4.1, based
on the survey sample, I estimated that weak versus strong national identification
predicts a corresponding 0.56 versus 0.70 duty to vote—a 14-percentage point
"increase." That number is nearly identical to the 13-percentage point treatment
effect that priming national obligation has on the civic duty to vote in the experiment. The survey evidence from the previous section also shows that such pattern extends to other manifestations of civic duty beyond voting, such as the
duty to pay taxes. Taken together, the survey and experimental findings paint

a consistent picture in South Korea. In democracies where national stories sustain widespread beliefs of strong nation-state linkage, national obligation exerts a powerful pull toward civic duty.

The notion of the Korean nation as a singular bloodline (*danilminjok*) was in many ways a survival response to Japanese colonialism in the early twentieth century. Yet as this national reimagination continued to frame the critical junctures leading up to South Korea's independent statehood, it also seeded another belief: that the South Korean people and their state were as if one body. Democratization based on such strong nation-state linkage led to a context where, in contrast to the more familiar story of nationalism as a source of instability in many Western democracies, nationalism supported powerful moral attachments in support of the democratic state. Through a complementary mix of survey and experimental data, this chapter demonstrated the democratic benefits of such strong nation-state linkage for contemporary South Korea.

When South Koreans lined up at the national gold drives during the Asian financial crisis, the international media were shocked. The managing director of the International Monetary Fund called the efforts "admirable,"[21] and the national gold drives are still described as "one of the most moving shows of patriotism and self-sacrifice."[22] When Greece faced similar fiscal challenges nearly two decades later and a similar collective effort failed to emerge, many were quick to cite the lack of "Confucian ethics" or the "special 'strength and power'" of Korean nationalism.[23]

Such answers capture only part of the story. What was "special" about Korea was not its Confucian culture or its minjok-based nationalism but the way that Korea's national stories framed the people and the state as if one. It was this active storytelling by both the state and the national people who lived in it that seeded the foundations for strong civic duty in South Korea. Cultural accounts paint an overly deterministic picture of this constructive and contested process and ultimately do a disservice to other societies hoping to replicate impressive feats of civic duty like the national gold drives.

To show how the same Confucian legacy and similarly ethnic nationalism can yield very different effects on civic duty, the next chapter turns the comparative lens to Taiwan. Anyone who has been to Taiwan can attest that there is no shortage of nationalist fervor on the island democracy. Weekends in Taipei are often loud with protestors waving the green independence flag, and down in Kaohsiung, one of the first things a visitor will notice is the multilingual subway signs written in Taiwanese dialect.

Yet Taiwan differs from South Korea in a pivotal, but nonobvious way. Due to political decisions made by the early ruling elites from mainland China, Taiwanese nationalism grew in opposition to the state in this neighboring democracy. As chapter 3 showed, many Taiwanese have come to see the democratic state as representing the national "other" and to associate being a good Taiwanese with counterstate citizenship. Then despite the cultural and structural similarities between South Korea and Taiwan, the theory predicts that a sense of obligation to the Taiwanese nation should pull citizens away from civic duty. The next chapter replicates the two empirical studies in Taiwan to see whether this is the case.

WEAK CIVIC DUTY AND FRAGMENTED NATION IN TAIWAN

The island democracy of Taiwan sits only a short distance from South Korea. On the surface it appears to be a similarly thriving democracy with vibrant manifestations of nationalism. Yet a very different nation-state landscape lies underneath. Unlike South Korea, Taiwan's democracy was born of an emerging nationalist conflict between pro-Taiwan islanders and pro-China mainlanders. The island formally democratized in 1996, but the Kuomintang (KMT)'s legacy of exclusive rule casts a long shadow over how the state is perceived. Many islanders still see the best interests of "my" Taiwanese nation as something to be protected from, rather than by, the state. This was especially the case in 2013, when most of the data for this study were collected. After a successful reelection campaign, the KMT incumbent Ma Ying-jeou was heading into his second term.

This chapter documents how widespread beliefs of fractured nation-state linkage have measurably negative consequences for Taiwan's maturing democracy. I predict that civic duty in Taiwan is much less rooted in nationalism than it is in South Korea. The empirical goal of the South Korea and Taiwan pairing is to keep constant the main aspects of the survey and experimental studies while varying the pivotal lever of nation-state linkage. Thus, while some specifics have been adapted to better fit Taiwan's nationalist context, the reader will find that the overall design of the empirical studies is the same as the South Korea chapter. I begin with a parallel survey analysis of the national effect on the civic duty to vote and the civic duty to pay taxes in a nationally weighted sample of Taiwan citizens. I complement that analysis with a survey experiment that, as in South

Korea, primes national obligation as the reason to contribute to the state, this time in the context of relief efforts for earthquakes—a real and recurring threat to the island.[1]

The key difference is that the predictions in this chapter are the opposite of those in South Korea. Given what I have shown to be Taiwan's largely fractured nation-state landscape, I expect national obligation to exert little to no pull toward civic duty for many citizens on the island. Indeed, despite my best efforts to detect a national effect in both studies, the evidence consistently suggests that a sense of obligation to "my" Taiwan plays almost no role in motivating civic duty for most citizens, save for a small and rapidly shrinking group that still identifies with a pro-China nationalist vision.

The Taiwanese are not any less committed to their nation than their South Korean counterparts. A deep love and sense of responsibility for an independent Taiwanese nation is palpable on the island. Yet for many this national obligation remains disconnected from the Republic of China and the pro-China legacy from the days of KMT rule that the official state name reflects. Taiwan still musters comparably high levels of civic duty to South Korea as measured through national surveys. But the data show that civic duty in Taiwan rests more heavily on political incentives, rather than a deep, identity-based commitment to the democratic state. The differing roots of civic duty in Taiwan, as compared to South Korea, have important implications for the durability of the civic foundations of Taiwan's democracy in the long run.

Survey Evidence

Given the paucity of off-the-shelf survey data on civic duty in Taiwan, I fielded my own online survey through the Election Study Center (ESC) at National Chengchi University, one of the leading survey research centers in Taiwan. The ESC runs the recurring Taiwan's Election and Democratization Study (TEDS) and over the years has amassed a nationally representative online panel from its face-to-face surveys. My survey was fielded to this panel for a week in July 2013. A total of 1,004 respondents chose to fill out the survey. As is the case with most opt-in online surveys, the sample is not representative. My online sample was younger, more educated, and more female than the national population. To address this selection bias, I weighted the online sample to the closest available face-to-face, nationally representative sample from the 2012 TEDS, also conducted by the ESC.[2] All analyses in this chapter are based on the nationally weighted sample.

Empirical Strategy and Predictions

The challenge of identifying the moral pull of the nation—an intrinsic motivation—in a survey context carries over from the South Korea analysis. To test for the presence (or in this case, the predicted absence) of the nation's moral pull toward civic duty, I follow the same intuition developed in chapter 4. Taking seriously what political theory says about the principled nature of moral obligation implies a trade-off with payoff-based motivations: as the pull of national obligation increases, payoffs should matter less to whether a person feels a sense of civic duty to contribute to her democracy. I showed in chapter 4 that this kind of relationship between two variables can be captured statistically through a negative interaction. The estimation model for civic duty in Taiwan, the same used in the South Korea analysis, is as follows:

$$civic\ duty_i = \beta_0 + \beta_1(national\ identification)_i + \beta_2(payoffs)_i$$
$$+ \beta_3(national\ identification \times payoffs)_i + \beta_4(controls)_i + \varepsilon$$

In contrast to South Korea, however, the main prediction in Taiwan is that the nation's moral pull toward civic duty should be negligible. When belief of nation-state linkage is fractured, as is the case for most citizens in Taiwan who still see the state as embodying the KMT's pro-China legacy, a sense of obligation to "my" Taiwan should have little to no effect on civic duty. Both β_1, the marginal national effect, and β_3, the interaction effect with payoffs, should therefore be close to null.

Yet null effects can be observed for many reasons. How can one distinguish between the real absence of national pull versus poor measurement? On this point the heterogeneity of national stories in Taiwan offers important clarity. National stories and the nation-state relationships they embed vary predictably across the different national groups in Taiwan. As chapter 3 traced in detail, self-identified Taiwan nationalists tend to pass down national stories that paint a fractured or opposed relationship to the former KMT state, whereas China nationalists are more likely to be socialized into a state-supportive relationship.

The within-case variation in national stories in Taiwan serves as an excellent validation check for the theory. If internalized beliefs about nation-state linkage most immediately shape the nation's moral pull toward civic duty, then even within the same democracy I should observe varying national effects across the distinct national groups. The national effect on civic duty should be null for Taiwan nationalists and New Taiwanese, who both see Taiwan as an independent nation from China. Most citizens in Taiwan fall into these two groups, and both β_1 and β_3 should be close to zero for them. But for China nationalists, the minority with strong beliefs of national linkage to the KMT legacy state, the theory predicts a strong national effect on civic duty that parallels the results in

South Korea. For this group only, we should see a positive estimate on β_1 and a negative sign on the interaction term β_3. The main axis of comparison remains at the case level, between a nationally unified democracy like South Korea versus a nationally fragmented one like Taiwan. Yet the comparison between national groups within Taiwan offers a valuable check on the validity of that pairing by illuminating why we observe a weaker national effect in Taiwan.

Measures

The survey questions were designed to mirror those used in the South Korea analysis as much as possible. The civic-duty-to-vote question used identical wording as follows:

> Different people think differently about voting. Some people think that voting is a responsibility, and you should vote even if you don't like any of the candidates or parties. Other people think that it is all right to vote or not vote, and the decision depends on how you feel about the candidates or parties. Do you think voting is a responsibility or that it is all right to either vote or not vote?

The only difference is that in the Taiwan survey, I included a follow-up question asking how strongly respondents believed that "voting is a responsibility." The item measures the strength of civic duty to vote, which I code by strong (=2), weak (=1), or none (=0). Most respondents—71 percent—saw voting as a matter of responsibility, and of those a third felt strongly so.

Civic duty to pay taxes was measured through a comparable question to the World Values Survey (WVS)'s "justifiability" battery that was used for South Korea, where respondents were asked to rank how justifiable it was to cheat on taxes when given the chance. The same wording does not translate appropriately in Taiwan, as the word "justifiable" implies a legal obligation and therefore would yield very little variation. I worked with native-speaking researchers at the ESC to develop an alternate wording that better captures the subjective morality aspect of the WVS battery: "Different people think differently about what it means to be a good citizen. As far as you are concerned personally, how important is it to never cheat on taxes, even if you have the chance?" Respondents who said it was "very important" were coded as feeling a strong civic duty to pay taxes (=2), "somewhat important" as weak duty (=1), and "not very important" or "not important at all" as no duty (=0). About half the Taiwan sample—55 percent—felt a strong duty to never cheat on taxes, 33 percent felt weak duty, and 12 percent felt no duty.

The main measurement challenge in Taiwan is the independent variable, strength of national identification. The standard wording used in most cross-national surveys—"how strongly do you identify with [nation]?"—quickly runs into problems. Because of Taiwan's bifurcated nationalist history, what "Taiwan" means depends on who you ask. Two respondents could answer the same question as "very strong" but feel that sense of identification toward two very differently imagined national communities. Thus, accurately measuring strength of national identification in Taiwan requires a two-step process: first, measure strength of identification with Taiwan, and then identify what "Taiwan" means for each respondent.

To do this, I designed the following question battery for the survey. Respondents first answered the generic national-identification question: "How strongly do you identify with Taiwan?" Following this, they were asked to define the boundaries of what they mean by "Taiwan" based on territory, countrymen, legitimate government, and cultural identity.[3] These components capture what Taiwan scholars have shown to be two distinct dimensions of contemporary Taiwanese identity: the political dimension of independence from China (territory, countrymen, legitimate government) and the ethnocultural dimension of distinctiveness from Chinese culture (cultural identity).[4]

The two dimensions reflect the evolution of Taiwanese nationalism. The origins of the Taiwan nationalist movement were rooted in an ethnocultural backlash against the KMT's aggressive re-Sinicization efforts. Based on significant differences in dialect, history, and customs, many islanders saw themselves as ethnically distinct from the mainlanders. But with generational turnover and intermarriage, the islander-versus-mainlander divide that once defined the nationalist landscape in Taiwan has started to fade, especially among the youth. With democratization the primary axis of Taiwanese nationalism has shifted toward civic notions of political independence vis-à-vis the People's Republic of China. Citizens today identify with the cultural and political dimensions of Taiwanese nationhood in distinct combinations depending on their personal histories. The question battery used here is a best effort to capture the variations in those subjective identifications by allowing each respondent to define "my" Taiwan.

Based on their answers, respondents were categorized into one of three distinct national groups, as shown in table 3: Taiwan nationalists, who identify with Taiwan as a politically and culturally independent nation from China; New Taiwanese, who identify with Taiwan as a politically independent nation from China but are culturally agnostic; and China nationalists, who identify with Taiwan as a nation that is politically and culturally part of China. These identity categories are logically coherent and based on the historical analysis of Taiwan's nationalist movement in chapter 3.[5] Combining the strength of identification measure with this identity battery, I now have a measure for how strongly each respondent identifies with "my" Taiwan.

TABLE 3   Categorization of national groups in Taiwan

	TAIWAN NATIONALISTS	NEW TAIWANESE	CHINA NATIONALISTS
	POLITICALLY AND CULTURALLY PRO-TAIWAN	*POLITICALLY PRO-TAIWAN, CULTURALLY NEUTRAL*	*POLITICALLY AND CULTURALLY PRO-CHINA*
Political dimension			
What territory constitutes "my nation"?	Taiwan only	Taiwan only	Mainland and Taiwan
Who are "my countrymen"?	Taiwanese people only	Taiwanese people only	Mainland and Taiwanese people
Where does "my legitimate government" govern?	Taiwan only	Taiwan only	Mainland and Taiwan
Cultural dimension			
Is Taiwanese culture part of Chinese culture, or are these two cultures different?	Different	Part of Chinese culture	Part of Chinese culture
N	247	345	83

With the key variables in hand, I now turn to a statistical analysis of what motivates the civic duty vote and civic duty to pay taxes in Taiwan. For both analyses, I first estimate the national effect for everyone in the sample, which serves as the main comparison to South Korea, and then separately by national groups, which serves as an additional check for the theory. Every effort was made to use the same set of controls and survey measures as in the South Korea analysis to generate a cross-national comparison.

One exception to this effort is the payoff variable I consider for the civic duty to vote in Taiwan. Using the same variable as in South Korea—how strongly one cares about which party wins the election—was problematic as the online survey in Taiwan was not fielded close to an actual election. I therefore consider an alternative, but equally compelling, source of payoff for voting: fairness of elections, or how much one trusts the state to collect and count the votes honestly. This variable comes from the contractual literature on procedural justice, where transparency and fairness of process signal the long-term returns from continued membership in that state.[6] In an electoral context no procedure is more important than fairness in counting votes. The sample is equally divided across people who believe elections to be fair most of the time, some of the time, and rarely.[7] Otherwise, the duty-to-vote model in Taiwan includes the same set of covariates as the South Korea analysis: collective values to account for generalized dutifulness, interpersonal trust, political interest, age, age-squared, and education.

For the civic duty to pay taxes, the predictive model is the same as in South Korea, save for a slight improvement on the measurement of the payoff variable.

In the South Korea analysis, I was limited by what was available in the World Values Survey and therefore used trust in national government. Admittedly, this is a vague measure of institutional trust as it relates to tax compliance. In the Taiwan survey I therefore asked more specifically about trust in how the government manages taxes. Respondents were generally weak on such trust, with 65 percent feeling "little to none," 18 percent feeling "moderate," and only 17 percent feeling "strong." Otherwise, the duty-to-pay-taxes model in Taiwan includes the same covariates as in the South Korea analysis: support for big government to account for ideological preference for tax and redistribution, interpersonal trust, female, income class, and age. Models were estimated using ordinary least squares (OLS) regression with all variables rescaled to range from 0 to 1, so that it is easy to compare the size of coefficients across the models.

Findings

Quite a different relationship between nationalism and civic duty emerges in Taiwan than the one we saw in South Korea, as shown in table 4. Starting with the duty to vote on the left side, we see that on average, stronger national identification in Taiwan is associated with a 15 percent higher duty to vote, less than half the size of the comparable national effect in South Korea.[8] The interaction with fairness of elections, the payoff motivation, is close to null, which suggests that for most respondents, the national effect we do observe is likely not based on a sense of obligation to "my" Taiwan.

The most eye-opening pattern, however, is revealed in the subgroup analysis by national groups in Taiwan. For Taiwan nationalists and New Taiwanese, the national effect on the duty to vote is negligible, as the theory would predict for citizens whose beliefs of nation-state linkage are largely fractured or opposed to the state. Interestingly, in the absence of a moral pull from the nation, political interest is the most powerful predictor of the civic duty to vote for these individuals. For the minority of China nationalists, however—the only group for whom strong beliefs of nation-state linkage persist—we see a robust national effect that parallels what we saw in South Korea. For this group stronger national identification predicts a 56 percent greater duty to vote, a nearly five to six times stronger association compared to the other national groups. The interaction coefficient, while noisy due to the smaller sample size of this group, is also directionally negative. As national identification strengthens, the fairness of elections matters less to these individuals' civic duty to vote. The pattern suggests that for China nationalists, a sense of obligation to "my" Taiwan exerts a moral pull toward the civic duty.

We see a parallel pattern with the duty to pay taxes on the right side. Overall, both the national coefficient and its interaction with trust in government are

TABLE 4 Estimates of national effect on civic duty in Taiwan

	DUTY TO VOTE				DUTY TO PAY TAXES			
	ALL	TAIWAN NATIONALISTS	NEW TAIWANESE	CHINA NATIONALISTS	ALL	TAIWAN NATIONALISTS	NEW TAIWANESE	CHINA NATIONALISTS
National identification	0.15*	0.10	0.12	0.56**	0.08	0.06	0.08	0.24
	(0.09)	(0.12)	(0.13)	(0.26)	(0.09)	(0.13)	(0.13)	(0.34)
Payoff								
Fairness of election	−0.003	−0.07	−0.005	0.43				
	(0.12)	(0.17)	(0.16)	(0.26)				
Trust in government					0.008	−0.07	−0.11	0.30
					(0.17)	(0.24)	(0.29)	(0.51)
Interaction								
National x payoff	0.007	0.04	0.06	−0.43	0.12	0.28	0.18	−0.10
	(0.16)	(0.22)	(0.23)	(0.37)	(0.21)	(0.31)	(0.34)	(0.61)
Controls								
Collective values	0.12**	−0.02	0.20**	0.51***				
	(0.06)	(0.09)	(0.09)	(0.18)				
Political interest	0.30***	0.39***	0.25***	0.10				
	(0.05)	(0.07)	(0.07)	(0.14)				
Interpersonal trust	−0.11	−0.13	−0.05	0.01	0.04	0.07	0.01	0.05
	(0.08)	(0.11)	(0.13)	(0.26)	(0.04)	(0.05)	(0.06)	(0.10)
Support big government					0.01	0.04	0.04	−0.18*
					(0.04)	(0.08)	(0.06)	(0.10)
Demographic controls	yes	yes	yes	yes	yes	yes	yes	yes
Constant	0.30***	0.30*	0.40***	−0.38*	0.48***	0.45***	0.48***	0.58**
	(0.10)	(0.16)	(0.14)	(0.21)	(0.08)	(0.11)	(0.14)	(0.27)
R-squared	0.13	0.17	0.13	0.35	0.05	0.06	0.04	0.18
N	666	244	342	80	666	244	342	80

Estimates are based on ordinary least squares regressions, with all variables rescaled 0 to 1.

*** p < .01
** p < .05
* p < .10

statistically indistinguishable from zero. This null effect holds across the Taiwan nationalists and New Taiwanese. The China nationalists are again the exception. The relative size of the national coefficient stands out. Stronger national identification in this group predicts a 24 percent greater duty to not cheat on taxes—a nearly three-fold stronger association compared to the other national groups. China nationalists are also the only group for whom a negative interaction between national identification and trust in government emerges, which suggests a moral pull.

Figure 5.1 plots how predicted civic duty changes with strength of national identification for the different national groups in Taiwan. The graphs starkly visualize the overall absence of a national pull in Taiwan, as well as the important contrast between the national groups. Starting with the duty to vote in the upper

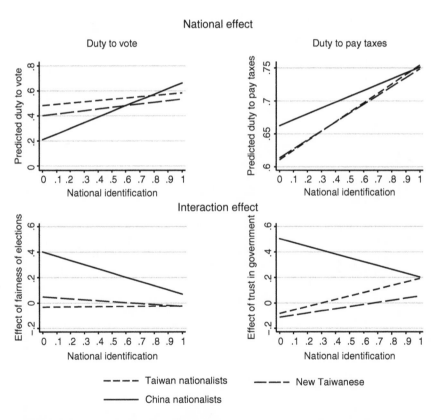

FIGURE 5.1. Predicted civic duty by national identification in Taiwan. Predicted values are based on estimates from table 4, holding covariates at their actual values versus their means. Confidence intervals are not shown in order to make visual comparisons between the groups easier.

left, the lines for Taiwan nationalists and New Taiwanese are relatively flat, meaning that stronger national identification has little relation to the duty to vote for these groups. For China nationalists, however, stronger national identification takes the predicted duty to vote from 0.20 to almost 0.70 on a 0 to 1 scale, from "weak" to "strong."

The bottom left shows the interaction relationship: how the effect of fairness of elections on the civic duty to vote changes with strength of national identification. For Taiwan nationalists and New Taiwanese, stronger national identification makes no difference in how much fairness of elections matters, again shown by the flat lines. For China nationalists, however, the predictive power of fairness of elections steadily declines as national identification strengthens, from a 0.4 percentage point effect on the duty to vote to zero. In other words, for a China nationalist who strongly identifies with "my" Taiwan, how fair or unfair the election process is no longer matters to her sense of civic duty to vote.

The patterns are similar for the civic duty to pay taxes, shown on the right side of figure 5.1. Initially, the upper right quadrant seems to suggest that stronger national identification predicts greater civic duty to pay taxes for all groups. But the bottom right quadrant, which graphs the interactions, shows a clear difference in how that national identification matters. For Taiwan nationalists and New Taiwanese, the estimated effect of trust in government on the duty to pay taxes is relatively flat, regardless of strength of national identification. This suggests that while national identification might matter in other ways for these individuals, a moral pull toward civic duty is likely not one of them. Only for China nationalists does a meaningful negative interaction emerge, where stronger national identification more than halves the estimated effect that trust in government has on the civic duty to pay taxes.

Overall, Taiwan exhibits very different national effects on civic duty compared to its "most similar" democratic neighbor, South Korea. Despite nearly identical model specifications and survey measures, I find at best a negligible national effect on the sense of civic duty to vote and to pay taxes for most citizens in Taiwan. The only group for whom I find evidence of a nation-based civic duty is the China nationalists—the only group in Taiwan that, for reasons of nationalist history on the island, still harbors strong beliefs of nation-state linkage.

The differing national effects across the groups are not due to the fact that Taiwan nationalists or New Taiwanese are any less "nationalists" than their China nationalist counterparts. The mean and distribution of the national identification variable is essentially the same across the three groups. Those familiar with Taiwanese society might wonder whether the typically higher proportion of civil servants among China nationalists confounds the results, but in my online sample, civil servants similarly make up 15 to 17 percent of each national group.

One may wonder if the results simply reflect a KMT incumbency effect. The data for this study were collected in 2013, during the heyday of KMT president Ma Ying-jeou. The singular national effect among China nationalists, who are overwhelmingly KMT supporters, may therefore be a temporal "rally around the party" effect, rather than reflecting deeper patterns of nation-state linkage. If that were the case, then we would expect the patterns to be reversed under a DPP president. To check this, I examined turnout rates in the 2001 and 2004 TEDS Legislative Election Surveys, which were conducted during the first DPP incumbency under Chen Shui-bian. These surveys do not include a question on the duty to vote, so to isolate turnout that is likely driven by a sense of civic duty, I only compare turnout rates among respondents who expressed no preference in the election outcome. I find that the pattern remains the same, even under a DPP incumbency. In both legislative elections, duty-based turnout was higher among China nationalists by about 5 percentage points. Thus, the results in table 4 more likely capture historicized differences in the basis of civic duty across national groups in Taiwan, rather than an ephemeral incumbency effect.

Another way to test whether the positive national effect among China nationalists only is real is to see whether it holds up against potential costs. To do so, I asked the following question in the survey: "How much do you approve or disapprove of some of your tax money being spent to improve air pollution in mainland China?" This may appear to be a strange question. Tax resources are limited, and since the beneficiaries of this policy are residents of the mainland, supporting it diverts funds away from the island. Based strictly on payoff considerations, everyone on the island should oppose such a policy.

Curiously, however, the level of disapproval varies significantly by national group. Whereas nearly nine of ten Taiwan nationalists and New Taiwanese oppose the policy, only six of ten China nationalists do, which is to say that nearly half of them support it. How do we make sense of this puzzle? For Taiwan nationalists and New Taiwanese, a state policy that benefits individuals living on the Chinese mainland—clear national "others" in both the political and cultural sense—should elicit no moral obligation whatsoever. For China nationalists in Taiwan, however, the beneficiaries are broadly "co-nationals" as they are part of the greater imagined Chinese nation. If China nationalists are indeed motivated by a moral pull to "my" Taiwan that is part of China, then for this group only we should see a positive national effect on support for the state policy.

The results in table 5 suggest that the nation's moral pull is real for China nationalists. Stronger national identification has no effect on policy support among Taiwan nationalists. But for China nationalists, it predicts 30 percent greater support for a state policy that takes tax money away from themselves. It is quite difficult to square these findings with explanations based solely on

TABLE 5 National effect on support for tax policy to improve China's pollution

	TAIWAN NATIONALISTS	CHINA NATIONALISTS
National identification	0.07	0.30*
	(0.05)	(0.18)
Controls		
Collective values	0.04	−0.18
	(0.07)	(0.20)
Interpersonal trust	−0.06	−0.03
	(0.05)	(0.11)
Demographic controls	yes	yes
Constant	−0.11	−0.28*
	(0.08)	(0.16)
R-squared	0.09	0.14
N	244	80

Estimates are based on ordinary least squares regressions, with all variables rescaled 0 to 1. Demographic controls, not shown, include income class, female, and age.

*** p < .01

** p < .05

* p < .10

self-interest. Even an argument based on the regional spillover effects of pollution fails. Bad air quality would negatively affect everyone on the island, not just China nationalists. My interpretation is a more parsimonious one: when it comes to supporting the state, China nationalists are motivated by a real moral pull to support "my" nation that includes imagined co-nationals on the mainland.

In sum, the survey evidence from Taiwan paints quite a different picture from South Korea. For most citizens who identify as either Taiwan nationalists or New Taiwanese, voting or paying taxes to what many still see as a KMT-legacy state invokes little sense of national obligation to "my" Taiwan. Such individuals may still feel a civic duty to vote or pay taxes for other reasons, as the larger coefficients on political interest or income class suggest. But fulfilling a moral obligation to their nation is likely not one of them.

The implications for Taiwan's maturing democracy, however outwardly vibrant and participatory, are worrisome. Levels of civic duty in Taiwan, as measured through surveys, remain comparably high to those in South Korea. Yet for most citizens in Taiwan, civic duty appears to be a matter of give and take with the state, rather than something based on an intrinsic identity attachment. The consequences of this difference are likely less visible and less serious during good times. The real costs of weakly underpinned civic duty often do not manifest until the worst of times, when democracies are unable to promise future returns, such as during war, economic recessions, or natural disasters, but nevertheless need citizen sacrifice.

How serious are the stakes in Taiwan? To examine this I turn to an experimental study of civic duty in a crisis setting. The context is a real and recurring natural threat to the island democracy: earthquakes. Because of their indiscriminate and largely unpredictable nature, earthquakes represent a crisis where the state depends a great deal on spontaneous citizen compliance and sacrifice. The survey experiment tests whether nationalist appeals increase the sense of civic duty to help the state in its earthquake recovery efforts.

A Survey Experiment on Civic Duty and Crisis

Taiwan sits near the junction of two tectonic plates in a zone tellingly named the Pacific Rim of Fire. Taiwan's Central Weather Bureau estimates that in the past century there have been more than a hundred earthquakes on the island, with at least half resulting in human casualties. Of all the earthquakes in Taiwan's public memory, the 921 earthquake—named after its fatal date of September 21, 1999—was by far the deadliest and most damaging.[9] The 7.5-magnitude earthquake killed an estimated 2,145 people and seriously injured more than 11,000 in its wake. Emergency recovery efforts by the military and several international organizations, which lasted for weeks, focused on digging out people who had become trapped under the rubble after more than 51,000 buildings had collapsed. Taiwan's stock market was forced to close for a full week, and total damages added up to NT$300 billion.

I chose the 921 earthquake as the topic of the survey experiment for two reasons. First, earthquakes are a recurring threat that requires the state to dig into the moral reserves of the citizenry in order to conduct efficient relief and recovery efforts. Because the exact timing and scale of earthquakes is hard to predict, in the immediate aftermath of a natural disaster, states often need voluntary donations and aid from citizens on site. Earthquakes are therefore a realistic crisis context for the island democracy where a sense of civic duty matters tremendously. Second, scholars have argued that large-scale crises often serve as moments of exigency where the "moral glue" within a community is heightened.[10] A natural disaster such as an earthquake, which for the small island poses an indiscriminate threat to all residents, is certainly one such collective crisis. If nationalism exerts any moral pull toward contributing to the state in Taiwan, earthquakes offer a ripe context in which to find it.

The crisis experiment in Taiwan serves as an illuminating comparison to the turnout experiment in South Korea. Methodologically, the two experimental studies serve the same purpose: to complement the survey findings by pressure testing the theory in a controlled, randomized setting. But the two experiments also dialogue with each other. South Korea's turnout experiment tested the effectiveness of nationalist appeals on civic duty in ordinary times for a citizen act that is routine and expected in most democracies. The Taiwan experiment extends the same methodological approach to civic duty in extraordinary times for a citizen act that is much less routine and reciprocal. Together, the pair of experiments covers two ends of the various forms that civic duty takes in democracies.

Design

The experiment came at the very end of the same online survey used in the previous section, fielded with the Election Study Center at National Chengchi University. The 1,004 recruited participants were randomly assigned to control and treatment groups and asked to read one of two versions of a news article about the 921 earthquake. The control group (N=504) read a "neutral" frame article that described only historical facts about the event. The treatment group (N=500) read a "national obligation" frame article that also included anecdotes and quotes that emphasize sacrifice and obligation to the national community in the aftermath of the disaster. Table 6 shows the full text of each article.

TABLE 6 News frame treatment for earthquake experiment in Taiwan

CONTROL "NEUTRAL" FRAME	TREATMENT "NATIONAL OBLIGATION" FRAME
921 SHAKES THE ISLAND	**921 SHAKES ISLAND, BUT STRENGTHENS COMMUNITY**
On September 21, 1999, a 7.5 magnitude earthquake hit the island at 1:47 in the morning. The disaster, called the "921 earthquake," did permanent damage to the island's economy and landscape.	The "921 earthquake," which hit the island with a force of 7.5 magnitude in 1999 and killed 2,145 people, was a tragedy, but also a moment that brought the national community together.
A total of 2,145 people died, with another 11,305 injured. 51,711 buildings collapsed entirely into the ground, contributing to the high death toll. The Taiwan Stock Exchange was also closed for almost a week, and several big factories were damaged, causing the country to take a serious economic hit. Nantou County was shaken the most, leaving the landscape in ruins.	"In my head, any person under that rubble is my own father, mother, or child," said a soldier who had not slept for several days digging the ruins for survivors. Citizens from all over the island donated food and water for victims, some even opening their homes. Many different charity groups raised a total of NT$34 billion from individual donations.
In total, the damages added up to NT$300 billion. It was the second deadliest earthquake in the island's history.	Despite being the second deadliest earthquake in the island's history, many remember 921 as the rebirth of national community. It showed the world that people on the island can become one in dark times.

The aim of the treatment, as with the South Korea experiment, was to prime a sense of moral obligation to "my" nation. The treatment article was careful not to cue any specific nationalist vision of Taiwan but simply to highlight examples of sacrifice by members of the national community at large in the wake of the collective disaster. The assumption was that any priming effects would be directed toward "my" nation as imagined by each subject. The experiment then tests whether, all else equal, priming national obligation increases a sense of civic duty to help the state in the context of a crisis. After reading the respective news articles, all subjects were asked whether they saw contributing to state efforts on earthquake prevention and relief as a matter of duty or personal choice.

Unlike most experiments, where the prediction is to find a treatment effect, here the theoretical prediction is a null effect. Most individuals in the experimental sample, which has been weighted to match Taiwan's population distribution, identify as Taiwan nationalists or New Taiwanese. For these individuals, there is little reason to expect that priming a sense of obligation to "my" Taiwan should translate into greater civic duty to contribute to a state that most see to represent the best interests of a national "other."

Yet a null effect can also be the result of a weak treatment. Here, the presence of distinct national groups in Taiwan, each with different beliefs of nation-state linkage, helps adjudicate between the two scenarios. If what I observe is a "true" null effect of nationalist appeals due to widely fractured beliefs of nation-state linkages in Taiwan, then I should see predictably heterogeneous treatment effects when the sample is divided by national groups. For those who identify as Taiwan nationalists and New Taiwanese, the null effect should hold, whereas for the minority who identify as China nationalists—the only group with strong beliefs of linkage—I should see a positive treatment effect. On the other hand, if the null effect is due to an ineffective treatment, then it should hold across all national groups, regardless of their beliefs about nation-state linkage.

The distinct national groups in Taiwan also serve as a check on the validity of the experimental design. Experimental treatments based on news articles or vignettes are prone to spillover effects, where the multifaceted treatment ends up affecting other emotions or attitudes in addition to the specific one targeted. Spillover can muddy inference by making it less clear why we observe a treatment effect. In the current experiment, for example, the anecdotes and quotes in the "national obligation" article might also prime altruism or empathy. Yet only the intended part of the treatment—the priming of national obligation—predicts divergent treatment effects across the national groups, as I theorized that the national effect on civic duty is moderated by the belief of nation-state linkage. In contrast, altruism or empathy should increase civic duty across all national groups, as earthquake relief helps all individuals on the island regardless of their national identification. Spillover therefore predicts convergent treatment effects across the groups, whereas the theory predicts divergent effects. Thus, analyzing the treatment effect separately by national groups serves as a way to check for spillover in the experimental design.

Results

Figure 5.2 shows how priming national obligation affects civic duty in a crisis context in Taiwan. The top line is the average treatment effect for the entire sample, followed by the treatment effects by national group. As predicted, on average, priming national obligation has a null effect on the sense of civic duty to contribute to the state's relief efforts. This null effect holds across Taiwan nationalists and New Taiwanese, who together comprise the majority of the sample. Less than half of each group—47 percent and 49 percent, respectively—see contributing to the state's earthquake efforts as a matter of duty, and priming national obligation makes no difference to those numbers. But for the minority of China nationalists,

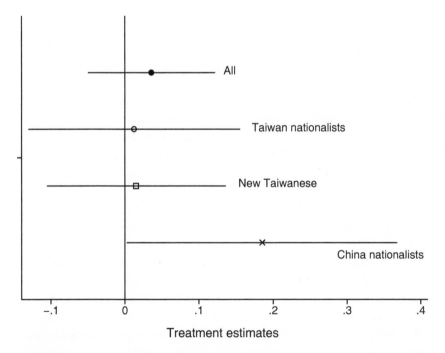

FIGURE 5.2.   Treatment effects in Taiwan's survey experiment. Estimates are the treatment effect of reading the "national obligation" frame news article on sense of civic duty to contribute to the state's earthquake relief efforts. Error bars mark the 95% confidence intervals.

there is a positive and statistically significant treatment effect. Priming a sense of national obligation for this group increases the sense of duty to contribute to the state's earthquake efforts by 19 percent ($p < 0.047$), from 51 percent in the control group to 70 percent in the treatment group.

The uniquely positive treatment effect for China nationalists withstands the most obvious alternative explanations to a nationally motivated civic duty. One possibility is that the memory of the 921 earthquake emotionally affects some national groups in Taiwan more than others. The island's political geography back in the 1990s was more segregated, such that the north was heavily pro-KMT, whereas the south was the birthplace of the pro-Taiwan opposition movement. If damages from the 921 earthquake were concentrated in the north, then the treatment may have been disproportionately effective on China nationalists. In fact, however, the 921 earthquake hit central Taiwan the hardest, especially Nantou and Taichung counties, which have typically been more mixed in partisan and national leaning.

To more explicitly test for uneven effectiveness of the treatment, I included a manipulation check question. After reading their assigned news article, all subjects were asked how much closer they feel to "my" Taiwan. Reading the treatment article similarly increased feelings of national closeness by about 5 percentage points for both Taiwan nationalists and China nationalists. In other words, the singularly positive effect for China nationalists holds despite a treatment that appears to have been equally effective across the groups. This check further supports the uniquely strong beliefs of nation-state linkage among China nationalists as the most sensible explanation for the results.

In democracies where beliefs of nation-state linkage remain fractured or opposed for many, the Taiwan experiment shows that calls for civic duty in the name of the nation tend to fall on deaf ears. Among pro-Taiwan citizens, less than half felt a civic duty to contribute to the relief efforts of what they see to be a KMT legacy state. Invoking national obligation did nothing to move them. The practical consequences of this finding in the wake of another massive earthquake in Taiwan are tragic and alarming.

The implications of the experimental findings extend beyond natural disasters. As Beijing's pressure on the island democracy intensifies through trade exclusions, diplomatic isolation, and even military threat, supporting Taiwan's democracy will become increasingly costly, as Hong Kong's recent extradition crisis glaringly demonstrated. Defending Taiwanese democracy against such pressures may mean having to forgo large company profits or knowingly sending one's son to serve in a risky military situation. Under such circumstances the state's inability to fully harness the powerful pull of its most widespread

Taiwanese nationalism will undoubtedly carry high political stakes for the island democracy.

Ask almost any young person from Taiwan if they are Chinese, and they will quickly correct you that they are, in fact, Taiwanese. While some may have cultural reasons and others political reasons for answering that way, an attachment to the idea of a Taiwanese nation, as separate from China, runs deep for many on the island. On the surface, the coexistence of such strong nationalist sentiments alongside a developing democracy in Taiwan easily invites parallels to neighboring South Korea.

Yet I have shown that very different beliefs of nation-state linkage in Taiwan yield a significantly weaker national basis for civic duty than in South Korea. In South Korea the forced shift into modernity under the Japanese bore a national narrative that, by necessity of survival, took an inclusive approach to all Koreans as part of a singular bloodline. This reimagination of the Korean nation powerfully bonded the nation and state as one through pivotal moments in democratization.

In contrast, Taiwan's hasty modernization under the helm of mainlander KMT elite, who were singularly focused on taking back the Chinese mainland, forced a China nationalist vision over subcultures and dialects that had been fostered on the island for generations. Taiwanese nationalism grew as a backlash to this exclusive approach and wedged a divide between "my" nation and the KMT state for many islanders. While there has been partisan turnover and institutional reform since democratization, many aspects of the Taiwan state—officially still the Republic of China—remain steeped in the KMT's pro-China legacy. As this chapter found, ordinary citizens' perceptions of the state have been even slower to change. Beliefs of nation-state linkage, once internalized, become a durable lens through which individuals filter the political world around them.

Contemporary survey data from this chapter show that fractured beliefs of nation-state linkage in Taiwan effectively cut off civic duty's nationalist roots. Many citizens of Taiwan still vote and pay taxes, but I find that except for self-identified China nationalists, few do so out of a sense of national obligation. The survey experiment bleakly illustrates the consequences of such weaker identity attachment to the state, which are brought into stark relief in times of crisis. Even in the face of earthquakes—a threat to everyone on the island—civic duty to contribute to the state's relief efforts remains weak and unaffected by national appeals for most citizens.

The contrasting findings from the "most similar" pairing of South Korea and Taiwan demonstrate how distinct beliefs of nation-state linkage, internalized

from different kinds of national stories, matter pivotally for the civic foundations of democracies. The pairing has the advantage of naturally controlling
for many confounding factors, but it also leaves open important questions. For
instance, how representative are South Korea and Taiwan of nationally unified
versus nationally fragmented democracies elsewhere? Does the moral pull of the
nation extend beyond ethnic nationalisms, which form the primary basis of both
Korean and Taiwanese national stories?

I therefore widen the empirical lens to examine civic duty and nationalism in
an entirely different cultural and geopolitical context: postunification Germany.
Germany obviously differs from the two East Asian democracies on most background factors, from cultural values and regional history to the explicitly civic
basis of its contemporary nationalism. Yet at the same time, Germany's nationalist division and the contested national stories between the former East versus West maintain important parallels to nationally fragmented Taiwan and the
divided-states situation of the Korean nation. It therefore serves as a compelling
case for externally validating the theory.

Germany is often touted as an exemplary case of democratization by way of
national integration. While it has certainly made impressive strides, I focus on
how a national theory of civic duty can shed light on a less obvious and less
optimistic aspect of its democracy: a sizeable turnout gap between East and West
Germans that has persisted since reunification. Why, despite gains in democratic
experience and generational turnover, has the regional turnout gap stubbornly
remained? What does it signal about the civic foundations of German democracy? The next chapter applies the theoretical lens to this German puzzle and tests
how well it explains patterns of civic duty outside the East Asian democracies,
halfway across the world.

Part III

6

STUNTED CIVIC DUTY IN REUNIFIED GERMANY

On midnight of November 9, 1989, Berliners from both sides rallied around the fall of the Wall. Amid rumbling *Tor auf* ("open the gate") chants, many citizens brought their own hammers and picks to chunk away at the wall as bulldozers knocked down the concrete slabs that had divided Germany for nearly half a century. While the fall of the Berlin Wall symbolized many things—the thawing of the Cold War, an ultimate triumph for the Allies—to most Germans that night it symbolized a new beginning for the divided German nation. As Willy Brandt famously said, "Now what belongs together can grow together."

Less than a year afterward, the two Germanys had reunified under a single state. By most obvious measures Germany's democracy has fared quite well, keeping stable through exchanges of power, party transitions, and massive developmental challenges. Yet a curious regional gap persists, which is the subject of this chapter. Since reunification in 1990, East Germans have always voted less than West Germans in federal elections. A turnout gap in the beginning is unsurprising, since West Germans had a head start with democratic elections for more than four decades during the division. Yet why the gap has persisted for so long, and so stably, is a puzzle. Everything we know from political socialization predicts that such a gap should narrow over time as a new generation of East Germans gain in democratic experience. But even after three decades since reunification—the typical length of a generational turnover—the regional turnout gap remains.

Existing answers for the regional turnout gap focus on the democratic deficit or economic deprivation of the East. Yet Germany's divided past and bifurcated national story suggest a potentially different answer based on unequal development of civic duty between Easterners and Westerners. Reunification was a critical juncture in the evolution of Germany's nation-state relationship. Seeing Germany through this theoretical lens, I pay close attention to how divergent national stories of the former East versus West interacted with reunification to produce contrasting legacies of nation-state linkage—and contrasting civic duty—by region.

Before delving further into the civic foundations of German democracy, it is helpful to situate Germany in comparative perspective. Germany differs from the two East Asian democracies in ways that significantly broaden the appeal of the theory. At the time that South Korea and Taiwan gained independence from Japan and began their nation-building processes, Germany was torn by ideological divisions over how to address its Nazi past. Contemporary German nationalism was a conscious move away from ethnocentrism, in contrast to the predominantly ethnic basis of nationalisms in East Asia.[1] Democratization was also achieved quite differently in Germany. Unlike South Korea and Taiwan's organic and bottom-up process, Germany democratized in a top-down manner, first externally established in the West by the Allied victory and then expanded to the East through reunification. Germany also falls far outside the purview of Confucianism and is subject to different geopolitical pressures as it sits in the middle of Western Europe. In terms of the basis of nationalism, pathway to democratization, cultural values, and geopolitical constraints—the key macro-level variables that were naturally controlled for in the "most similar" East Asia pairing—Germany stands as a clear outside case. It therefore serves as an excellent test for how the theory travels beyond South Korea and Taiwan.

Why do East Germans vote less than West Germans? I begin by demonstrating through the German General Social Survey (GGSS) that, in fact, there is a regional gap in the civic duty to vote that mirrors the turnout gap. Using historical analysis, I trace this civic-duty deficit back to the very process that was meant to bring Germans together: reunification. A speedy reunification led by the West suddenly left many Easterners, who had been socialized into a distinctly Eastern identity over a past century, under a new state that they viewed as representing the best interests of "the other" Germany. This abrupt shift fractured beliefs of nation-state linkage for many Easterners while solidifying strong linkage for Westerners, producing regionally contrasting national stories and, in turn, divergent potential for civic duty to the unified state.

I complement the historical analysis with contemporary GGSS survey data, which reveal strikingly different national effects on civic duty by region. While stronger national identification with "Germany as a whole" predicts a greater sense of civic duty to vote for most West Germans, it exerts no such pull among East Germans. This contrasting national effect holds through multiple robustness checks, including Land fixed-effects and matching to account for regional differences. The survey findings are consistent with the explanation that fractured nation-state linkage stunted civic duty for many East Germans, of which lower turnout is an easily observable consequence.

A stark regional gap exists in the development of civic duty in contemporary Germany. The very event that was meant to mark the beginnings of democratic development in the East ironically sowed the identity schism that impedes that process for many East Germans today. A weaker sense of civic duty is not the only reason why East Germans participate less in their democracy. But it is a powerful one that, judging from recent statistics on regional integration, remains largely unrecognized or unaddressed by the state.

The findings point to a worrisome trend, as lower turnout is arguably the least pernicious consequence of stunted civic duty in the East. As Germany faces mounting socioeconomic costs from the influx of migration—the country is one of the leading host democracies for refugees—it increasingly relies on native citizens to make sacrifices in the form of sharing resources, higher taxes, and support for newcomer assistance. In response, Germany's ultranationalist political party, Alternative für Deutschland (AfD), has quickly gained popularity in the former East. Crime rates against immigrants are also significantly higher in the East than in the West. Is it that Easterners are more xenophobic? In fact, the root of the problem runs deeper. Many Easterners feel less civic connection to the German state for identity reasons that predate contemporary migration challenges. They are therefore much less willing to respond to the state's demands, especially when doing so is seen as costly. When the consequences of regionally stunted civic duty are brought into full view, I argue, they carry troublesome implications for the resilience of Germany's democracy going forward.

The Regional Turnout Gap in Germany

Now over three decades old, reunified Germany appears to be a well-functioning and stable democracy in many ways. Since reunification in 1990, the state has had nine successful rounds of federal elections, developed a stable multiparty system, and undergone peaceful exchanges of power between the leading Social Democratic Party (SDP) and Christian Democratic Union (CDU) coalitions. Turnout rates in federal elections have hovered around 70 percent, which is at the higher end of advanced democracies. Despite the massive economic challenges that came with reunification, there has been no serious secessionist movement to date. By such common indicators of democratic success, German democracy appears in good health.

Upon closer inspection, however, remnants of the country's division for nearly half a century prior to reunification are still visible. When the federal turnout rates are divided by region, a sizeable turnout gap between East and West emerges. Figure 6.1 shows that since the first unified Bundestag elections in 1990, East Germans have always voted less than West Germans.[2] The regional turnout gap averages to about 5.5 percentage points, with the widest gaps reaching nearly 8 percentage points in the election years 1994, 2002, and 2009.

The curious part about the regional turnout gap is not necessarily its size but its persistence over time. An initial gap in 1990 is not surprising: East Germans were participating in democratic elections for the first time, whereas West Germans had been doing so for decades.[3] But as East Germans gain in democratic experience and build partisan attachments, political socialization suggests that children should "soak up" such resources to start at a higher baseline of participation.[4] Even if the authoritarian-parent generation is resistant to change, the youth generation should internalize democratic norms through civic education. Then with generational turnover, we should expect the regional turnout gap to steadily narrow over time. Yet figure 6.1 shows no signs of catching up in the East.

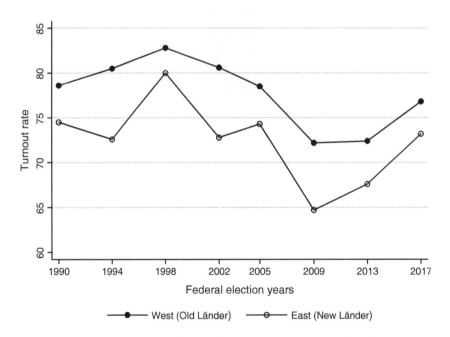

FIGURE 6.1.   Regional turnout gap in federal elections of reunified Germany. "West" includes the former Federal Länder and West Berlin, East includes the new Länder and East Berlin. Official turnout statistics are from the Federal Returning Officer.

Existing explanations for the regional turnout gap tend to paint a picture of politically disillusioned East Germans. One line of argument focuses on the region's democratic deficit. The claim is that due to Communist socialization, many East Germans harbor a deep skepticism toward democratic principles. Scholars have shown that East Germans are weaker in political efficacy, and political dissatisfaction is one of the strongest predictors of vote abstention among this group.[5] Such patterns broadly mirror other post-Communist societies, where scholars have found political cynicism to be a consistent predictor of low turnout after democratization.[6]

Another line of argument focuses on economic disillusionment. East Germans expected great economic benefits from reunification. At the time of reunification, the belief that a unified Germany would increase economic prosperity was nearly twice as high among East Germans as it was among West Germans.[7] Yet the rapid transition into capitalism that accompanied reunification proved rocky. Many East Germans found themselves less than competitive in the newly expanded market economy, and an extended period of economic stagnation and high unemployment rates plagued the region. Scholars have argued that disappointment in the state's ability to deliver on its economic promise led many East Germans to withdraw from politics more generally, including voting in federal elections.[8] This "depressing disenchantment" theory of low political participation is a common one in post-Communist societies, although empirical evidence for it has been mixed.[9]

When examined over time, however, both explanations quickly lose their luster. Figure 6.2 plots, from the years 1990 to 2017, the mean levels of economic

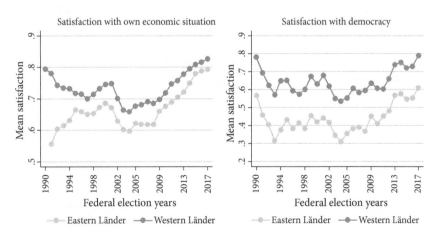

FIGURE 6.2. Trends in democratic and economic satisfaction by region in Germany. Annual estimates are based on Germany's *Politbarometer* time-series survey.

and democratic satisfaction by region. Data come from the *Politbarometer* times-series survey, which has asked both questions every year.[10] The economic disenchantment thesis on the left quickly falls apart. The regional gap in economic satisfaction has steadily narrowed over the years, but the turnout gap has remained. On the right side, the regional gap in democratic satisfaction appears quite stable over time. But in most years, satisfaction with democracy trends in the opposite direction as turnout. In the critical first decade after reunification, for example, democratic satisfaction fell in both regions, whereas the turnout rate peaked between 1990 and 1998 for both East and West Germans. And while turnout since then has fallen nearly in a straight line in both regions until 2009, democratic satisfaction oscillated back and forth during that period. Thus, existing explanations offer little purchase on the puzzle of the persistent turnout gap between the regions. Economic or democratic satisfaction may strongly predict turnout at a given point in time, but neither tracks very well changes in the regional turnout gap over time.

My claim is that the regional turnout gap primarily reflects a different kind of deficit in the East—one of weaker civic connection to the democratic state of unified Germany. I argue that the issue is not really disillusioned East Germans who see little benefit from voting, as it is disconnected East Germans who feel little sense of obligation to contribute to the democracy in which they live.

Indeed, the GGSS data suggest that East Germans feel weaker civic duty to vote than West Germans. The survey only asked a duty-to-vote question in the years 1998 and 2008, which rules out a similar time-series graph as in figure 6.2, but the two years nevertheless provide important snapshots of short- versus long-term checkpoints after reunification.[11] In 1998, nearly a decade after reunification, 70 percent of West Germans felt a civic duty to vote, whereas only 54 percent of East Germans did—a 16-percentage-point gap. Another decade later, in 2008, that duty-to-vote deficit had actually widened to 20 percentage points: while 77 percent of West Germans now felt a duty to vote, still only 57 percent of East Germans did.

This civic-duty deficit among Easterners matters significantly to the regional turnout gap. Pooling GGSS data from 1998 and 2008, I used logistic regression to estimate the effect of feeling a duty to vote on predicted turnout in the East versus the West. I find that a sense of duty to vote strongly predicts turnout in both regions, even after accounting for democratic and economic satisfaction, political interest, education, age, gender, and year effects. In fact, the duty-to-vote effect is nearly twice as strong in the East: whereas feeling a sense of duty to vote is associated with 4.2 times higher odds of turnout in the West, it is associated with 7.1 times higher odds in the East. These results suggest that an explanation for the regional turnout gap in Germany is not complete without an account of why the sense of civic duty to vote has lagged in the East.

The National Identity Politics of German Reunification

A national theory of civic duty shifts the focus away from socioeconomic differences between the regions and toward their divergent nationalist histories. The crux of the theory is that national stories internalize beliefs about the relational linkage between the national people and the democratic state in which they live. These beliefs then serve as the pivotal levers that harness or stunt the nation's moral pull toward civic duty. I therefore focus on a critical juncture in Germany's nation-building process that was likely a seismic shock to the nation-state landscape: the reunification of 1990. Unlike existing explanations for the turnout gap, which focus on reunification's political and economic losses for the East, this section highlights a different kind of identity loss for East Germans—that of fractured beliefs of nation-state linkage.

Perhaps what is most remarkable about Germany's reunification is just how quickly it happened. In late 1989 mounting economic unrest within the German Democratic Republic (GDR) in the East culminated in the fall of the Berlin Wall, opening a window of opportunity that Chancellor Helmut Kohl of the Federal Republic of Germany (FRG) in the West seized immediately. Under the banner of economic urgency, his party ran in and won the first free *Volkskammer* elections in the GDR. With his party in power, Kohl aggressively pushed for a speedy unification under Article 23, which would preserve the Western Constitution and simply append the Eastern territory as new Länder. The measure ultimately passed, and on October 3, 1990—less than a year after the fall of the Wall—the GDR went from a troubled state to a nonexistent one.

The rapid pace of reunification meant that East and West Germans each entered the new union with their different nationalist socializations very much intact. While both states claimed to represent the German nation, they defined the boundaries and basis of that nation quite differently. The nationalist rhetoric of the FRG was always one of a singular German nation, of which the FRG was the sole legitimate representative. Official speeches and publications by Western leadership were imbued with language of pan-German solidarity, referring to the East German people as "the brothers and sisters over there."[12] Even as the FRG actively contested and discounted the ideology of the GDR state, the Western vision of a German nation was always inclusive of the people in the East.

In contrast, for nearly half a century, the GDR went to aggressive lengths to socialize its people into a uniquely East German national identity, defined by differentiation from the West. To make a clear break from fascist legacy and Nazi guilt, the GDR touted itself as the "better" Germany and actively sought to construct a new, socialist vision of the German nation. Textbooks recast the most

renown German cultural icons as specifically Eastern heroes and omitted historical events and political figures that challenged this national redefinition. In contrast to the FRG, which discounted the GDR state but claimed the Eastern people as part of its nation, the GDR reimagined the German nation—through the
means of cultural reproduction, education, and socialist branding of everyday
life necessities—as exclusively of the East. In these ways, each state had "[strived]
to create their own version of the German nation, hence two separate nations."[13]

In principle, reunification was meant to bridge this bifurcating German
nation. In practice, however, the near exclusive Western dominance over the process deepened the identity schism for many East Germans. East Germans were
suddenly the minority, comprising only one-fifth of the newly expanded citizen
population. The sudden and unilateral imposition of Western institutions and
norms cut deeply for many Easterners, and it bore national stories of inferiority,
victimization, and exclusion by the unified state they now called home. Such stories told of the loss of cherished Eastern community customs such as the *Jugendweihe* coming-of-age ceremony, which lost state funding due to its Communist
roots. Trabants and other DDR products that were part of everyday life in the
East and integral symbols of East German national identity were discontinued
due to privatization. Many Eastern fathers who lost their jobs in an open capital-
ist market lamented the unfulfilled economic promises of reunification. Stories
of Eastern politicians being emasculated by Western party leaders, even when
they were representing Eastern districts, were well known.[14] Such stories of alien-
ation from the state were only bolstered by accounts of resentful and discriminat-
ing West Germans who, now burdened with the solidarity tax to finance the costs
of integration, saw *Ossies* as free riders and a burden.

The Wall had fallen, but the "wall in the mind" had grown. The one-sidedness
of reunification left many East Germans feeling as if they were being "colonized,"
rather than united with the West.[15] Through the 1990s, such sentiment was so
widespread among Easterners that it earned the moniker *ostalgie*—a nostalgia for
the Eastern life. In fact, the GGSS shows that between 1991 and 2000, the percentage of East Germans who strongly identified with former East Germany actually
increased, from 43 to 69 percent. Such statistics suggest that the psychological
process of reunification, or what some have called "inner unification," lags far
behind the territorial unification of the two Germanys.[16] "On the level of social
and personal relations, of customs and everyday life, integration and incorpora-
tion of the East are clearly limited. In these respects, one can still speak of two
different societies, and awareness of this split seems to grow."[17]

Beliefs of nation-state linkage therefore remain deeply divided along former regional lines in contemporary Germany. For most West Germans, unified

Germany is both constitutionally and communally the continuation of the FRG and its pan-German nationalist vision. Thus, there was little reason for reunification to alter the belief of strong nation-state linkage that Western national stories had internalized for half a century. In contrast, East Germans had many reasons to see the reunified state as representing the best interests of the "other" German nation. Eastern national stories took a dramatic turn at this critical juncture to reflect the fractured and even opposed nation-state relationship created by a West-led reunification. I argue that this has stunted many Easterners' sense of civic duty to the unified state. For such Easterners voting in federal elections or otherwise contributing to the democracy of unified Germany invokes little sense of obligation to "my" Germany—a national community that disappeared by way of reunification. As a result, fewer East Germans feel a civic duty to vote in federal elections and fewer make it to the polls.

An Empirical Test

I turn to the 2008 GGSS—the only year that the survey includes questions on both the civic duty to vote and national identification—to assess the nationalist roots of the regional gap in civic duty. Given the contrasting beliefs of nation-state linkage by region, a sense of obligation to "my" Germany should exert a powerful pull toward civic duty in the West but not in the East. The empirical prediction is contrasting national effects by region: all else equal, we should expect to see a strong and positive national effect on the duty to vote in the West, but close to a null effect in the East.

To specify that the national effect is driven by a moral pull toward civic duty and not some other motivation, I return to the statistical model of moral motivations developed in chapter 4. The model mathematizes a key insight about moral obligation from political theory: its principled nature. For an individual who sees voting as an obligation to her nation—as a matter of intrinsic commitment—other payoff-based considerations, such as how much she cares about who wins the election, should not matter to her sense of civic duty to vote. I showed that this principled and ordered relationship between moral versus nonmoral motivations can be captured statistically by a negative interaction between them. For individuals who see voting as a national obligation, as their national identification strengthens, the effect that expected payoffs from voting have on the sense of civic duty to vote should decrease to zero. Whether a negative interaction emerges from the data serves as a test for the presence or absence of the nation's moral pull, even if we cannot directly observe intrinsic motivations in a survey context. The model predicting the civic duty to vote in Germany is as follows:

$$civic\ duty\ to\ vote_i = \beta_0 + \beta_1(national\ identification)_{e,w} + \beta_2(payoffs)_i$$
$$+ \beta_3(national\ identification \times payoffs)_{e,w} + \beta_4(controls)_i + \varepsilon$$

Individual i's sense of civic duty to vote is modeled as a function of three key variables: strength of national identification with Germany, which I predict to be imagined differently for most East versus West Germans (indexed e, w); expected payoffs from voting; and the interaction between the two variables. For most West Germans, for whom beliefs of nation-state linkage should be strong, I predict the national effect to be positive and significant ($\beta_1 > 0$), and for the accompanying interaction effect with payoffs to be negative ($\beta_3 < 0$). For many East Germans, for whom I argue that beliefs of nation-state linkage should be largely fractured, the national effect should be close to null ($\beta_1 = 0$) and exert no significant moral pull ($\beta_3 = 0$) toward the duty to vote.

The key variables are measured in the GGSS as follows. The dependent variable, the civic duty to vote, is measured by asking respondents how strongly they agree or disagree with the following statement: "In a democracy, every citizen has the duty to vote in elections." Those who answered that they "strongly agree" were coded has feeling strong civic duty, "somewhat agree" as weak duty, and all other categories ("neither agree nor disagree," "somewhat disagree," "strongly disagree") as not feeling a duty to vote.

The key independent variable, strength of national identification, is measured by asking respondents how strongly they identify with "Germany as a whole and its population." The question appears in a battery asking about identification with different levels of community and uses the same wording in both regions, thus offering a fair test of whether "Germany as a whole" is imagined differently by East versus West Germans. On average, both East and West Germans feel "pretty strong" levels of national identification (0.63 on a 0–1 scale) and the variances are similar, such that any regional difference in the national effect is unlikely to be due to differences in measurement.

For a payoff-based motivation to vote that is particularly salient in post-Communist contexts, I consider satisfaction with government performance. In the "depressing disenchantment" thesis about low political participation in post-Communist societies, the argument is that dissatisfaction with state performance reduces the expected material and psychic payoffs from turnout, resulting in disillusioned citizens who cannot be bothered to vote. Greater satisfaction with government performance, then, should incentivize turnout by increasing the perceived returns from voting.

The model also controls for political interest, frequency of church attendance, party identification—known predictors of the duty to vote from prior studies—and well-established demographic controls in turnout studies: female, education, age, and age-squared. Table 7 shows the estimates from ordinary least squares (OLS) regression separately for individuals in the West versus the East. All variables have been rescaled from 0 to 1 and standard errors are clustered by Land.

A striking contrast in the national effect emerges between the regions. Stronger identification with "Germany as a whole," as understood by respondents in the East versus the West, matters very differently for their sense of civic duty to vote. For West Germans all of the empirical signs suggest that a moral obligation to the nation motivates the duty to vote: the national effect is strong and positive, and its interaction coefficient with satisfaction with government performance is directionally negative and of a substantial magnitude.

TABLE 7   Estimates of national effect on duty to vote by region in Germany

DUTY TO VOTE	WEST	EAST
National identification	0.20***	−0.07
	(0.05)	(0.04)
Payoff		
Satisfaction with government performance	0.24***	0.27
	(0.08)	(0.19)
Interaction		
National identification x performance	−0.17*	0.05
	(0.09)	(0.30)
Controls		
Political interest	0.19***	0.28**
	(0.04)	(0.08)
Church attendance	0.09***	0.14**
	(0.03)	(0.07)
Party identification		
SPD	0.12***	0.16*
CDU	0.05**	0.15***
Greens	0.07*	0.18
PDS	0.02	0.10**
Other	0.06*	0.13*
Demographic controls	yes	yes
Constant	0.35***	0.20**
	(0.04)	(0.07)
R-squared	0.11	0.16
N	1907	938

Estimates are based on ordinary least squares regressions, with all variables rescaled 0 to 1 and standard errors clustered by Land.
*** $p < 0.01$
** $p < 0.05$
* $p < 0.10$

For East Germans, I predicted that fractured beliefs of nation-state linkage from reunification would likely block this national impetus for civic duty. Indeed, the national effect on the duty to vote among Easterners is essentially zero, and no meaningful interaction emerges with how much satisfaction with government performance matters. The regional contrast in the national effect holds up even when I substitute alternative payoff-based motivations to vote, such as satisfaction with the economy or trust in government, and even when Land-fixed effects are included to account for any unobserved particularities of each Land.

Figure 6.3 plots the model predictions by region. For an average West German in the top left, stronger national identification takes her predicted duty to vote from 0.68 to 0.85—from "weak" to "strong." The bottom left quadrant plots the interaction. We see a pattern that is indicative of a moral pull from the nation: as national identification strengthens, the predicted effect of government performance on the duty to vote gradually reduces from 0.25 toward zero. For a West German who strongly identifies with her nation, how satisfied she is with the government's performance no longer matters to her sense of duty to vote. In stark contrast, both lines are essentially flat for an East German on the right side, for whom national identification has little relation to her sense of civic duty to vote.

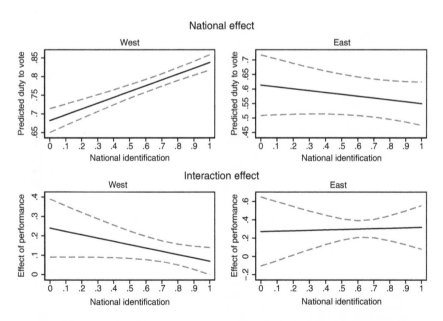

FIGURE 6.3. Predicted duty to vote by national identification in Germany. Predictions based on regression estimates from table 7, holding all covariates at their actual values, not means. Error bars mark 95 percent confidence intervals.

The average predicted duty to vote hovers around 0.60 or "weak," regardless of strength of national identification.

The GGSS also asks about identification with the former national communities of the FRG and GDR to West and East Germans, respectively. Neither nation technically exists anymore. But if the main results are driven by the legacies of nationalist socialization during the division and how they responded differently to reunification, then we should expect identification with the former national communities to elicit patterns that are parallel to those in table 7. For many West Germans, lingering identification with the former FRG community should still motivate a civic duty to vote under the unified state that historian Jürgen Kocka once described as "an enlarged version of the old Federal Republic."[18] In contrast, for many East Germans, enduring ties to the GDR community should exert no moral pull to participate in the federal elections of a state that many see to represent the "other" Germany.

In fact, East Germans who still strongly identify with the former GDR community are likely individuals who were socialized into East German national stories that embedded opposed nation-state linkage. When the state in which one lives is seen as not only representing a national "other" but also threatening the best interests of "my" nation, national obligation should motivate a kind of anti-civic duty to reject or resist the demands of that state. It is possible that a subset of East Germans holds such beliefs, since the vision of the East German nation as a separate community from the West was effectively eradicated by a West-led reunification. For such individuals, stronger national identification with the former national community of the GDR should predict a weaker civic duty to vote in the federal elections of unified Germany.

TABLE 8   Former national ties and the duty to vote in Germany

DUTY TO VOTE	WEST	EAST
National identification (Former FRG/GDR communities)	0.08*	−0.10*
	(0.04)	(0.06)
Satisfaction with government performance	0.14**	0.21*
	(0.07)	(0.12)
National identification × performance	−0.005	0.12
	(0.10)	(0.18)
Controls	yes	yes
Constant	0.41***	0.18***
	(0.04)	(0.05)
R-squared	0.10	0.16
N	1793	929

Estimates are based on ordinary least squares regressions, with all variables rescaled 0 to 1 and standard errors clustered by Land. Controls include the same set of covariates as in table 7.

*** $p < .01$

** $p < .05$

* $p < .10$

Table 8 shows that identification with the former national communities elicits a parallel regional contrast to the results in table 7. As predicted, for West Germans, strongly identifying with the former FRG community predicts an 8 percent greater duty to vote. For East Germans, the national effect is opposite: strongly identifying with the former GDR community predicts a 10 percent weaker duty to vote. This dampening effect is consistent with beliefs of opposed nation-state linkage. These findings suggest that one important reason why East Germans still vote less than West Germans is due to national stories that have internalized a moral disconnect between the nation of their past and the state of their present.

Communism's Shadow?

Being an Easterner carries a great deal more baggage than simply identifying with a different national community. For nearly half a century, East Germans were also governed under a Communist state, a fact that shaped every detail of their daily lives. The Communist experience left enduring imprints on the region's socioeconomic landscape. East Germany emerged significantly poorer and less religious than the West, having endured a sustained period of economic stagnation at the hands of a heavily controlling and largely closed-off state. It is quite possible that such cumulative experiences reshaped East Germans' views of government and citizenship in ways that fundamentally differ from those of West Germans. Such deep-seated differences in worldviews between the regions cannot be fully captured through individual-level controls for frequency of church attendance or even Land fixed-effects in regression models.

In their book about the different types of Communist legacies, Grigore Pop-Eleches and Joshua Tucker distinguish between two kinds of Communism's shadows.[19] The first is psychological: how the experience of "living through" Communism impressionably shapes the way that individuals approach their political worlds thereafter. The second is structural: how the result of "living in" Communist institutions leaves enduring imprints on the socioeconomic landscape. Both kinds of shadows certainly still hang over the Eastern region of Germany today, but they relate to the national explanation told in this chapter in different ways. Whereas the structural shadow is a possible confounder that negates the nationalist explanation, the psychological shadow is in many ways a complementary part of the story. I first assess how much of the main findings can be attributed to Communism's structural shadow before circling back to address the legacies of the psychological shadow.

As a result of living under Communist institutions, East Germans tend to be poorer, less educated, and less religious than their West German counterparts.

Given that education and church attendance are known predictors of the duty to vote, and income and education are strong correlates of national identification, the structural counterargument would be that such socioeconomic legacies of Communism explain the regional gap in the duty to vote instead. The regionally contrasting national effects observed in tables 7 and 8 may simply reflect these socioeconomic differences between East and West, rather than the result of socialization into different kinds of national stories.

One way to account for Communism's structural legacy is to use matching between the regions. Matching weights the regional samples such that they are conditionally identical in their socioeconomic compositions. I designate being from the East as the treatment category and predict the propensity of being an Easterner based on the socioeconomic variables that the regional samples differ significantly on: income, highest education, and church attendance. Weights are generated by taking the inverse of the probability of selection to the East.[20] If the main finding in table 7 is primarily an artifact of Communism's socioeconomic imprint in the East, then matching should largely wash out the regionally contrasting national effects on the duty to vote. Instead, if the main findings are due to socialization into different kinds of national stories in the East versus the West—a psychological rather than a structural phenomenon—then even after socioeconomic adjustments between the regions, the national effects should remain largely unchanged.

Table 9 shows the matched estimates based on the same duty-to-vote model in table 7. We see unequivocal support for the latter scenario: the regional contrast in the national effect appears to be, as far as the data show, mostly an identity

TABLE 9 Assessing Communism's structural shadow through matching

DUTY TO VOTE	WEST	EAST
National identification	0.19***	−.09
	(0.03)	(0.11)
Satisfaction with government performance	0.21**	−0.12
	(0.08)	(0.22)
National identification × performance	−0.14	0.56
	(0.10)	(0.34)
Controls	yes	yes
Constant	0.34***	0.28**
	(0.04)	(0.10)
R-squared	0.11	0.17
N	1907	938

Matched estimates are based on ordinary least squares regressions, with all variables rescaled 0 to 1 and standard errors clustered by Land. Controls include same set of covariates as in table 7.

*** p < .01

** p < .05

* p < .10

effect. Even after matching the regional samples on socioeconomic differences, stronger national identification still predicts a 19 percent greater duty to vote in the West, while it has a null effect in the East.

The socioeconomic imprints of Communism may still account for Easterners' lower political participation in other ways. For instance, one of the most noticeable changes with matching is how, for East Germans, the effect of satisfaction with government performance goes from positive in table 7 to a null effect in table 9. Yet the national coefficients for both East and West Germans remain essentially unchanged, which suggests that they are not reducible to the socioeconomic differences between the regional samples. These results lend support for the original interpretation: that the contrasting national effects reflect differing levels of moral commitment to unified Germany, internalized from divergent national stories sown by reunification.

What of the first kind of Communism's shadow—the psychological effects of "living through" Communism? In many ways, the story told in this chapter of how the legacies of GDR nationalist socialization still fracture beliefs of nation-state linkage for many East Germans is wholly compatible with this kind of Communist shadow. Communist ideology was the very basis of a uniquely Eastern nationalist claim and served as the organizing principle for the everyday practices and rituals that helped internalize that identity among Easterners. Trabants, Rondo coffee, Zeha shoes, and other DDR brands—all products of the Communist state—were woven into the fabric of the daily life of Easterners. State-funded socialist ceremonies, such as the Jugendweihe, were a cherished part of what it meant to grow up in the East. Indeed, it is an emotional attachment to these seemingly mundane, quotidian experiences of "living through" Communism that fuels ostalgie. The stickiness of Eastern nationalist socialization, the effects of which are still visible among many East Germans three decades after reunification, is deeply intertwined with this kind of Communist shadow.

To say that the stunted civic duty to vote among East Germans is a Communist legacy, however, would be inaccurate. The claim here is not that Communism is intrinsically opposed to civic life or that all post-Communist societies are disadvantaged in achieving a vibrant democracy. No empirical test from this chapter substantiates such a blanket conclusion. Rather, Communism matters to the extent that it served as a particularly enduring basis for an East German national identity as distinct from the West. What ultimately positioned this nationalism to be counter to the democratic state was the abrupt and unilateral way that reunification absorbed the Eastern national community into the West. It is the fractured beliefs of nation-state linkage from this sudden transition, not an unyielding devotion to Communist ideology, that still stunts a sense of civic duty to German democracy for many Easterners today.

Willy Brandt may have taken too much for granted when he famously said, "Now what belongs together can grow together." The Wall fell over three decades ago, but the civic consequences of the identity schism sown by reunification still remain. If anything, this chapter has shown that in order to grow together, we must first belong together.

Broader Implications for German Democracy

In the grand scheme of democratic life, is a regional turnout gap of a few percentage points that important? The issue is that lower turnout is most likely just the tip of the iceberg. The persistence of fractured beliefs of nation-state linkage among many East Germans, and the resulting civic-duty deficit, has worrisome implications for German democracy that extend beyond electoral turnout.

The reason that such beliefs have been so sticky among Easterners is partially because there has been little reason for change in the national stories that sustain them. More than three decades into reunification, East Germans are still severely underrepresented in the state and society of unified Germany. Angela Merkel was the first head of state from the East, but she was an anomaly: even during her third term as chancellor, Merkel herself was the only Easterner in her cabinet. According to a 2016 study by the University of Leipzig, among federal agencies that are not specifically designated for East German affairs, only one is headed by an Easterner.[21] The same study estimates that across politics, business, and education, only 1.7 percent of leadership positions are held by individuals of Eastern origin. In short, there has been little reform—both to the representational architecture of the state and to the reach of social opportunities—to spur new, reparative kinds of national stories for Easterners.

This identity disconnect in the East metastasizes in many ways. One area where such effects are particularly acute is the German nativist response to the migration crisis. In 2017 the United Nations estimated the global refugee population to be 68.5 million, and Germany has emerged as a leading host democracy, housing over 970,000 refugees.[22] There is no doubt that the social and economic integration of these refugees will be one of the defining challenges for German democracy going forward.

Native reactions to the dramatic influx of foreigners have been understandably mixed, but a parallel regional pattern to the turnout gap has emerged: negative reactions, such as violence against foreigners, are disproportionately concentrated in the East. In 2014, for example, the Federal Ministry of the Interior reported that nearly 50 percent of the 130 antiforeigner crimes were committed in former GDR states, even though only 17 percent of the national population lives there.[23] Similarly, a study by the Leibniz Centre for European Economic Research estimates that, all else equal, a refugee faces ten times higher odds of becoming a hate crime victim in the East versus the West.[24] The regional skew in xenophobic violence has certainly sharpened with the refugee surge between 2013 and 2015, but it is a pattern that actually dates back to at least the 1990s, since reunification.

Are East Germans more xenophobic than West Germans? Some see the regional skew in anti-immigrant violence as the ideational product of right-wing extremism that has grown popular in the East, such as the rapid rise of AfD. The classic chicken-versus-egg problem plagues this explanation, however, and importantly, the AfD cannot explain regional differences in the early days after reunification, when the party had yet to exist. Others have argued that the nativist reaction in the East is a side effect of the GDR's failure to confront Nazism. Whereas West Germany forced itself to reckon with Nazi guilt, explicating norms against ethnic discrimination and xenophobia, East Germany's distancing from this past may have implicitly tolerated antiforeigner sentiments.[25] But the most common explanation is an economic one: relatively deprived Easterners are more likely to see immigrants and refugees as a threat and feel more hostility toward them.

Yet empirical support for the economic argument remains thin. It is true that on average the East has been relatively poorer than the West. But one of the earliest studies on the regional skew in antiforeigner violence found that, when crime rates are examined locally within each region, they do not correlate at all with level of development. Economists Alan Kreuger and Jörn-Steffen Pischke summarized their null finding: "In general, our results are difficult to reconcile with simple economic theories of crime against foreigners. . . . A more complex process seems to be at work, perhaps a repercussion of the difficult issues arising from the unification of east and west Germany."[26]

One such "complex process" stemming from reunification that this chapter highlights is fractured beliefs of nation-state linkage in the East. The issue is not an "us versus them" mentality that typically defines antiforeigner violence, but rather, an "us versus the state" problem in the East. Germany's decision to accept the influx of refugees entails a high ask of its citizens. The state is implicitly asking citizens to help finance integration, expend efforts toward social inclusion, and otherwise make sacrifices to uphold what Germany wishes to stand for. Yet Merkel's *wir schaffen das* ("we can do this") slogan clearly backfires for many in the East who have long felt excluded from the national "we" espoused by the state. For such individuals the state's calls for further sacrifice on behalf of even more national "others" incites backlash rather than cooperation. Higher rates of violence against immigrants and refugees in the East is a long-standing and tragic side effect of such civic disconnect dating back to reunification.

The troubling part about this explanation is that improving nativist backlash to the migration crisis is not really about economic incentives, which can be offered, or even about xenophobia, which can be policed. The regional skew in xenophobic violence illustrates the perverse ways in which a deficit of national linkage to the democratic state manifests. And there is no quick fix for restoring severed moral connections, an issue that poses a much deeper problem than lower turnout rates for Germany's democratic future.

Lags in levels of democratic participation are common in post-Communist societies. The dominant picture behind such patterns is that of the "disadvantaged and powerless" citizen.[27] The argument generally follows that, disillusioned by poverty and the failed ideologies of their past, these individuals withdraw from politics because they see little value in or prospect of a return from their participation.

Yet a national theory of civic duty paints quite a different picture of the post-Communist citizens of East Germany. The empirical evidence shows that lower turnout among East Germans has a great deal more to do with a deficit in civic duty, rooted in fractured beliefs of nation-state linkage, than a deficit in income or political trust. For many East Germans, the reunification of 1990—the very event that was meant to bring Germans together—produced national stories that framed the unified state as standing for a national "other," severing moral attachments to the new democracy. The civic repercussions of a rapid and one-sided reunification led by the West are still traceable in survey data two decades later. Whereas stronger national identification predicts a greater sense of civic duty to vote in federal elections for most West Germans, this identity-based pathway to civic duty remains almost entirely blocked for East Germans.

So far, across five distinct national groups in three democracies, a remarkably consistent empirical pattern has emerged. National stories and the beliefs of nation-state linkage they embed matter powerfully for how the nation's moral pull sometimes supports, but at other times stunts, a sense of civic duty to one's democracy. Germany demonstrates that the national theory of civic duty is not just an East Asia story. By varying almost every macrolevel confounder that was naturally controlled by the South Korea and Taiwan pairing, Germany served as a particularly powerful third case for generalizing the theory.

But democracies vary in all sorts of other ways as well. How systematic and consequential is the national effect on civic duty when seen from a bird's-eye view, across a cross-section of the world's democracies? The next and final empirical chapter expands to a global analysis of the relationship between nationalism and civic duty in democracies. Across the widest possible set of democratic citizens for whom reliable cross-national data exist, I examine how the moral pull of the nation shapes a sense of civic duty to vote, pay taxes, and defend one's country in the event of war.

NATIONALISM AND CIVIC DUTY ACROSS THE WORLD

Nationalism has always had an uneasy relationship with democracy. Nationalism's capacity to unite people of different backgrounds within its boundaries makes it an invaluable political asset for democracies. Yet the pitfalls of such homogenizing power are also glaringly clear. History attests that the line between love for the national "us" and hatred for the national "them" is easily thinned and crossed during times of strain. The atrocities of World War II tragically demonstrated how insecure variants of nationalism could be weaponized by demagogues to fuel support for violence, persecution of minorities, and even mass genocides. Nationalism, especially of the ethnic kind, became stained as antiliberal and antidemocratic as scholars tried to salvage the "good" kind of civic nationalism from the ruins.

This book does not argue for negating the potential dangers of nationalism. It argues instead that the Manichean focus on good versus bad nationalisms has evaded deeper inquiry into the nuanced push and pull between nationalism and democracy. Nations are built on definitions of who "we" are, but nationalisms— the actions, expressions, and commitments made in the name of the nation—are based on the relationships that connect a national people to each other, national others, and importantly, the state. It is this relational aspect of nationalism that most immediately shapes how a nationalism manifests in support of or against the democracy that houses it.

National stories do the work of connecting "who we are" to "how we should live" based on the lived experiences of a national people. I have argued that a specific relationship embedded in national stories—that between a national people and the state in which they live—shapes people's beliefs about what they owe to their democracy. When this historicized linkage is one of mutual support, nationalism—even of the ethnic kind—can generate important benefits to democracy in the form of greater civic duty and willingness to sacrifice on its behalf. It is the context, rather than the content, of nationalism that shapes its relationship to democracy.

The final empirical chapter of the book turns to the most expansive test of this contextual argument. The national theory of civic duty was inspired by the impressive show of civic duty in the unlikely setting of South Korea's young and fragile democracy during the Asian financial crisis. I carefully vetted the theory's logic about national stories and beliefs of linkage through a paired comparison of civic duty in South Korea and Taiwan. Germany's enduring regional gap in civic duty between the former East and West offered an important extension to the theory's generalizability. In an entirely different cultural and historical setting from East Asia, the German case externally validated the civic effect of national stories. This chapter pushes a step further. Using the largest sample of democratic citizens for whom reliable survey data on civic duty exist, I test how consequential the national pull toward civic duty is in democracies across the world. The cross-national findings offer a strong basis for rethinking the common and one-sided assumption that strong nationalism is detrimental to democracies.

Data

Among the major cross-national surveys with a political focus, the World Values Survey (WVS) best fits the data criteria for this study. First, the paucity of off-the-shelf survey data on civic duty means that most cross-national surveys include at best only one question on civic duty, usually the duty to vote.[1] The most recent sixth wave of the WVS includes three measures of civic duty toward voting, paying taxes, and defending the state. Second, the dataset needs to concurrently ask questions about both civic duty and strength of national identification. Of the major cross-national surveys that cover more than one region of the world, the WVS is the only one that includes both questions in the same survey wave.[2] Any large-N cross-national analysis faces a trade-off between maintaining comparability of the questions across sample countries versus maximizing the number of countries for generalizability. For the empirical purpose of this test, I prioritized the latter and have taken multiple steps to address the comparability issues in the WVS.

I focus on the sixth wave (2010–2014) of the WVS, which covers 90,350 individuals from sixty countries. Each participant country in the WVS collects its own nationally representative, face-to-face data based on a shared root question-naire, and the country samples are later combined into a cumulative dataset. I use only the sixth and most recent wave because several notable changes to the root questionnaire vastly improve measurement of the key variables in the analy-sis. For instance, to measure strength of national identification, the independent variable in the analysis, the WVS changed from a relative measure—"To which of these geographical groups would you say you belong first of all?"—to an abso-lute one in the fifth wave, which asks how strongly one agrees with the following statement: "I see myself as part of the [French] nation." The new version of the question much more closely taps a sense of psychological identification with the national community.

As for civic-duty measures, a wording change in the root questionnaire enables a proxy measure for the civic duty to vote for the first time. In the sixth wave the WVS changed from asking only about most recent turnout—"Did you vote in your country's recent elections to the national parliament?"—to turnout behav-ior in general: "When elections take place, do you vote always, usually, or never?" The prior wording simply measures self-reported turnout in the last election, which is not necessarily indicative of a sense of duty to vote. Individuals may have voted in that election for many different reasons, only one of which is civic duty. However, the new wording captures habitual voting (those who "always" vote), which prior studies find to be a behavioral indicator for feeling a sense of duty to vote. This wording change, along with existing questions for the civic duty to pay taxes and defend the country, makes the sixth wave of the WVS the cross-national survey with the most diverse list of civic-duty measures.

The WVS sample includes thirty-two democracies based on the dichotomous Boix-Miller-Rosato democracy index from 2010, the start year of the sixth wave.[3] The index codes democracies versus nondemocracies based on two factors: 1) whether there are free and fair elections for the legislature, and 2) whether at least half the male population is eligible to vote. The index is radically minimal-ist when compared to multidimensional indexes such as the Polity score, but its advantage lies in parsimony and transparency.[4] A binary indicator based on the functional minimum for a democratic rule-making process avoids researcher subjectivity in deciding the appropriate cut point for what makes a real or con-solidated democracy. The index yields a sample of 50,733 democratic citizens across the world.

Moving from in-depth case studies to large-N, cross-national analysis inevita-bly comes with growing pains. The most important for this analysis is whether the key variables carry the same meaning across the sample countries. Does agreeing with "I see myself as part of the . . . nation" tap a sense of psychological identifi-cation with the national community in Ukraine as it does in South Korea? Does "always" voting in elections reflect a sense of duty to vote in Australia as it does in Taiwan? When someone says that cheating on taxes is "never justifiable" in Colombia versus Sweden, can we reliably infer a sense of duty to pay taxes in both places? The answer to some of these questions is obviously no. I address these comparative challenges through a mix of statistical and commonsense strategies.

For comparability of the national identification measure, prior research offers a useful benchmark. Sociologist Eldad Davidov distinguishes between two kinds of comparability issues: conceptual comparability versus scalar comparability.[5] The former has to do with consistency in meaning—whether the national identification measure taps the same construct across countries. The latter has to do with consistency of scale—whether ticking "strongly agree" in Ukraine corresponds to the same strength of identification as it does in South Korea. Using factor analysis on nationalism measures in the International Social Survey Program (ISSP) across thirty-four countries, Davidov finds strong support for conceptual comparability: "In spite of cultural differences, people appear to understand the meaning given to nationalism and patriotism by their indicators in a similar manner . . . These findings justify employing the proposed scale of nationalism and [constructive patriotism] to compare their relations to other theoretical constructs of interest in several countries."[6] There is little support for scalar comparability, however. In fact, Davidov finds wide scalar inconsistencies for national measures across countries. I address this in the analysis by including country fixed effects in the regressions, so that strength of national identification is only compared among individuals within, not between, countries. Doing so is not just an empirical fix but also stays true to the theoretical logic, a point to which I return in the following section.

Cross-country comparability for civic-duty measures is most immediately shaped by different compliance contexts. For instance, some democracies enforce compulsory voting while others do not; some have military conscription that requires young men to fulfill mandatory service while others do not; and some are known to have high levels of tax evasion while others are leading examples of fiscal compliance. These institutional settings vary what it means to "always" vote, say "yes" to defending the country in time of war, or respond that cheating on taxes is "never justifiable" in one democracy versus another.

For each kind of civic duty examined in this analysis, I therefore only compare individuals in similar compliance settings. The duty to vote is analyzed only among democracies with no compulsory voting, such that "always" voting in elections serves as a proxy for the sense of duty to vote rather than obedience to the law. The duty to pay taxes is analyzed only within democracies where reasonable evidence exists that most citizens do pay their taxes, such that saying cheating on taxes is "never justifiable" is not just cheap talk. I limit the tax sample to individuals in democracies that fall within the fifty smallest shadow economies in the world based on the World Bank's estimates.[7] The shadow economy "typically entails the production and distribution of services that are themselves not illegal, but become unlawful either by tax evasion or the bypassing of regulations" and is a commonly used estimate for the level of tax evasion.[8] The duty to defend the state is analyzed only among democracies with no military conscription, since saying "yes" to defending the country in the event of war carries different meaning in democracies where doing so is constitutionally mandated versus voluntary for male citizens.[9]

Variables and Measurement

The main prediction from the theory for the cross-national sample is straightforward: on average, stronger national identification should predict greater civic duty to vote, pay taxes, and defend the state. What really distinguishes the theory from vague accounts about nationalist passions, however, is the moral logic that underpins that prediction. Stronger national identification generates greater moral pull, but what harnesses that national pull in support of civic duty are beliefs about the nature of nation-state linkage. When national stories embed strong linkage, as they often do in nationally unified democracies, we should expect a positive national effect on civic duty. However, when national stories embed fractured or opposed linkages, as they often do in nationally divided or contested democracies, we should expect the national effect on civic duty to be negligible or even negative. The theory generates an important second prediction: the national effect on civic duty should vary conditionally with the strength of nation-state linkage.

NATION-STATE LINKAGE

Beliefs of nation-state linkage are internalized from national stories. These stories embed historicized knowledge about the state's role in the lifecycle of the nation—how it aided, protected, threatened, or betrayed the national people through moments of change or crisis. Told across generations in the form of parables based on lived experiences under a particular state, national stories cue whether the state should be seen as inclusive or exclusive to the boundaries of national obligation. Previous chapters identified beliefs of linkage by closely analyzing nationalist histories and the personal narratives of citizens in each case country. Testing the conditional effects of linkage cross-nationally requires finding a creative way to quantify and standardize that kind of in-depth case analysis.

Nation-state linkage is a constructed belief about the state's representational intent toward "my" national people, not a descriptive fact about ethnic or even national diversity. Strength of linkage can correlate with ethnic heterogeneity within a state, but the two are not the same. Strong beliefs of nation-state linkage can exist in ethnically diverse democracies, where the state supports an inclusive nationalist vision. Conversely, linkage can be fractured in ethnically homogeneous democracies with histories of state exploitation or exclusion of nonethnic minorities. Thus, standard measures of diversity in the literature, such as the ethnolinguistic fractionalization (ELF) index, the cultural fractionalization index (Cdiv), or the politically relevant ethnic group fractionalization index (PREG), do not accurately capture nation-state linkage. Moreover, while such measures generate a diversity indicator for each democracy, they tell us little about the variation of beliefs across groups and individuals within democracies.

As an alternative, I turn to an institutional proxy for belief of nation-state linkage: the degree to which "my" national group is represented in positions of power in the democratic state in which one lives. National stories are based on historical experiences of nationalist inclusion or exclusion by the state. For instance, in the narrative analysis in chapter 3, fractured beliefs of nation-state linkage among Taiwanese youth were based on national stories about discrimination from leadership positions in the military and government. Many youth described the top military generals as all *waishengren*. Even if not factually true today, such perceptions are based on institutional history, where islanders were systematically excluded from positions of power during the KMT martial law period. Similarly, in chapter 6, the feeling among many East Germans of being "colonized" by the West through reunification can be traced to practices of institutional exclusion, where Western party leaders dictated how Eastern representatives should vote and barred them from positions of power within the party.

A national group's power status in the state is therefore an institutional proxy that should reflect historicized beliefs about the nation-state relationship. Where national members hold positions of power in the state and wield real political clout, beliefs of nation-state linkage will tend to be strong within that group.[10] In contrast, where national members are only marginally included in the state or, worse, systematically excluded from positions of power, beliefs of nation-state linkage will tend to be fractured or opposed within such groups.

The Ethnic Power Relations (EPR) dataset codes the institutional inclusion status for 758 ethnic groups across 157 countries, from 1946 to 2010.[11] For each country, the dataset identifies all ethnic groups with minimal political relevance,[12] and for each group, it codes their degree of inclusion or exclusion from positions of power in the national-level government based on eight levels of "access to power": monopoly, dominance, senior partner, junior partner, regional autonomy, powerless, discrimination, and irrelevant.[13] The EPR categorizes a group to "rule alone" in a monopoly or dominance status, to "share power" in senior or junior partner status, and to be "excluded" from power if in a regional autonomy, powerless, discrimination, or irrelevant status. The EPR therefore maps out the relative power status between different ethnic groups within a state.[14]

For all respondents in my WVS sample, I generate a binary indicator for nation-state linkage by matching the person's self-identified ethnic group, which the WVS asks in nearly all countries, to that group's inclusion status in the state based on the EPR's access to power index. Individuals identifying with groups in monopoly, dominance, or senior-partner status, where the group "rules alone" or "shares power" over the state from a position of dominance, were coded as having strong nation-state linkage (=1).

All other levels of power access in the EPR imply varying degrees of exclusion from the state. Groups in junior-partner or regional autonomy status share power over the state—but from a position of nondominance. Individuals who identify with these groups are most likely to hold fractured beliefs of nation-state linkage. Individuals who identify with groups in discriminated, powerless, or irrelevant status are systematically excluded by the state and likely harbor beliefs of opposed nation-state linkage. For the sake of analytical simplicity, I combine individuals who experience any degree of exclusion from the state as having weak nation-state linkage (=0), combining the fractured and opposed linkage categories.

My logic for designating the cutoff at junior-partner status is that this is the first level at which individuals in the group have at least a minimal potential for holding fractured beliefs of nation-state linkage. Junior partners are still included in the state but do not rule from a position of power. They are typically made up of groups who, prior to democratization, were discriminated against or marginalized by the ruling elite of the state. For instance, junior partners include African Americans in the United States, the Colored in South Africa, Muslims and other backward castes in India, and the Maori in New Zealand.

Table 10 shows the estimated proportion of the citizenry in strong nation-state linkage contexts for each democracy in my sample.[15] A "1" indicates that all individuals in that democracy are in contexts of strong nation-state linkage, whereas a "0" hypothetically indicates that no one is. Most individuals in most democracies in my sample belong to groups in strong nation-state linkage positions. The list passes some quick sanity checks: nationally unified democracies, such as Japan, South Korea, and Sweden, all score a value of "1," whereas democracies with known histories of nationalist division or contestation, such as Taiwan, India, South Africa, or Ukraine, all score below "1."

Taiwan's score of 0.05 may raise some eyebrows. Taiwan is nationally fragmented, but it is hardly an exclusionary democracy. It is important to remember,

TABLE 10   Nation-state linkage by country

COUNTRY	PROPORTION OF NATIONAL SAMPLE IN CONTEXTS OF STRONG NATION-STATE LINKAGE
Argentina	1
Estonia	1
Germany	1
Japan	1
South Korea	1
Sweden	1
Poland	0.99
Romania	0.99
Mexico	0.99
Uruguay	0.95
Peru	0.94
Australia	0.92
Ecuador	0.92
Chile	0.92
Netherlands	0.89
New Zealand	0.87
Colombia	0.87
Ukraine	0.82
South Africa	0.75
United States	0.72
Ghana	0.59
Trinidad and Tobago	0.58
Brazil	0.47
India	0.30
Taiwan	0.05

however, that the score captures perceptions of nation-state linkage based on the EPR coding, not actual exclusion. Taiwan's low score is mostly a function of how the ethnic groups are defined and coded in the surveys. The WVS distinguishes four ethnic groups in Taiwan: Hakka from Taiwan, Minnan from Taiwan, China, and Aborigine. Of these, only China identifiers, who comprise a minority of the population, are coded as "senior partners" in the corresponding year's EPR and therefore receive a "1" for strong linkage in my dataset; Minnan and Hakka identifiers, who comprise the majority, are coded as "junior partners" in the EPR and receive a "0" for weak linkage based on my coding. Thus, Taiwan's low score should be seen as reflecting widespread beliefs of weak nation-state linkage, rather than an objective measure of an exclusionary state.

Taiwan's case also highlights an important caveat to codifying nation-state linkage using the EPR. The EPR uses ethnic, rather than national, groups as the unit of analysis. Not all national groups are based on ethnic lines, and the EPR will not capture linkage very well for such cases. For instance, in table 10, Germany receives a "1" because the EPR codes both East and West Germans as part of the same German ethnic group that occupies dominant status. But as chapter 6

shows, two contested visions of nation have long coexisted within that ethnically homogeneous polity and matter tremendously for people's perceived exclusion from the state, especially for East Germans. The EPR is still the best cross-
national dataset for measuring the relative power status of groups within states,
but using it to codify nation-state linkage will miss such nuances. In most cases,
the measurement error will run conservatively. That is, the EPR is more likely to
miscode weak linkage individuals as strong when ethnic and national lines do
not align, as in the German case, and dilute the true national effect on civic duty.
Thus, the results in this chapter are likely underestimates of the nation's civic pull
in democracies.

Operationalizing something like belief of nation-state linkage across democracies is difficult, and this method is by no means perfect. But an important
advantage of using a publicly available and vetted index like the EPR is that it
offers a clear blueprint for replication and basis for improvement through future
research.

STRENGTH OF NATIONAL IDENTIFICATION

How strongly an individual feels the moral pull of her nation is measured by
her strength of national identification, its source. The WVS asks all respondents
how strongly they agree or disagree with the following statement: "I see myself as
part of the [French] nation."[16] The wording "I see myself as" captures the subjective aspect of psychological identification with the nation, rather than objective
membership. Those who "strongly agree" were coded as feeling strong national
identification, "agree" as weak identification, and "disagree" or "strongly disagree" as no identification.

CIVIC-DUTY MEASURES

The WVS includes measures for three common manifestations of civic duty in
democracies that have been analyzed throughout the book. The first, the duty
to vote, is measured by the following question: "When elections take place, do
you vote always, usually, or never?" Habitual voting—the act of "always" voting despite changes in incentives or costs—implies a principled commitment
and is often taken as the behavioral proxy for the sense of duty to vote in prior
studies.[17] The duty to vote is analyzed among democracies without compulsory
voting. Respondents who answered that they "always" vote were coded as feeling
a duty to vote, whereas "usually" or "never"—answers that imply any degree of
conditionality—were coded as no duty.

Duty to pay taxes is measured by a WVS battery on the "justifiability" of a list
of morally ambiguous actions, of which "cheating on taxes if you have a chance"
is one. Paying taxes is a legal obligation in all democracies, but monitoring is
never universal and the severity of penalty for cheating is relatively low. Thus in

practice, it is a form of "quasi-voluntary" compliance, where a sense of duty to not cheat matters a great deal.[18] The WVS question taps that gray area: "if you have a chance" implies whether one feels a civic duty to pay taxes honestly, even when one can presumably get away with cheating. Respondents were asked to rank how justifiable cheating is on a scale of 1 to 10, from "never justifiable" to "always justifiable." Those who said it was "never justifiable" were coded as feeling a duty to pay taxes, while all other shades of justifiability were coded as no duty. To minimize social desirability bias, I analyze the duty to pay taxes in democracies within the top fifty smallest shadow economies, where there is reasonable evidence that most citizens do, in fact, pay their taxes.

Finally, the duty to defend the state is measured through the following question: "Of course, we all hope that there will not be another war, but if it were to come to that, would you be willing to fight for your country?" An unconditional willingness to fight, particularly in democracies without military conscription, reflects a sense of duty to defend one's state. Respondents who answered "yes" were coded as feeling a sense of duty to defend, whereas those who answered "don't know/not sure" or "no" were coded as not feeling such duty.

The final compiled dataset includes measures for three kinds of civic duty, strength of national identification, and a binary indicator for strong versus weak nation-state linkage for over 27,000 unique individuals across twenty-seven democracies.

Empirical Strategy

The cross-national analysis tests two predictions from the theory. First, is the moral pull of the nation a strong predictor of civic duty for democratic citizens around the world? Second, does that national effect vary conditionally and predictably based on people's beliefs of nation-state linkage?

To test these predictions, I return to the statistical model of moral motivations developed in chapter 4. Demonstrating that stronger national identification predicts greater civic duty across the board is a start, but the model goes an extra step to test whether it is the nation's moral pull that drives the relationship. For individuals who see voting, paying taxes, or defending their democracies as an intrinsic obligation to "my" nation, how much or little they expect to gain from doing so should not matter to their sense of civic duty. Then as national identification strengthens, the effect of expected payoffs should decrease for such individuals. Statistically, this kind of trade-off relationship between two variables can be captured through a negative interaction. Whether or not such a negative interaction emerges from the cross-national data serves as a test for the presence (or absence) of the nation's moral pull toward civic duty.

For individual i in democracy j, the sense of civic duty to vote, pay taxes, and defend her state is therefore modeled as a function of her strength of national identification, expected payoffs, and their interaction:

$$civic\ duty_{ij} = \beta_0 + \beta_1(national\ identification)_{ij} + \beta_2(payoffs)_{ij}$$
$$+ \beta_3(national\ identification \times payoffs)_{ij} + \beta_4(controls)_{ij}$$
$$+ \beta_5(country\ fixed\ effect)_j + \varepsilon_{ij}$$

The model also includes country fixed effects for two reasons. The empirical reason is to account for the lack of cross-national scalar comparability in nationalism measures documented in prior research. But more importantly, the national theory of civic duty is ultimately a story about within-state identity politics: how different national groups within a given democracy see their relationship to the state differently, and how those beliefs motivate a sense of civic duty for some but not others. A hierarchical fixed-effects model, which estimates the national effect within, but not across, countries, is most consistent with that theoretical logic.

Across all three manifestations of civic duty the prediction is the same. In the full sample, given that most individuals are in contexts of strong nation-state linkage, I predict on average a positive national effect ($\beta_1 > 0$) and a negative interaction with expected payoffs ($\beta_3 < 0$). Then, when I divide the sample by strong versus weak linkage individuals, a bifurcated pattern should emerge. For the strong-linkage group, the national and interaction coefficients should be in the same direction as in the full sample, but both larger in size and more precisely estimated ($\beta_{1\_strong} > \beta_{1\_all}$ & $|\beta_{3\_strong}| > |\beta_{3\_all}|$). In contrast, for the weak-linkage group, both the national and interaction coefficients should be significantly smaller in size compared to the full sample and close to a null effect ($0 \leq \beta_{1\_weak} < \beta_{1\_all}$ & $0 \leq |\beta_{3\_weak}| < |\beta_{3\_all}|$).

For the duty to vote analysis, I consider fairness of elections as the payoff-based motivation to vote. The variable comes from the literature on procedural fairness as a gauge for the long-term payoffs from continued membership in the state. It is measured by the WVS question that asks respondents how often votes are counted fairly in the country's elections. Following the duty-to-vote analyses in previous chapters, I also control for political interest and frequency of church attendance—known predictors of the duty to vote—as well as the demographic correlates of turnout—education, gender, age, and age-squared. The sample is limited to individuals in democracies without compulsory voting who are between eighteen and seventy-five years of age, so that they are both legally eligible and physically able to vote.[19] This yields just over 20,000 individuals across fifteen democracies.

The model for the duty to pay taxes includes confidence in the government as the payoff-based motivation, again following prior analyses in the South Korea and Taiwan chapters. The measure is based on the WVS institutional-trust battery that includes "the government (in your nation's capital)." I also control for support for big government to account for differences in fiscal ideology, female for gendered norms around fiscal responsibility, marital status as a key life event that changes tax burdens in most democracies, and a subjective measure of class.[20] To minimize overreport bias on the duty to pay taxes, the sample is limited to democracies that fall within the fifty smallest shadow economies in the world, where relative evidence for high tax compliance exists. This yields nearly 10,000 individuals across seven democracies.

For the duty to defend, I consider confidence in the military as the main payoff motivation, which comes from the same institutional-trust battery mentioned above in which "the armed forces" is listed. The measure does not distinguish between confidence in the military's capability to win wars versus confidence in the military as a fair institution. For the purposes of this analysis, such ambiguity does not matter as long as the measure serves as a cumulative index for all expected payoffs from defending the state. I control for the perceived likelihood of war to account for differences in stakes, as well as marital status and education to account for the opportunity costs of fighting. Across the nineteen democracies in the WVS without military conscription, I further limit the sample to men younger than forty years old—the subset of the population that would most realistically be expected to fight in the event of war.[21]

A Cross-national Test

Table 11 shows the estimates of the national effect on the civic duty to vote, pay taxes, and defend the country across the cross-national sample of democratic citizens. Estimates are from hierarchical logistic regressions with country fixed effects, so that the coefficients represent the average national effect within a given democracy. All variables are rescaled 0 to 1 so that the size of the coefficients can be easily compared and standard errors are clustered by country.

The most striking pattern in table 11 is the positive coefficients on national identification across the board, shown in the first bolded row. Because of the interaction in the model, these are marginal effects—how much national identification matters for someone who sees no payoff-based reason to contribute to her democracy. Strong identification with the nation more than doubles—and in the case of the duty to defend, nearly triples—the odds of feeling a sense of civic duty to contribute to one's democracy. The consistently negative interaction coefficients, shown in the second bolded row, suggest that this national effect is mostly due to the nation's moral pull. The interactions imply that the more

TABLE 11 Cross-national estimates of national effect on civic duty

	DUTY TO VOTE	DUTY TO PAY TAXES	DUTY TO DEFEND
National identification	0.86***	1.02***	1.18***
	(0.09)	(0.29)	(0.24)
Payoffs			
Fairness of elections	0.64***		
	(0.15)		
Confidence in government		0.35***	
		(0.07)	
Confidence in military			1.87***
			(0.25)
Interaction			
National identification x payoffs	–0.07	–0.33***	–0.90***
	(0.14)	(0.10)	(0.32)
Controls			
Political interest	0.93***		
	(0.23)		
Religious attendance	0.40***		
	(0.07)		
Support for big government		0.20	
		(0.19)	
Class		–0.25	
		(0.15)	
Likelihood of war			0.57***
			(0.18)
Demographic controls	yes	yes	yes
Constant	–1.92***	–0.30	–1.44***
	(0.37)	(0.19)	(0.14)
N	20,542	9,990	6,848
Country N	15	7	19
Countries	Colombia	Australia	Argentina
	Estonia	Japan	Australia
	Georgia	Netherlands	Chile
	Germany	Poland	Ecuador
	Ghana	Spain	Ghana
	India	Sweden	India
	Mexico	United States	Japan
	Netherlands		Netherlands
	Pakistan		Pakistan
	Philippines		Peru
	Poland		Philippines
	Romania		Romania
	South Africa		Slovenia
	Taiwan		South Africa
	Ukraine		Spain
			Sweden
			Trinidad Tobago
			United States
			Uruguay

Estimates are based on hierarchical logistic regressions with country fixed effects, with all variables rescaled 0 to 1 and standard errors clustered by country.

*** $p < 0.01$

** $p < 0.05$

* $p < 0.10$

strongly one identifies with the nation, the less important considerations such as fairness of elections, trust in government, or confidence in the military become to whether that person feels a civic duty to vote, pay taxes, and defend her democracy, respectively. The interaction effect is greatest for the duty to defend, where strong national identification reduces the effect of payoffs by nearly half.

The model predictions are shown in figure 7.1. The top row shows that across varying democratic contexts, on average, strongly identifying with the nation is associated with a 15 to 20 percent higher probability of feeling a civic duty to vote, pay taxes, and defend the state. That predicted increase occurs at a substantively important threshold. For the average democratic citizen who does not identify with the nation, her predicted probability of feeling a sense of civic duty is about fifty-fifty, essentially a coin toss. Strong national identification takes that probability to near or over 70 percent across all three manifestations of civic duty. In other words, strong national identification is the difference between a citizen who sees voting, paying taxes, or defending the state as a matter of duty only half the time versus most of the time.

The cross-national results challenge the idea that strong nationalism is necessarily bad for liberal democracy. In fact, for many democratic citizens, nationalism

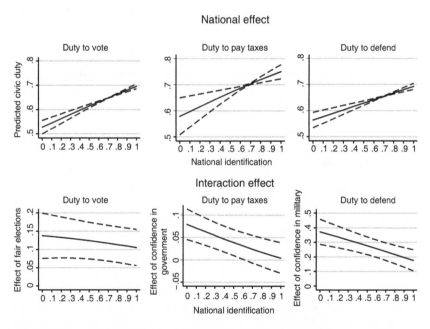

FIGURE 7.1. Predicted civic duty by national identification across the world. Predictions based on regression estimates from table 11, holding all covariates at their actual values, not means. Error bars mark the 95 percent confidence intervals.

appears to be an important part of what sustains their sense of civic duty to support their democracies. This is not due to cherry picking "good" types of nationalisms. The sample includes individuals in predominantly civic nationalist countries like the United States and Germany but also heavily ethnic nationalist countries like Japan and Ukraine.

My claim is that the results attest to the relational aspect of nationalism: when "my" nation is seen to be in a mutually committed relationship with the democratic state in which one lives, this linkage harnesses the nation's moral pull toward prodemocratic ends, such as civic duty. The positive national effect owes to the fact that most individuals in the cross-national sample are in contexts of strong nation-state linkage, as shown in table 10. One way to check if this relational logic holds is to divide the full sample by individuals in strong versus weak linkage contexts. The theory predicts a bifurcated pattern. Compared to the full-sample estimates in table 11, the national effect should be larger among the strong-linkage group, whereas it should be significantly weaker to null in the weak-linkage group.

Table 12 shows the new estimates for the strong- versus weak-linkage groups, respectively. Overall, there is visible divergence. The national coefficients for the

TABLE 12 Cross-national estimates of national effect on civic duty by strength of linkage

	DUTY TO VOTE		DUTY TO PAY TAXES		DUTY TO DEFEND	
	STRONG	WEAK	STRONG	WEAK	STRONG	WEAK
National identification	**0.87*****	**0.45**	**1.07*****	**1.08*****	**1.44*****	**−0.11**
	(0.09)	**(0.28)**	**(0.37)**	**(0.39)**	**(0.24)**	**(0.69)**
Payoffs						
Fairness of elections	0.73***	0.04				
	(0.17)	(0.27)				
Confidence in government			0.37**	0.05		
			(0.17)	(0.11)		
Confidence in military					2.18***	0.82
					(0.20)	(0.55)
Interaction						
National identification ×	**−0.10**	**0.80**	**−0.35**	**0.35**	**−1.58*****	**0.94**
payoffs	**(0.15)**	**(0.50)**	**(0.25)**	**(0.30)**	**(0.33)**	**(0.89)**
Constant	−2.01***	−1.46***	−0.28	−0.74	−1.48***	−0.34
	(0.46)	(0.40)	(0.23)	(0.42)	(0.14)	(0.56)
N	14,237	2,762	7,899	785	3,983	1,482

Estimates are based on the same models and covariates (not shown) as in table 11 but separately estimated for strong- versus weak-linkage groups.
*** p < 0.01
** p < 0.05
* p < 0.10

strong-linkage group are generally larger than the original estimates in table 11 across all manifestations of civic duty. In contrast, the national effect is significantly diminished for the weak-linkage group. Compared to individuals in contexts of strong linkage, national identification matters only half as much for the civic duty to vote and not at all for the civic duty to defend. The exception is the civic duty to pay taxes, where stronger national identification predicts equally greater duty to pay taxes for both linkage groups. But the interaction coefficients suggest that what appear to be similar national effects are produced through different mechanisms in the two groups.

Figure 7.2 plots the interaction for strong- versus weak-linkage groups, where the contrast is stark. For individuals with strong linkage, marked by the solid lines, stronger national identification systematically "pulls down" the effect of payoffs on civic duty. This pattern is consistent with morally motivated, thick civic duty: as national identification strengthens, expected returns from contributing to the state matter less to these individuals' sense of civic duty. In contrast, for individuals with weak linkage, marked by the dashed lines, stronger national identification generally "pulls up" the effect of payoffs on civic duty. For the civic duty to pay taxes, the more one identifies with the nation, the more that confidence in government also matters. This pattern better describes a citizen for whom evaluations of state performance and the expected payoffs from that success drive both her sense of national identification and civic duty. The result is a thin civic duty that more easily waxes and wanes with perceptions of national status, rather than being rooted in an intrinsic identity linkage to the state.

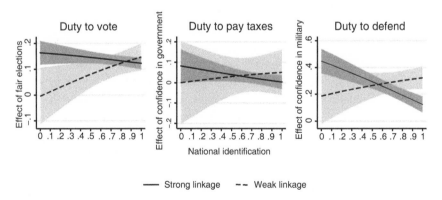

FIGURE 7.2. How nations' moral pull toward civic duty varies by strength of linkage. Predicted interactions are based on estimates from table 12, holding all covariates at their actual values, not means. Shaded areas mark the 95 percent confidence intervals.

A national theory of civic duty was inspired by the surprising case of South Korea's national gold drives during the Asian financial crisis. One of the motivating questions for the book was whether Mrs. Han and the estimated 3.5 million South Koreans who gave up their personal possessions to save their young democracy were simply outliers—a unique reaction to an acute crisis—or whether they reflected something deeper about why citizens sacrifice for their democracies that was missing from our theories about democratic citizenship.

Each chapter has taken a systematic step toward answering that question. Through a "most similar" comparison between South Korea and Taiwan, I was able to isolate the power of national stories and the relational linkages to the state that they embed by triangulating across multiple methods. The German case provided a critical extension outside of East Asia, showing that parallel mechanisms of national linkage and civic duty hold up in an entirely different cultural and historical context. This cross-national study is the most extensive effort toward generalizability. I find that across more than 27,000 citizens in twenty-seven democracies around the world, many see contributing to their democracies—by giving their time, money, and even potentially their lives—through a similar lens of national obligation as did Mrs. Han.

The cross-national evidence in this chapter offers significant empirical legs to the debate on whether nationalism helps or hinders democracy. Nationalist rebellions, wars, and secessionist movements—common topics of contemporary studies on nationalism—are certainly detrimental to democratic stability. But stability is more than the absence of conflict. It also has a constructive side that relies on conscious input from citizens to buttress the political, fiscal, and military needs of their democracy. This chapter shows that, when it comes to that aspect of democratic stability, nationalism is more often than not a positive moral resource.

The civic benefits of nationalism do not depend on having a particular kind of national identity or character. Rather, the data suggest that they are products of the national identity politics within a given democracy. Even within the same democracy, the positive national effect on civic duty was limited to individuals in contexts of strong nation-state linkage and did not extend to those in weak linkage contexts. Thus, when it comes to strengthening democracy's civic foundations, the answer is not simply more nationalism. The context of nationalism matters. The findings imply that more nationalism in strong linkage contexts will generate collective will to support the democracy, whereas intensifying national attachments in weak- or opposed-linkage contexts can fuel anti-civic commitments that destabilize the democracy.

The final chapter turns to how the cumulative findings in this book speak to several big debates about nationalism and democracy. At minimum, they cast doubt on the common assumption that strong nationalism hinders democracy or that particular kinds of nationalisms are incompatible with vibrant civic life. Neither claim is supported by the evidence in this book. The findings also pose a new set of questions. Given the national roots of civic duty, how should we think differently about what makes strong democracies? What are the primary threats to democratic resilience in an increasingly globalized, "post-national" world, and how can democracies bolster their own civic foundations in the face of dramatic socioeconomic change? Coming full circle, I take up such questions in the context of East Asia's democratic future.

CIVIC CHALLENGES TO DEMOCRACY IN EAST ASIA

The evidence amassed in this book builds toward what is bound to be a surprising claim to many scholars of democracy: that nationalism—the "dangerous and powerful passions"[1] that are better known to tear democracies apart—also motivates a sense of civic duty for many citizens in democracies. How do we explain this apparent contradiction?

Nationalism refers to the deep psychological and emotional attachment to one's national community. This book has shown that such attachments are rarely learned in a vacuum. The national stories that instill belonging to a particular nation also embed critical know-how about that nation's past and present relationships to co-nationals, other nations, and the state it calls home. It is this relational aspect of nationalism, and specifically its historicized relationship to the state, that shapes its civic or uncivic manifestations in democracies.

When pundits or policy experts say that "nationalism" is a threat to democracy—from Narendra Modi's revival of exclusionary Hindu nationalism in India to Donald Trump's stoking of American white supremacist nationalism—what they are actually referring to are the effects of oppositional national stories. In such cases, demagogues have married national attachments with stories of exclusion and inferior treatment by the state, deliberately seeding beliefs of opposed nation-state linkage among the marginalized in order to destabilize the establishment and justify their own rule. These are consequences of opportunistic politics, not nationalism per se.

This book has documented a quieter, but brighter side to the use of nationalism in democracies. When national attachments are married with other kinds of stories—stories that tell of a mutually committed relationship between the national people and the democratic state—they can produce important civic benefits for that democracy. Thick civic duty that is rooted in an identity attachment to the state is less reliant on payoffs and performance and is therefore uniquely important to democracies, especially during hard times. In times of need, when the usual perks of state membership begin to wane, authoritarian states can rely on coercion to force their citizens to comply and contribute. Democracies have strict limits against most forms of coercion. Instead, they must fall back on the voluntary sense of obligation by citizens to stand up for their democracy, even when it is costly to do so. National stories and the beliefs of nation-state linkage they embed shape the depth of that civic reservoir.

The key findings in the book speak to several big questions about the relationship between nationalism and democracy. In light of globalization and claims about the thinning of national boundaries, what would a "post-national" democracy be like? How does the evidence urge us to rethink the foundations of strong and resilient democracies and the kinds of threats that weaken them? I explore such questions in the context of East Asia's democratic future.

Nationalism and Democracy

The book comes at a particularly fragile moment for nationalism. Demagogues have used nationalism to promote exclusionary or illiberal ideologies in order to seize power, even in long-standing democracies like the United States that were once thought to be immune to such backsliding. At the same time, the COVID-19 pandemic has exacerbated existing national tensions, with the human toll laid bare as countries compete for vaccine procurements. In response to such developments, democratic leaders around the world have called for the containment of nationalist impulses and so-called "vaccine nationalism,"[2] citing nationalism's divisive force as a threat to democratic stability during a global health crisis.

Meanwhile, another global development has been gradually eroding the dominance of the nation-state model from the bottom up. One of the most significant social changes in the past half century is the dramatic increase in global migration, whether by voluntary choice or forced displacement. The persistent effort of migrants to claim basic political rights in their host states by appealing to humanitarianism and international organizations has granted them access to what was once the exclusive merits of national citizenship. In *Limits of Citizenship*, Yasemin Soysal argues that a different kind of "post-national" citizenship is emerging in its wake: "As an identity, national citizenship—as it is promoted, reinvented, and reified by states and other societal actors—still prevails. But in terms of its translation into rights and privileges, it is no longer a significant construction."[3]

The confluence of such forces has amplified the chorus for moving beyond nationalisms and toward cosmopolitanism—the conscious thinning of national and ethnic identities for "the person whose allegiance is to the worldwide community of human beings."[4] Cosmopolitans see the ridding of particularistic allegiances as the cure for the many ills that plague contemporary democracies, such as chauvinism, discrimination, and xenophobia. They argue that cosmopolitanism can serve as the foundation for a more egalitarian and inclusive liberal government—a kind of "post-national" democracy.

The evidence in this book unequivocally rejects such an idea. There may be strong normative reasons for why cosmopolitanism is an ideal worth pursuing. But on empirical grounds my findings suggest that liberal democracy without nations and nationalism would mostly fail to produce the very thing that it needs to flourish: citizens who feel a strong sense of civic duty to contribute to "my" democracy.

Democratic citizenship entails the claiming and exercising of rights, but it also requires the keeping of duties and obligations. Without individuals who are willing to practice both sides of citizenship, democratic states—or any kind of state, for that matter—would struggle to sustain themselves in the long run through inevitable crises and hardships. The basis for rights claiming and political inclusion may have expanded beyond national boundaries, as Soysal points out. But in terms of political obligations and what commits citizens to one democracy over another, I find that the nation still remains an enormously significant construction.

What is needed for stronger and more resilient democracies is not less nationalism, then, but more nationalism of a specific kind—nationalism that is grown within the context of strong linkage to the democratic state. Whether nationalism is good or bad for democracy turns out to be the wrong question. This book shows that nationalism can be both things for democracy, not based on its definitional character, but its relational context to the state it calls home.

Taking seriously the national roots of civic duty inspires a new set of questions about democratic quality. During the Third Wave of democratization, the largest wave yet in the world's history, the overwhelming focus of democracy scholars was on democratic transitions and consolidation. Democratic success was gauged by a state's ability to remain democratic and avoid reversion or breakdown into authoritarianism. The most widely used democracy indexes today reflect this priority. For instance, the core metrics of the Freedom House or V-dem indexes remain a set of ratings for factors such as an independent judiciary, electoral transparency, partisan turnover, and protection of civil and press freedoms. Such formal institutional aspects of democracy have long been seen as the pillars for its survival.

Democracies should not only aim to survive, however, but also thrive. This book highlights a distinct, yet complementary dimension to what makes strong democracies. For democracies to be resilient against inevitable setbacks, they need more than institutional safeguards. In the face of shocks, crises, and performance failures—factors that open vulnerabilities and weaken public trust in those very institutions—democracies need an intrinsically committed citizenry that is willing to sacrifice for "my" democracy. In bad times, such informal civic norms are the last bastion against democratic breakdown when institutions fail. In good times, they are the oil that keeps the democratic engine running smoothly with minimal coercive effort.

That civic foundation of democracies, this book shows, is largely a product of national identity politics. Liberal democratic theory has always shied away from thick identities and too much groupness as sources of irrationality and political instability. Nationalism can certainly have such effects when it is antagonized against the state. But I have shown that when the boundaries of national obligation encompass the state, nationalism can also generate intrinsic loyalty in support of that democracy. While the emotions invoked by the nation can feel deep and almost primal, the moral logic of how those feelings are mobilized in support of civic duty for some individuals, but not others, is rational and predictable. Better connecting nationalism to the state, as opposed to containing nationalism, is what helps democratic stability.

The centrality of nationalism to the civic strength of a democracy also suggests a novel way to think about threats to democracies. In the post–Cold War era, the prevailing assumption among democracy scholars was that the greatest threat to democracy's survival was external pressure from authoritarian regimes. In East Asia, for instance, North Korea's nuclear prowess and China's aggressive trade tactics are typically seen as the primary security threats to the regional democracies of South Korea, Taiwan, and Japan.

The book suggests, however, that deeply destabilizing threats to democracies come not only from the outside but also grow from within. National stories and the linkages they embed toward the state are not static. They respond to real changes in the way that the state defines and treats its national people. Dramatic socioeconomic shifts, such as worsening income inequality or increasing foreign migration, create new divisions and opportunities for "othering" within a national community. Such shifts can destabilize a democracy through economic stagnation or social unrest. But beyond these obvious effects, they can also fundamentally weaken a democracy's civic foundation in the next generation by disrupting and fragmenting a previously unifying national story.

The recent intensification of nationalist-driven partisan polarization in many democracies is a canary in the coal mine. Nationalist polarization is a specific form of party polarization, where partisan factions are primarily divided on mutually exclusive nationalist visions. The differences can be definitional—about "who we are"—or directional—about "where we ought to go." Extreme partisan polarization of any kind is usually detrimental to democracies, but what sets apart nationalist polarization is that nationalism is inherently state-seeking. As a political community that sees itself as deserving of self-rule, achieving nation-state congruency lies at the heart of any nationalist movement.[5] When political parties see exclusive state ownership as the end of democratic competition, the ripple effects on beliefs of nation-state linkage and the long-term health of the democracy can be disastrous.

Nationalist polarization turns the democratic state into an object of all-or-nothing capture and the opposition into an existential threat to "my" nationalist vision that needs to be eliminated. Accusations among party elites that the other side is "un-American" are reflective of this phenomenon.[6] When a given party is in power, voters who identify with the opposition and its nationalist vision may begin to see the state as standing for the best interests of the national "other." At the same time, the incumbent party is incentivized to aggressively pursue its nationalist agenda, even at the expense of free speech or civil liberties, to imprint its nationalist vision into the institutional core of the state. In these ways, nationalist polarization can lead to the impression on both sides that the state in which one lives is no longer "my" democracy, gradually eroding beliefs of nation-state linkage for large swaths of the citizenry. It is no coincidence that some of the most prominent cases of democratic backsliding today, from the United States to India to Hungary, are cases where demagogues have deliberately tilted the axis of partisan polarization toward nationalist claims, either by resurrecting old nationalist divisions or creating new ones on the heels of massive socioeconomic upheavals.

National storytelling that fosters strong beliefs of linkage in the citizenry can serve as a powerful antidote to such political tactics and should therefore be at the center of any democratic enterprise. In their seminal work on the mobilization of the periphery, Stein Rokkan and Henry Valen highlighted the importance of party outreach to democratic inclusion.[7] Electoral turnout remained lower in the geographical peripheries of Norway because it was physically difficult for party workers to reach these areas. This book highlights a different kind of "national periphery." Just like physical barriers to mobilization, stories of nationalist marginalization from the state pose real psychological barriers to developing a sense of civic duty toward one's democracy. As a result, such citizens are more likely to turn to candidates or parties that promise to serve "my" group in the short term, typically at the expense of the democracy's health in the long term.

In the next section I return to South Korea and Taiwan to examine the kinds of civic challenges faced by democracies in the twenty-first century. East Asia currently sits at the precipice of a dramatic sociodemographic shift. Unprecedented decline in birth rates across the region have necessitated an influx of migration and foreign labor in what have long been ethnically homogeneous democracies. The rapid pace of such change is challenging extant national stories and unhinging what were once strong bases of nation-state linkage for substantial parts of the citizenry, putting the regional democracies at risk of weakening from within.

In South Korea the influx of marriage migrants as a response to declining fertility is literally changing the ethnic face of the nation, raising questions about what it means to be Korean going forward. In Taiwan economic stagnation and an increasingly trade-aggressive Beijing have sowed a generational rift in the basis of Taiwanese nationalism that neither party captures very well, creating an identity disconnect to the state among youth. The discussion focuses on the specifics of the two East Asian democracies, but the civic challenges they face are shared by many other democracies currently under similar identity pressures from an unprecedented influx of migration or widening inequality.

What can democracies do to preserve their civic foundations in the face of change? In the closing section, I draw on prior work on nation-building to identify ways to maintain or restore beliefs of nation-state linkage through periods of socioeconomic upheaval. Democratic states hold a great deal more agency to shape their own resilience than democratic culture explanations would suggest. How the two East Asian democracies choose to respond to their internal identity pressures and reimagine their national stories will enduringly shape their capacities for civic duty going forward.

Contemporary Challenges to Democracy in East Asia

Beliefs of nation-state linkage are typically the "unmoved mover" behind civic duty. As deeply embedded products of socialization, they are usually quite stable over a person's lifetime. Such beliefs do evolve in windows of exigency, however. As the case of East Germans in the aftermath of Germany's reunification illustrates in chapter 6, sudden and seismic shifts to the makeup of the national community or the perceived national identity of the state can fracture beliefs of linkage in a relatively short window.

Knowingly or not, the East Asian democracies are at the cusp of such a critical juncture. The region is experiencing an unprecedented demographic crisis. The birth rate, defined as the average number of children a woman will bear in her lifetime, is less than 1 in South Korea—the lowest among OECD countries—and Taiwan trails close behind.[8] To put these numbers into perspective, the replacement rate needed to sustain the size of a population is 2.07. The negative economic effects of a shrinking population are the most immediate and obvious. But beyond economic stagnation, low fertility is also inverting the conventional age pyramid in these democracies. As one news article put it, "The Asian century is going to be gray."[9] As a shrinking young generation is saddled with the burden of providing for an oversized elderly population, a sense of economic insecurity and resentment is building.

While nearly all discussions of East Asia's mounting demographic crisis focus on the economic costs, in this section I highlight the potential democratic costs to South Korea and Taiwan. What connects changes in demography to democracy is national stories: how the demographic crisis challenges extant national stories and how those changes in turn strengthen or weaken the civic foundations of these democracies.

South Korea

With a birth rate of less than 1, the average South Korean woman is now more likely to remain childless than have at least one child in her lifetime. The acute decline in fertility is largely rooted in a skewed marriage market. In South Korea the typical rural to urban flight that comes with industrialization was asymmetrically composed of women, as Confucian tradition dictated that the men stay and carry on the family line. As a result, many rural men were left without brides, while many urban women who pursued professional careers found a work culture that was inhospitable to raising a family.

The fertility decline is arguably the most serious twenty-first-century problem that South Korea faces, as the repercussions extend far beyond economic stagnation.[10] As of 2019, the elderly outnumber youth by 1.2 million in South Korea, and nearly half of that aging population lives in poverty.[11] The suicide rate among the South Korean elderly is nearly ten-fold higher than the average of 19.3 per 100,000 persons in OECD countries. Thus, the declining birthrate has wide-ranging ramifications for South Korea's economy, welfare burden, and quality of life.

The South Korean government's long-standing solution to the issue has been marriage migrants. More than thirty-five municipal governments offer "marriage subsidies" to rural men in at-risk industries to marry foreign brides, usually from China or Southeast Asian countries. As of 2019, the Ministry of Gender Equality and Family estimated that over one million people in South Korea—about 2 percent of the overall population—are part of such multicultural families.[12] Babies born from such multicultural unions accounted for 5.5 percent of all newborns in 2018.[13] As these mixed-race Koreans—whom Katharine Moon has called the "New Koreans"—become a larger portion of the citizenry, South Korea's once ethnically homogeneous nation is changing: "The [Republic of Korea] is in a transitional moment from what Anthony Smith describes as the 'ethnic-genealogical' model of national identity to the 'civic-territorial' model."[14]

So far, the South Korean government has taken an inconsistent approach to reconciling the country's new demographic reality with its ethnonationalist legacy. In principle, the government has actively promoted a multiculturalist (*damunhwa*) nationalist vision.[15] The progressive Roh Moo-hyun administration made the integration of marriage migrants a hallmark of its 2006 Grand Plan. In 2008 the Support for Multicultural Families Act doubled the budget for multicultural programs, bringing it to nearly $200 million in 2012. Since then, over 200 multicultural centers have been established across the country to teach Korean language and customs to migrant wives.

In practice, however, strong traces of ethnonationalism remain in how such policies are implemented.[16] The multicultural centers for migrant wives mostly function as cultural assimilationist centers, where foreign newcomers are expected to learn and conform to Korean traditions.[17] A landmark revision to the National Citizenship Law in 2010 grants migrant wives a pathway to naturalization, but that right is limited to those who remain married to their Korean-blood husbands, leaving wives vulnerable in abusive situations and reifying an ethnocentric view of citizenship.[18] Moreover, despite the multicultural banner, the South Korean government does not treat its foreign migrants equally. North Korean refugees—the only group with putatively co-national status by way of history—are given selective treatment, with effectively guaranteed citizenship and state aid. Other migrants, even co-ethnic Korean Chinese, are given significantly weaker rights and protections.[19]

Meanwhile, South Koreans are increasingly divided on the question of what it means to be "Korean." According to the 2020 Korean Identity Survey by the East Asia Institute, support for Korea as a "multicultural country" among South Koreans was only 44 percent, a notable decline from 60 percent in 2010.[20] Support for Korea as an ethnically homogeneous country was 39 percent. The largest shift over the past decade was in a third category of South Koreans who answered "I don't know" when asked what kind of country Korea ought to be. That segment grew from 2 percent in 2010 to 13 percent in 2020, with the largest jump among youth respondents. Such changes reflect South Korea's growing national fragmentation.

The splintering of Korea's nationalist landscape has worrisome implications for its democracy. For South Koreans who identify with an ethnonationalist narrative, the government's expansion of multicultural programs at the perceived expense of tax dollars for native Koreans can gradually seed the belief that the state now serves a national "other." For South Koreans and newcomers who identify with a multicultural narrative, the government's repeated shortfalls to deliver on this promise can cast doubt on whether the state really holds the best interests of "people like us." Over time, national stories based on such lived experiences with the state can sow fractured beliefs of linkage, weakening many South Koreans' sense of civic duty to sacrifice on behalf of their democracy just when the state most needs it.

The recent anti-Yemeni refugee protests in South Korea offer a glimpse into a potential future. In 2018 hundreds of Yemeni refugees fled to South Korea using the no-visa entry policy at Jeju Island, a popular international tourist destination. In response, thousands of South Koreans protested on the streets in what was described by international media as "a wave of anti-immigrant sentiment, leading to what has been considered South Korea's first organized anti-asylum movement."[21]

It is easy to paint such reaction as nativist xenophobia, especially in a country known for its strong ethnic nationalism. I argue, however, that the anti-Yemeni protests were driven by something deeper. A closer look at the signage and slogans suggests that they were, in fact, not anti-refugee protests, but anti-state protests fueled by fraying beliefs of nation-state linkage. The protestors quickly rallied around a set of common slogans that were displayed at each demonstration. Key slogans included: "Citizens Pay Taxes, Foreigners Benefit, Stop This Reverse Discrimination," "Abolish Refugee Laws Without Citizen Consent," "It's Not About Hate, It's About Safety," and "Don't Be Like Europe." As these slogans attest, the protests were not really about xenophobia against Yemeni refugees. Rather, they were driven by concerns over slipping representation—the uneasy sense that what used to be the state of "my" nation now serves the best interests of a growing national "other." As previous chapters showed, such beliefs can drive a kind of anti-civic duty to resist and reject the demands of one's state. South Korean democracy's weakening civic foundation is a less visible, but no less alarming, fallout from its worsening demographic crisis.

The question is not simply what kind of national identity—ethnic, multicultural, or something else—is better for South Korea's democratic future. What matters is how well beliefs of nation-state linkage are preserved through periods of change. Too precipitous of a top-down shift in nationalist vision by the state, without parallel shifts in the lived experiences of the people, risks alienating parts of the citizenry. A delicate sequencing act is needed between how the state redefines the national community and how that intent is received by the people. For a long time since independence from Japan, South Korea's ethnonationalist narrative effectively produced unifying national stories that tied the national people and state as one and generated widespread civic duty to the young democracy. But as the country's demographic crisis ushers in a new era of immigration and multiracial Koreans, that narrative has run its course. How South Korea decides to evolve its ethnonationalist legacy, and the kinds of national stories that are produced in its wake, will ultimately shape the civic strength of its democracy going forward.

Taiwan

The island democracy has long lived under the shadow of the KMT's pro-China legacy over the state, deeply entrenched from the days of authoritarian rule. Indeed, fervent Taiwanese nationalism often manifests against the state, typically through a moral imperative to resist the agenda of the incumbent KMT. Tsai Ing-wen's victory in the 2016 presidential election was therefore widely regarded as a watershed moment. The DPP—the party of Taiwanese nationalism—was back in power after a tumultuous first-time incumbency under Chen Shui-bian, and this time under the helm of the first Hakka-origin president. Tsai's presidency opened a real window to shift public perceptions about the national identity of the state, from the right arm of the KMT to a truly home-grown Taiwanese democracy.[22]

Yet a generational shift in the basis of Taiwanese nationalism complicates this window. In chapter 5 I argued that it makes sense to think of Taiwanese national identity as having two dimensions: an ethnic dimension of distinctiveness from Chinese culture and a political dimension of independence from the People's Republic of China (PRC). For most generations in Taiwan, the two dimensions typically went hand in hand, as two sides of the same coin. Identifying as Taiwanese was synonymous with supporting political independence from the PRC.

For the younger generation, however, the demographic crisis and worsening economic pressures are decoupling the two dimensions of Taiwanese nationalism. For the "born independent" generation[23]—individuals born in the late 1980s who came of age in a democratized Taiwan—being "Taiwanese" is no longer a cultural or political statement, but simply a matter of fact: "Those who are born in Taiwan are Taiwanese."[24] This generation came of age under distinct political and economic circumstances. With the legitimization of the liberal order following the Cold War, Beijing shifted tactics from military threat to trade aggression, squeezing its economic hold over the island. As a result, Taiwan's early economic boom had significantly stalled by the early 2000s, leaving fewer jobs. The youth unemployment rate has hovered around 10 percent for the last few years. Taiwan's birthrate of just over 1, while not as low as South Korea's, is gradually distorting the standard population pyramid into a bell shape, where an oversized middle-aged generation sits on top of a shrinking youth population. The fertility decline shows no signs of reversing and only stands to add to the economic burden of the rising generation.

As a result of such economic pressures, what it means to be "Taiwanese" is shifting for the born-independent generation. Whereas many in the older generation saw an independent Taiwan as the hill to die on, for the younger generation separating from China is no longer the sine qua non to being a proud Taiwanese. Instead, this generation is increasingly drawn to a nationalist vision of Taiwan based on economic self-reliance, rather than political independence.[25]

Yet it appears that the DPP, the party of Taiwanese nationalism, has failed to capture this generational turn. The 2018 midterm elections were a wakeup call for the party. Referendum 13—a proposal to change the name of Chinese Taipei to Taiwan in international sporting events—was put on the ballot as the DPP's hallmark nationalist policy. Such symbolic identity claims, which would often draw Beijing's ire, were long the bread and butter of the DPP. Voters, however, overwhelmingly rejected the referendum. The incumbent DPP lost all but six of the twenty-two mayoral seats, even losing in Kaohsiung, the birthplace of the Taiwan nationalist movement and home base of the DPP.

Is it that Taiwanese nationalism is in decline? Recent survey data from National Chengchi University show the opposite: Taiwanese identification in the population is at an all-time high.[26] What, then, explains the paradox of declining support for the DPP amid strengthening Taiwanese nationalism?

I argue that the answer is a growing identity disconnect between party elites and voters. The DPP is still campaigning based on a Taiwanese nationalism of the past, based on ethnic identity and antagonism against China. Meanwhile, the newest generation of voters is shifting away from that nationalist vision, which it sees as a threat to an economically independent vision of Taiwan.

The 2014 Sunflower Movement protesting the Cross-Strait Services Trade Agreement (CSSTA) by KMT president Ma is an illustrative example of this national shift. On the surface the movement may have appeared as a typical pro-Taiwan identity backlash against China and the KMT. But the Taiwanese youth leaders who protested at the Legislative Yuan did not oppose CSSTA purely on identity grounds. Rather, they disputed the economic merits of the CSSTA, arguing that closer economic connections to China, while a stimulus in the short term, would leave too much of Taiwan's long-term developmental trajectory in the hands of Beijing. As Ming-sho Ho of National Taiwan University writes, the movement was driven by "a generational sense of relative deprivation among young activists, as the rapid economic growth and upward class mobility that their parents' generation enjoyed have been denied to them."[27]

The DPP's mayoral loss in Kaohsiung, in an upset victory to the KMT's fringe candidate Han Kuo-yu, tells a similar story. Campaigning as a business outsider, Han heavily criticized the DPP for its staunch anti-China trade policies, accusing the DPP of threatening the economic security of the hardworking citizens of Taiwan. This message appealed to the farmers and laborers of the largely blue-collar district of Kaohsiung, who had long borne the brunt of Taiwan's stagnating economy.[28] Han's unexpected victory in the birthplace of the DPP is testament to the fact that "growing numbers of Taiwan voters appear to be rejecting traditional party politics."[29]

It is not that identity has given way to the economy. Identity and economy have merged in a new way. For the rising generation, achieving economic self-reliance has become an integral part of what it means be an independent Taiwanese nation. Whereas Taiwanese nationalism of the older generation drew a hard political and economic line against China for the sake of identity, the younger generation sees strategic compromise as the only way to protect the longevity of a Taiwanese nation. Playing the "identity card" increasingly risks estranging many youth by seeding national stories that paint the state as tone deaf to the best interests of the rising generation of the national people.

Tsai's legacy on Taiwan's democracy will therefore be less about her Hakka ethnic-islander background and more about her administration's ability to capture this generational turn in Taiwanese nationalism. For rising youth, representing the best interests of Taiwan demands a move away from symbolic identity claims like Referendum 13 that incite economic retribution from Beijing and a greater focus on prudent policies that can address Taiwan's unemployment and stalling economy. If Tsai can unite both DPP and KMT factions under this new mission, then her presidency offers a genuine opportunity—perhaps the first of its kind since Lee Teng-hui's landmark presidency—to inspire new kinds of national stories that can repair deeply fractured beliefs of nation-state linkage for many islanders. A Taiwan that can fully harness the moral pull of its Taiwanese nationalism in support of the democratic state would be a formidable force against its mounting demographic and economic crisis.

Reimagining National Stories

As South Korea and Taiwan find themselves at the cusp of dramatic sociodemographic change, the key challenge is how to sustain strong beliefs of nation-state linkage in the citizenry. This is a challenge shared by many democracies at the moment. In the face of global migration, rising income inequality, and populist upheavals, many democracies are dealing with new kinds of "us" versus "them" divisions that threaten a unifying national basis for civic duty. How can national stories be reimagined to adapt to change?

Sociologist Andreas Wimmer has studied nation-building extensively. He argues that like any other large organization, a nation is built on relational alliances across different groups.[30] Three factors are particularly important for nation-building alliances: widespread voluntary associations, public-goods provision, and communicative integration. As the nature of these factors suggests, "Nation-building is a generational project. . . . One cannot fix failed states or build nations within the time span of an American presidency or two." The *longue-durée* historical conditions that gave rise to vibrant community associations or unified language systems in some places but not others cannot be willed into existence. But as Wimmer himself puts it, what is history if not "the sedimented consequences of myriads of individual actions taken in the past?"[31]

Of course, nation-building from scratch is not the same as reimagining an existing nation-state relationship. Wimmer was looking at the rise of nations from tribes, cities, or cantons, where the key was building alliances where they did not exist before. Those lessons do not always carry over neatly. For instance, communicative integration can backfire in existing nation-states that are trying to become more inclusive toward newcomers. The imposition of English-only elementary education for German Americans after World War I further alienated them from American society and the state, instead of bringing them closer.[32]

What we can learn from this research, however, is that the state can play a proactive role in the reimagination of national stories. States are one half of the nation-state relationship embedded in national stories. Through political rhetoric and public policies, democratic states can draw new relational alliances by defining who belongs to the nation and how it treats them. Such state-led shifts in the lived experience of a national people can, over time, gel into new kinds of national stories. I discuss three policy areas that can help lay strong and inclusive identity foundations for civic duty in democracies.

First, access to positions of power in the state should mirror the national community that the state claims to represent. As I discussed in prior chapters, fractured beliefs of nation-state linkage among many islanders in Taiwan or East Germans in reunified Germany centered on national stories of exclusion from state leadership. A democratic state that does not actively promote the inclusion of every group that belongs to its nationalist vision is bound to fray beliefs of linkage for the marginalized groups over time. The issue is a deeper one than simply achieving descriptive representation. It matters how a democracy gets there. Because beliefs of linkage center around the perceived intent of the state toward the best interests of the national people, the initiative toward representation needs to come from the state, rather than from the excluded group.

State-sponsored policies such as inclusive eligibility to run for office, campaign subsidies for minority candidates, or quota systems, are all bases for national stories that signal the state's commitment to inclusive national representation.

Second, building on Wimmer's point about voluntary associations, I argue that state-sponsored youth programs can be an effective means for seeding strong beliefs of nation-state linkage in the rising generation. Common examples include mandatory military service, youth scout programs, or a public-service requirement as part of civic education. Such programs foster attachment on both sides of the nation-state relationship. Programs that bring together youth from different silos within the national community build bridging social capital and can extend a sense of national belonging to newcomers.[33] At the same time, by contextualizing this togetherness within collective acts of public service, such programs direct feelings of co-nationality in support of the state. State programs can therefore produce the kinds of national stories that naturally link national membership with ideals of state-supportive citizenship, as we saw in the Korean personal narratives in chapter 3. French president Emmanuel Macron's plans to revive a national service program for all French youth is a prescient move in this regard.[34]

Yet South Korea's multicultural centers for foreign wives illustrate the complexities of implementing such state programs. National stories exist at the contested nexus between state policy and intent and the national people's perceptions and lived experience. The multicultural centers offer foreign wives Korean language and culture lessons, such as how to make kimchi and host traditional holidays. The state's intent in establishing them was to ease the integration burden of foreign wives.

The way that the multicultural centers are experienced by foreign wives, however, is quite different. Rather than building bridging social capital that brings foreign wives into the national fold of native wives, such centers reify a kind of "hierarchical nationhood" within the population that designates foreign wives as culturally inferior.[35] The unilateral expectation of having to assimilate to Korean customs can reinforce feelings of nationalist exclusion for migrant women—at the hands of the host state no less—and stunt a nascent belief of nation-state linkage before it can solidify.[36] Thus, when it comes to state programs geared toward national newcomers, emphasis on bridging experiences between natives and newcomers is key.

Third, for democracies striving for national stories that can build strong beliefs of linkage, access to citizenship for all purported members of the nation is the most basic form of public good that the state needs to provide. Wimmer argues that equitable public-goods provision contributes to nation-building by preempting the rise of factions. In the context of citizenship, this sounds much simpler than it is. In many democracies, even with purportedly civic nationalist foundations, there has been a great deal of nativist backlash against expanding naturalization criteria. The reversion to an "us" versus "them" mentality is strong, especially in places where migrants are screened for specific skill sets and are therefore seen as an economic threat.

State efforts to expand access to citizenship despite such public concerns will likely incur electoral backlash in the short term. But doing so will secure important civic benefits for the host democracy in the long term. Migrant newcomers typically come without any national linkage to their host democracy. In this vacuum, state policies that legally affirm their status as a national member can be a foundational basis for building such belief of linkage and serve as a powerful antidote to experiences of social discrimination.

In this view, South Korea's tenuous citizenship pathway for foreign wives, where access is conditional on married status,[37] or Taiwan's weak welfare and employment protections for Southeast Asian migrants,[38] are glaring shortcomings given the demographic crisis that both democracies face. The state's failure to offer the most basic kind of public good can entrench the kinds of national stories that paint the host state as exclusionary or worse, predatory. Fractured or even opposed beliefs of nation-state linkage that result from such stories lead to weak civic duty at best and at worst a kind of anti–civic duty against the democratic state. As South Korea and Taiwan's reliance on foreign migrants increases, such problems are due to amplify.

None of these policy suggestions are quick fixes. New kinds of national stories take time to become sedimented and idiom-ized. The shifts in beliefs of nation-state linkage that they seed will likely manifest with generational turnover, given the time that deep socialization takes. But democracies have a great deal more agency in shaping the duration of that time, and the direction of change, than explanations based on democratic culture or maturity alone would suggest. For South Korea, Taiwan, and other democracies facing similar socioeconomic challenges, consciously designed policies and political rhetoric can lay the identity foundations for widespread civic duty in the generations to come, rather than entrenching identity barriers against it.

I began the book with a conversation with Mrs. Han in South Korea. Her unhesitating willingness to donate her wedding rings to the national gold drives during the devastating Asian financial crisis defied a great deal of conventional wisdom about civic duty. Civic duty was largely seen as a part of democratic culture—something possessed by societies with mature liberal values and a good "fit" with democracy. Very few things about South Korea at the time fit those criteria. It was still a very young and uncertain democracy, just coming out of the shadows of its military authoritarian past and deeply steeped in Confucian traditions and ethnic nationalism—both widely seen as impediments to democratic culture. Mrs. Han's own answer to why she donated, however, hinted at something else: "It was the only right thing to do. . . . It's what we have always done for Korea."

Many observers of the South Korean gold drives described the phenomenon as the result of an Asian collectivist ethos or something unique about Korea's postwar crisis mentality. I have shown that Mrs. Han's sense of civic duty to her flailing democracy was most immediately the result of a particular set of national stories that powerfully bound the Korean people and the South Korean state as if one. I found parallels to Mrs. Han in democratic citizens who were socialized into similar national stories, from China nationalists in Taiwan, West Germans in reunified Germany, to the majority of over 27,000 democratic citizens sampled across the world. Across these cases, the basis of the imagined linkage between "my" nation and the state called home varied from ethnic bloodline to democratic values to shared Communist experience. The civic benefits of nationalism were not tied to a particular type of nation. Instead, it was the boundary of national obligation as defined by national stories, as either inclusive or exclusive of the democratic state, that was pivotal to these peoples' sense of civic duty to vote, pay taxes, defend, and otherwise sacrifice for their democracies.

Still, the assumption of civic duty as something uniquely rooted in Western democratic culture has been hard to shake. South Korea's impressive handling of the COVID-19 pandemic based on exceptional citizen compliance with rigid masking, testing, and tracking rules by the state was once again heralded as a triumph of Confucian collectivism, rather than a show of strong civic duty.[39] On the other hand, as Third Wave democracies such as the Philippines, Turkey, and Venezuela show signs of democratic regress, observers were quick to point to their illiberal political cultures or ethnonationalist legacies. Recep Erdoğan's autocratic stronghold in Turkey, for example, has been attributed to "a political culture that is willing to accept 'big man' rule," whereas Hugo Chávez's populist overtaking of Venezuela is often described as a Bolivarian nationalist phenomenon.[40] An exclusively cultural approach to civic duty has evaded important questions about why it survives in the unlikeliest of places and why it wanes even in mature democracies such as the United States. As prominent Western democracies continue to fall prey to democratic backsliding, the chorus among global leaders for a civic revival and the tempering of nationalist resurgences has grown to a deafening pitch.

Nationalism can certainly take on antidemocratic manifestations. But the evidence amassed in this book shows that for many citizens it also instills a sense of obligation to contribute and sacrifice for "my" democracy. Nationalism's capacity to help or hinder democracies depends not on its ethnic or civic content or even the maturity of a democratic culture but on its relational context: how national stories weave the moral boundaries between the national people and the democratic state in which they live.

In the wake of World War II, nationalism left such a ghastly wound in world history that few wanted to look too closely at it anymore. How nationalism is intimately experienced by everyday members—how it becomes a deeply integral part of many people's identities through personal stories of family, generations, and friends and foes—became almost taboo to admit. But unpacking the basis for nationalism's enduring emotional pull revealed a fascinating insight about how the stories that bring the nation to life can also work to the benefit of democracies. National stories are fundamentally relationship stories that define the nation's ties to its members, other nations, and importantly, the state it calls home. This book has shown that when national stories draw strong linkages between a national people and the democratic state, stronger nationalism—even of the ethnic kind—can provide the moral impetus for deeper civic duty to that democracy.

Civic duty in democracies is largely a nationalist phenomenon. And because nations and their boundaries are imagined, civic duty is rarely a given. It is something that can be had and lost, but also grown. For all democracies, but particularly those in East Asia and other places long seen as hindered by their cultural or ethnic legacies, the book points to a ray of optimism.

Notes

1. DUTY, AGAINST THE ODDS

1. Author interview, June 21, 2013. Interviewee's real name has been modified.

2. "Collecting Gold Campaign Raises 225 Tons of Gold, Foreign Exchange Rate Worth of $1.8 Billion," *Yonhap News*, March 14, 1998.

3. "Koreans Give Up Their Gold to Help Their Country," *BBC News*, January 14, 1998.

4. "National Survey of Public Opinion 20 Years After the IMF Foreign Debt Crisis" *Korea Development Institute*, November 14, 2017.

5. William H. Riker and Peter C. Ordeshook, "A Theory of the Calculus of Voting," *American Political Science Review* 62, no. 1 (1968), 25–42. The civic duty to vote also appears as a powerful predictor of turnout in the following works: Angus Campbell et al., *The American Voter* (Chicago: University of Chicago Press, 1960); André Blais, *To Vote or Not to Vote? The Merits and Limits of Rational Choice Theory* (Pittsburgh, PA: University of Pittsburgh Press, 2000); David E. Campbell, *Why We Vote: How Schools and Communities Shape Our Civic Life,* (Princeton, NJ: Princeton University Press, 2006).

6. Margaret Levi coined the term to describe citizen obligations such as tax compliance. Most citizens choose to comply, but "it is quasi-voluntary because they will be punished if they do not and are caught" (23). See Margaret Levi, *Of Rule and Revenue,* (Berkeley: University of California Press, 1988). In such cases, a sense of civic duty or "tax morale" motivates compliance. See John T. Scholz and Neil Pinney, "Duty, Fear, and Tax Compliance: The Heuristic Basis of Citizenship," *American Journal of Political* Science 39, no. 2 (1995), 490–512.

7. Alexis de Tocqueville, *Democracy in America*, trans. Gerald Bevan (New York: Penguin Books, 2003), 276.

8. Albert Hirschman, *Exit, Voice, and Loyalty: Responses to Decline in Firms, Organizations, and States* (Cambridge, MA: Harvard University Press, 1970), 78–80.

9. David Easton, "A Re-assessment of the Concept of Political Support," *British Journal of Political* Science 5, no. 4 (1975), 444.

10. Larry Diamond, "Facing Up to the Democratic Recession," *Journal of Democracy* 26, no. 1 (2015), 141–55.

11. Patrick Kingsley, "How Viktor Orban Bends Hungarian Society to His Will," *New York Times*, March 27, 2018; Ted Piccone, "Latin America's Struggle with Democratic Backsliding," *Brookings Foreign Policy Report*, 2019.

12. Robin Wright, "Is America Headed for a New Kind of Civil War?" *New Yorker*, August 14, 2017.

13. Nancy Bermeo, "On Democratic Backsliding," *Journal of Democracy* 27, no. 1 (2016), 5–19.

14. Steven Levitsky and Daniel Ziblatt, *How Democracies Die* (New York: Crown, 2018); Matthew Graham and Milan Svolik, "Democracy in America? Partisanship, Polarization, and the Robustness of Support for Democracy in the United States," *American Political Science Review* 114, no. 2 (2020), 392–409.

15. See Lucian Pye, *Asian Power and Politics: The Cultural Dimensions of Authority* (Cambridge, MA: Harvard University Press, 1985); Francis Fukuyama, "Confucianism and Democracy," *Journal of Democracy* 6, no. 2 (1995), 20–33.

16. Fareed Zakaria, "Culture Is Destiny: A Conversation with Lee Kuan Yew," *Foreign Affairs* 73, no. 2 (1994), 113.

17. Samuel Huntington, *The Third Wave: Democratization in the Late Twentieth Century* (Norman: University of Oklahoma Press, 1991), 307. Huntington characterized the young East Asian democracies as the "adaptation of Western democratic practices to serve Asian or Confucian political values" (306) and doubted whether they would survive without being buttressed by continued economic development.

18. The civic versus ethnic dichotomy can be traced back to Friedrich Meinecke, who made the distinction between *Staatsnation* and *Kulturnation*. Later, Hans Kohn overlaid regionality to this distinction, comparing the civic nationalisms of "the West" to the ethnic nationalisms of "the rest" in *The Idea of Nationalism: A Study of the Origins and Background* (New York: Macmillan, 1944).

19. A quick survey of the titles of leading books on nationalism is revealing. See David D. Laitin, *Nations, States, and Violence* (Oxford: Oxford University Press, 1995); Michael Hechter, *Containing Nationalism* (Oxford: Oxford University Press, 2000); Jack Snyder, *From Voting to Violence: Democratization and Nationalist Conflict* (New York: W.W. Norton, 2000); Charles King, *Extreme Politics: Nationalism, Violence, and the End of Eastern Europe* (Oxford: Oxford University Press, 2010).

20. Turnout in the 1946 general election was 72 percent—higher than that of most advanced democracies today—and an impressive 66 percent for women, who had never voted before. Susan Pharr notes that in a 1951 survey of Japanese women, 73 percent answered that they voted because "not voting is a bad thing." See Susan Pharr, *Political Women in Japan: The Search for a Place in Political Life* (Berkeley: University of California Press, 1981), 27. Notably, this phrasing is almost identical to the way that contemporary studies of the civic duty to vote define it, as "the belief that not voting in a democracy is wrong." See Blais, *To Vote*, 93.

21. Gregg A. Brazinsky, "South Korea Is Winning the Fight Against COVID-19. The U.S. Is Failing," *Washington Post*, April 10, 2020; Derek Thompson, "What's behind South Korea's COVID-19 Exceptionalism?" *Atlantic*, May 6, 2020.

22. Gabriel A. Almond and Sidney Verba, *The Civic Culture: Political Attitudes in Five Western Democracies* (Princeton, NJ: Princeton University Press, 1963).

23. See, for instance, Ronald Inglehart and Christian Welzel, *Modernization, Cultural Change, and Democracy: The Human Development Sequence* (Cambridge: Cambridge University Press, 2005); Russell J. Dalton and Christian Welzel, *The Civic Culture Transformed: From Allegiant to Assertive Citizens* (Cambridge: Cambridge University Press, 2014); James Alm and Benno Torgler, "Culture Differences and Tax Morale in the United States and Europe," *Journal of Economic Psychology* 27, no. 2 (2006), 224–46.

24. David E. Campbell, *Why We Vote*; John B. Holbein and D. Sunshine Hillygus, *Making Young Voters: Converting Civic Attitudes into Civic Action* (New York: Cambridge University Press, 2020).

25. For important counterarguments to this prevailing dichotomy, see Rogers Brubaker, "The Manichean Myth: Rethinking the Distinction between <Civic> and <Ethnic> Nationalism," in *Nation and National Identity: The European Experience in Perspective*, ed. Hanspeter Kriesi et al. (Zurich: Rüegger, 1999), 55–72; Yael Tamir, "Not So Civic: Is There a Difference between Ethnic and Civic Nationalism?" *Annual Review of Political Science* 22 (2019), 419–34.

26. Harris Mylonas and Maya Tudor, "Nationalism: What We Know and What We Still Need to Know," *Annual Review of Political Science* 24 (2021): 109–32; Bart Bonikowski, "Nationalism in Settled Times," *Annual Review of Sociology* 42 (2016): 427–49.

27. Benedict Anderson, *Imagined Communities: Reflections on the Origin and Spread of Nationalism* (London: Verso, 1983).

28. National stories are best understood as the *popularized interpretation* of historical events, seen through the eyes of a particular national people. As I elaborate in chapter 2, national stories closely resemble the concept of "collective imaginaries" coined by Gérard Bouchard in the context of Québécois national consciousness. See Gérard Bouchard, *Social Myths and Collective Imaginaries*, trans. Howard Scott (Toronto: University of Toronto Press, 2017).

29. John Dunn, *Western Political Theory in the Face of the Future* (Cambridge: Cambridge University Press, 1993), 57.

30. Lars-Erik Cederman, "Blood for Soil: The Fatal Temptations of Ethnic Politics," *Foreign Affairs* 98, (2019).

31. The book joins a growing body of work on the positive effects of nationalism. See Edward Miguel, "Tribe or Nation? Nation Building and Public Goods in Kenya and Tanzania," *World Politics* 56, no. 3 (2004), 327–62; Prerna Singh, *How Solidarity Works for Welfare: Subnationalism and Social Development in India* (Cambridge: Cambridge University Press, 2015); Andreas Wimmer, *Nation Building: Why Some Countries Come Together While Others Fall Apart* (Princeton, NJ: Princeton University Press, 2018); Maya Tudor and Dan Slater, "Nationalism, Authoritarianism, and Democracy: Historical Lessons from South and Southeast Asia," *Perspectives on Politics* 19 no. 3 (2021), 706-22.

32. Emmanuel Macron, President of the Republic of Paris, "Commemoration of the Centenary of the Armistice Speech," November 11, 2018. Translated text accessed from the Permanent Mission of France to the United Nations.

33. See Jill Lepore, "A New Americanism: Why a Nation Needs a National Story," *Foreign Affairs* 98, (2019), 10–19, on the importance of continuously reimagining the national story.

34. Theda Skocpol and Eric Schickler, "A Conversation with Theda Skocpol," *Annual Review of Political Science* 22 (2019), 15.

35. See David C. Kang, *China Rising: Peace, Power, and Order in East Asia* (New York: Columbia University Press, 2007); Jessica Chen Weiss, "A World Safe for Autocracy? China's Rise and the Future of Global Politics," *Foreign Affairs* 98 (2019), 92–108.

2. A NATIONAL THEORY OF CIVIC DUTY

1. Max Weber, *The Theory of Social and Economic Organization*, ed. Talcott Parsons (New York: Free Press, 1964), 115.

2. For works on contractual approaches to citizen compliance, see Margaret Levi, *Consent, Dissent, and Patriotism* (Cambridge: Cambridge University Press, 1997); Valerie Braithwaite and Margaret Levi, *Trust and Governance* (New York: Russell Sage Foundation, 1998); Tom Tyler, *Why People Obey the Law*, (Princeton, NJ: Princeton University Press, 2006). As Tyler explains: "If there is a mechanism to assure that outcomes are distributed fairly, long-term membership in the group will be rewarding; evidence that procedures for allocation are fair provides a basis for a continued belief in the value of organizational loyalty in the face of negative decisions" (174).

3. Blais, *To Vote*, 111.

4. David Halbfinger, Wendy Ruderman, and Corey Kilgannon, "Displaced by Hurricane, but Returning Home, Briefly, to Vote," *New York Times*, November 6, 2012.

5. Weber, *Social and Economic Organization*, 115.

6. Michael Sandel, *Liberalism and the Limits of Justice* (Cambridge: Cambridge University Press: 1998), 179. See also Charles Taylor, *Sources of the Self: The Making of the Modern Identity* (Cambridge, MA: Harvard University Press, 1989); Michael Walzer, "The Communitarian Critique of Liberalism," *Political Theory* 18, no. 1 (1990), 6–23. Of course, communitarians are hardly a unified block. Each of these scholars has critiqued liberalism

for different reasons. What their works fundamentally share, however, is the concept of "the self" as located within and inseparable from community.

7. Clifford Geertz, "Thick Description: Toward an Interpretive Theory of Culture," in *The Interpretation of Cultures* (New York: Basic Books, 1973), 259. See also Edward Shils, "Primordial, Personal, Sacred, and Civil Ties: Some Particular Observations on the Relationships of Sociological Research and Theory," *British Journal of Sociology* 8, no. 2 (1957), 130–45.

8. For representative works on the politically constructed nature of identities, see David Laitin, *Identity in Formation: The Russian-speaking Populations in the Near Abroad* (Ithaca, NY: Cornell University Press, 1998); Daniel N. Posner, "The Political Salience of Cultural Difference: Why Chewas and Tumbukas are Allies in Zambia and Adversaries in Malawi," *American Political Science Review* 98, no. 4 (2004), 529–45.

9. Henri Tajfel and John C. Turner, "The Social Identity Theory of Intergroup Behavior," in *Psychology of Intergroup Relations*, eds. S. Worchel and L. W. Austin (Chicago: Nelson-Hall, 1986); Michael A. Hogg and Dominic Abrams, *Social Identifications: A Social Psychology of Intergroup Relationships and Group Processes* (New York: Routledge, 1988).

10. Anderson, *Imagined Communities*.

11. Ernst Renan, "Qu'est-ce qu'une nation?" in *Nation and Narration*, ed. Homi K. Bhaba (New York: Routledge, 1990), 19.

12. Ernest Gellner, *Nations and Nationalism* (Ithaca, NY: Cornell University Press, 1983); Charles Tilly, "States and Nationalism in Europe, 1492–1992," *Theory and Society* 23, no. 1 (1994), 131–46.

13. Katherine Verdery, "Whither 'Nation' and 'Nationalism'?" *Daedalus* 122, no. 3 (1993), 37–46.

14. Michael Billig, *Banal Nationalism* (London: Sage Publications, 1995), 8.

15. José Rizal, *Noli Me Tángere,* trans. Harold Augenbraum (New York: Penguin Books, 2006), chap. 3.

16. Robert E. Goodin, "What Is So Special about Our Fellow Countrymen?" *Ethics* 98, no. 4 (1988), 663–86. For works on the nation as "moral community," see also Cara J. Wong, *Boundaries of Obligation: Geographic, Racial, and National Communities* (New York: Cambridge University Press, 2010); Bernard Yack, *Nationalism and the Moral Psychology of Community* (Chicago: University of Chicago Press, 2012).

17. Anderson, *Imagined Communities*, 143–44.

18. Wong, *Boundaries of Obligation*, 5–6.

19. Leonie Huddy and Nadia Khatib, "American Patriotism, National Identity, and Political Involvement," *American Journal of Political Science* 51, no. 1 (2007), 65.

20. Miguel, "Tribe or Nation?"; Singh, *How Solidarity Works*; Volha Charnysh, Christopher Lucas, and Prerna Singh, "The Ties That Bind: National Identity Salience and Pro-Social Behavior toward the Ethnic Other," *Comparative Political Studies* 48, no. 3 (2015), 267–300.

21. Amelie Mummendey, Andreas Klink, and Rupert Brown, "Nationalism and Patriotism: National Identification and Out-group Rejection," *British Journal of Social Psychology* 40, no. 2 (2001), 159–72; Rui J.P. De Figueiredo, Jr., and Zachary Elkins, "Are Patriots Bigots? An Inquiry into the Vices of In-Group Pride," *American Journal of Political Science* 47, no. 1 (2003), 171–88.

22. Rogers Brubaker, "In the Name of the Nation: Reflections on Nationalism and Patriotism," *Citizenship Studies* 8, no. 2 (2004), 120. Andreas Wimmer makes a similar point in "Why Nationalism Works, and Why It Isn't Going Away," *Foreign Affairs* 98, no. 2 (2019): "Efforts to draw a hard line between good, civic patriotism and bad, ethnic nationalism overlook the common roots of both. Patriotism is a form of nationalism. They are ideological brothers, not distant cousins" (27).

23. Rogers Smith, "Citizenship and the Politics of People-Building," *Citizenship Studies* 5, no. 1 (2001): 73–96.

24. Gérard Bouchard, "The Small Nation with a Big Dream: Québec National Myths," in *National Myths: Constructed Pasts, Contested Presents*, ed. Gérard Bouchard (London: Routledge, 2013), 15–16.

25. Peter Hall and Michèle Lamont, *Successful Societies: How Institutions and Culture Affect Health* (Cambridge: Cambridge University Press, 2009), 12. The concept of "collective imaginaries" is developed from Gérard Bouchard's long-standing work on national myths of the Québécois. See Bouchard, *Social Myths*.

26. Rogers Brubaker, *Nationalism Reframed: Nationhood and the National Question in the New Europe* (Cambridge: Cambridge University Press, 1996), 17. Emphasis in original.

27. Brubaker, "Manichean Myth," 67.

28. Walker Connor also emphasized the need to better specify the relationship between nation and state in *Ethnonationalism: The Quest for Understanding* (Princeton, NJ: Princeton University Press, 1994): "The most fundamental error involved in scholarly approaches to nationalism has been a tendency to equate nationalism with a feeling of loyalty to the state rather than with loyalty to the nation" (91).

29. I use the term "best interests" to emphasize political intent over political performance, since even well-meaning states will sometimes fail to deliver.

30. A nationally homogeneous democracy is not the same as an ethnically homogeneous democracy. A singular national identity can be built from ethnically diverse populations, e.g., Miguel, "Tribe or Nation," and distinct national claims can emerge within coethnic populations, e.g., East versus West Germany during the division. Ethnic homogeneity is neither a necessary nor sufficient condition for strong beliefs of nation-state linkage.

31. Even in nation-states, extended periods of state abuse or negligence will eventually produce national stories that fracture beliefs of nation-state linkage over time.

32. Walker Connor, "Nation-Building or Nation-Destroying?" *World Politics* 24, no. 3 (1972), 335–36. Emphasis in original.

33. Rogers Brubaker, "Name of the Nation," 121.

34. Ora John Reuter, "Civic Duty and Voting under Autocracy," Journal of Politics 83, no. 4 (2021), https://doi.org/10.1086/711718.

35. Anna Stilz, *Liberal Loyalty: Freedom, Obligation, and the State* (Princeton, NJ: Princeton University Press, 2009).

36. Clifford Geertz, "The Integrative Revolution: Primordial Sentiments and Politics in New States," in *Old Societies and New States: The Quest for Modernity in Asia and Africa* (New York: Free Press, 1963), 108.

37. David Broockman, "Black Politicians Are More Intrinsically Motivated to Advance Blacks' Interests: A Field Experiment Manipulating Political Incentives," *American Journal of Political Science* 57, no. 3 (2013), 521–36.

38. For a discussion on the merits of the theory-driven controlled case study, see Dan Slater and Daniel Ziblatt, "The Enduring Indispensability of the Controlled Comparison," *Comparative Political Studies* 46, no.10 (2013), 1301–27: "Although simply choosing the cases that substantively interest one most is perfectly valid for comparativists pursuing internal validity, the pursuit of external validity requires that cases be selected precisely *to control for existing rival hypotheses*. This kind of 'folk Bayesian' perspective pushes scholars to choose cases whose variation simply cannot be accounted for by extant hypotheses, rather than seeking the chimerical goal of a perfectly paired comparison" (1313).

39. Evan Lieberman, *Race and Regionalism in the Politics of Taxation in Brazil and South Africa* (New York: Cambridge University Press, 2003); James Habyarimana et al., "Why Does Ethnic Diversity Undermine Public Goods Provision?," *American Political Science*

Review 101, no. 4 (2007), 709–25; Moses Shayo, "A Model of Social Identity with an Application to Political Economy: Nation, Class, and Redistribution," *American Political Science Review* 103, no. 2 (2009), 147–74; Gwyneth McClendon, *Envy in Politics* (Princeton, NJ: Princeton University Press, 2018).

40. Laura Stoker, "Interests and Ethics in Politics," *American Political Science Review* 86, no. 2 (1992), 376–77.

3. NATIONAL STORIES IN SOUTH KOREA AND TAIWAN

1. Ethnicity remains the primary basis for Korean identity, but generational shifts are occurring. Many youth identify with a "globalized cultural nationalism," for example, that emphasizes South Korea as a cosmopolitan nation. See Emma Campbell, *South Korea's New Nationalism: The End of 'One Korea'?* (Boulder, CO: First Forum Press, 2016). The decline in the singular importance of ethnicity is also evident in the low proportion of youth who see "shared ethnicity" as the reason for reunification with North Korea. See Jiyoon Kim et al., "South Korean Attitudes toward North Korea and Reunification," *Asan Institute for Policy Studies*, February 2015.

2. Max Fisher, "A Revealing Map of the World's Most and Least Ethnically Diverse Countries," *Washington Post*, May 16, 2013.

3. Chizuko T. Allen, "Northeast Asia Centered around Korea: Ch'oe Namsŏn's View of History," *Journal of Asian Studies* 49, no. 4 (1990), 787–806.

4. On the legacies of Japanese colonialism in South Korea, see Bruce Cumings, "The Legacy of Japanese Colonialism in Korea," in *The Japanese Colonial Empire*, ed. Ramon Myers and Mark Peattie (Princeton, NJ: Princeton University Press: 1984); Michael Edson Robinson, *Cultural Nationalism in Colonial Korea, 1920–1925* (Seattle: University of Washington Press: 1988).

5. For a comprehensive account of the origins of Korea's ethnic nationalism, see Gi-Wook Shin, *Ethnic Nationalism in Korea: Genealogy, Politics, and Legacy* (Stanford, CA: Stanford University Press, 2006).

6. As quoted from the *Doksasillon* prologue, first published in 1908.

7. Quoted from Shin, *Ethnic Nationalism*, 48.

8. Henry H. Em, "Nationalism, Post-Nationalism, and Shin Ch'ae-ho," *Korea Journal* 39, no. 2 (1999), 288.

9. Roland Bleiker, "Identity and Security in Korea," *Pacific Review* 14, no. 1 (2001), 123.

10. See Gi-Wook Shin, James Freda, and Gihong Yi, "The Politics of Ethnic Nationalism in Divided Korea," *Nations and Nationalism* 5, no. 4 (1999), 465–84, on how the principle of national homogeneity persists between the two Koreas: "Korea resembles Germany and Japan in that Korean ethnicity is perceived to be homogeneous. However, post-1945 territorial division has created the problem of who would represent the Korean ethnic nation, leading to a contested 'politics of representation' between the two Koreas" (466).

11. Paul Y. Chang, *Protest Dialectics: State Repression and South Korea's Democracy Movement, 1970–1979* (Stanford, CA: Stanford University Press, 2015).

12. Henry H. Em, "Minjok as a Modern and Democratic Construct: Sin Ch'aeho's Historiography," in *Colonial Modernity in Korea*, ed. Gi-Wook Shin and Michael Edson Robinson, 336–61 (Cambridge, MA: Harvard University Press 1999).

13. Sunyoung Park, "Introduction," in *Revisiting Minjung: New Perspectives on the Cultural History of 1980s South Korea* (Ann Arbor: University of Michigan Press, 2019), 3.

14. See Sheila Miyoshi Jager, *Narratives of Nation Building in Korea* (New York: M.E. Sharpe, 2003), 116: "Indeed, a close inspection of the internal logic of *chuch'eron* and the 'redemptive' narrative strategy that is used to tell the story of Korea's modern history reveals how its construction of the past was not unlike similar colonial and 'official'

post-war nationalist historiographies. . . . If dissidents sought to redeem their nation's past with the language of patriarchal renewal, they did so because benevolent fathers were deemed few, and filial sons had to, somehow, fill the void."

15. Namhee Lee, *The Making of Minjung: Democracy and the Politics of Representation in South Korea* (Ithaca, NY: Cornell University Press, 2007), 24.

16. Charles R. Kim, *Youth for Nation: Culture and Protest in Cold War South Korea* (Honolulu: University of Hawaii, 2017), 3.

17. On the link between inclusive national ideologies and successful democratic transitions, see Maya Tudor and Dan Slater, "The Content of Democracy: Nationalist Parties and Inclusive Ideologies in India and Indonesia," in *Parties, Movements, and Democracy in the Developing World*, ed. Nancy Bermeo and Deborah J. Yashar (Cambridge: Cambridge University Press, 2016): "An inclusive definition of the nation both provides a bulwark against antidemocratization forces and equips pro-democratization forces with a valuable legitimation resource during subsequent political struggles" (33).

18. Larry Diamond and Gi-Wook Shin, *New Challenges for Maturing Democracies in Korea and Taiwan* (Stanford, CA: Stanford University Press, 2014), 1.

19. Christopher H. Achen and T. Y. Wang, *The Taiwan Voter* (Ann Arbor, MI: Michigan University Press, 2017).

20. John Fuh-sheng Hsieh, "Ethnicity, National Identity, and Domestic Politics in Taiwan," *Journal of Asian and African Studies* 40, no. 1–2 (2005), 13–28.

21. Peter R. Moody, *Political Change on Taiwan: A Study of Ruling Party Adaptability* (New York: Praeger, 1992), 39.

22. Douglas Mendel, *Politics of Formosan Nationalism* (Berkeley, CA: University of California Press, 1970); Yun-han Chu and Jih-wen Lin, "Political Development in 20th Century Taiwan," *China Quarterly* 165 (2001), 102–29.

23. Robert Edmondson, "The February 28 Incident and National Identity," in *Memories of the Future: National Identity Issues and the Search for a New Taiwan*, ed. Stéphane Corcuff (Armonk, NY: M. E. Sharpe, 2002), 27.

24. Su Bing, *Taiwan's 400 Year History* (Washington, DC: Taiwanese Cultural Grassroots Association, 1986), 127.

25. Richard W. Wilson, *Learning To Be Chinese: The Political Socialization of Children in Taiwan* (Cambridge, MA: MIT Press, 1970).

26. Allen Chun, "From Nationalism to Nationalizing: Cultural Imagination and State Formation in Postwar Taiwan," *Australian Journal of Chinese Affairs* 31 (January 1994): 58. Emphasis in original.

27. Alan Wachman, "Competing Identities in Taiwan," in *The Other Taiwan: 1945 to the Present*, ed. Murray Rubinstein (Armonk, NY: M. E. Sharpe, 1994), 46.

28. For a detailed account of the DPP's rise and role in Taiwan's democratization, see Shelley Rigger, *From Opposition to Power: Taiwan's Democratic Progressive Party* (Boulder, CO: Lynne Reiner Publishers, 2001).

29. Aram Hur and Andrew Yeo, "Democratic Ceilings in East Asia: The Long Shadow of Nationalist Polarization," (American Political Science Association, 2020).

30. Yun-han Chu, Larry Diamond, and Kharis Templeman, *Taiwan's Democracy Challenged: The Chen Shui-bian Years* (Boulder, CO: Lynne Rienner Publishing, 2016).

31. Both the KMT and DPP have converged toward the status quo in recent years, producing extremist splinter parties like the New Party and Taiwan Solidarity Union in their wake. But the national identity issue vis-à-vis China still defines the "left-right" ideological spectrum in Taiwan (see Achen and Wang, *Taiwan Voter*, 108–48, 208–32). The "pan-blue" coalition led by the KMT supports a pro-China and pro-engagement vision, while the "pan-green" coalition led by the DPP supports a pro-Taiwan and pro-independence stance.

32. Lee Teng-hui strongly advocated for a shift toward civic nationhood, which he saw as indispensable to Taiwan's long-term survival. See Lee Teng-hui, "Understanding Taiwan: Bridging the Perception Gap," *Foreign Affairs* 78 (1999), 9: "To convey a sense of popular will on Taiwan today, I now refer to my fellow citizens as 'New Taiwanese,' meaning those who are willing to fight for the prosperity and survival of their country, regardless of when they or their forebears arrived on Taiwan and regardless of their provincial heritage or native language."

33. Stéphane Corcuff, "Taiwan's 'Mainlanders,' New Taiwanese?" in *Memories of the Future: National Identity Issues and the Search for a New Taiwan*, ed. Stéphane Corcuff, 163–95 (Armonk, NY: M.E. Sharpe, 2002), 19.

34. When I went into the field for data collection in 2013, the KMT's incumbent president Ma Ying-jeou had just begun his second term after handily beating the DPP challenger.

35. Sheena Chestnut Greitens, *Dictators and Their Secret Police: Coercive Institutions and State Violence* (New York: Cambridge University Press, 2016), 75–111.

36. Dan Slater and Joseph Wong, "The Strength to Concede: Ruling Parties and Democratization in Developmental Asia," *Perspectives on Politics* 11 no. 3 (2013), 717–33.

37. Kharis Templeman, "After Hegemony: State Capacity, the Quality of Democracy, and the Legacies of the Party-State in Democratic Taiwan," in *Stateness and the Quality of Democracy in East Asia*, ed. Aurel Croissant and Olli Hellman, 71–102 (Cambridge: Cambridge University Press, 2020).

38. Author expert interview, November 18, 2013.

39. In both democracies male citizens over eighteen years old are required to serve in the military. Military service is listed as one of the four constitutional duties of a citizen in South Korea and is typically two years or longer for specialized branches. In Taiwan a mandatory one-year service was recently reduced to four months of basic training for those born after January 1, 1994.

40. A landmark amendment to South Korea's Nationality Act, in effect since 2011, now permits dual citizenship. Previously, such individuals were forced to choose or renounce their Korean citizenship by the age of eighteen.

41. The transition to AVF began under Chen Shui-bian's administration as part of a comprehensive effort to "engineer the transformation for a modernized defense in order to ensure Taiwan's sufficient defense capability into the 21st century." See *Chen Shui-bian's Blueprint for State, vol. 1, National Security* (1999).

42. Michael Thim, "No Pain, No Gain: Successful AVF Transition Requires Greater Commitment from Government," *Strategic Vision for Taiwan Security* 3, no.18 (2014), 25.

43. Hsiu-chuan Shih and Yan-chih Mo, "Military Raises Wages to Lure Recruits," *Taipei Times*, December 27, 2013.

44. See Max Weber, "The Chinese Literati," in *From Max Weber: Essays in Sociology*, ed. H.H. Gerth and C. Wright Mills (Abingdon, UK: Routledge, 1948): 422. A soldier is not even in the Confucian category of occupations, as it was seen to be of even lower moral status than a merchant.

45. Author expert interview, November 12, 2013.

46. Author expert interview, November 16, 2013.

47. "Taiwan's Army Bloodied," *Economist*, August 10, 2013.

48. J. Michael Cole, "Forget the PLA, Taiwan's Military Threatens Itself," *Diplomat*, August 2, 2013.

49. On the merits and applications of personal narrative analysis to political science, see Molly Patterson and Kristen Renwick Monroe, "Narrative in Political Science," *Annual Review of Political Science* 1, no. 1 (1998), 315–31; Joseph P. Gone, Peggy J. Miller, and Julian Rappaport, "Conceptual Self as Normatively Oriented: The Suitability of Past

Personal Narrative for the Study of Cultural Identity," *Culture and Psychology* 5, no. 4 (1999), 371–98.

50. Robert Wuthnow, *American Mythos: Why Our Best Efforts to be a Better Nation Fall Short* (Princeton, NJ: Princeton University Press, 2006), 59.

51. Wuthnow, *American Mythos*, 60.

52. The phrase comes from the refrain of the South Korean national anthem and translates to "the Korean people, stay true to the Korean way."

53. In-jin Yoon, "Migration and the Korean Diaspora: A Comparative Description of Five Cases," *Journal of Ethnic and Migration Studies* 38, no. 3 (2012), 413–35.

54. College students in Taiwan were a convenience sample, but they are also the most relevant sample. Most men in Taiwan choose to fulfill their military service during or immediately after college. This population is the prime target for AVF recruitment.

55. See Matthew B. Miles, A. Michael Huberman, and Johnny Saldaña, *Qualitative Data Analysis: A Methods Sourcebook*, 3rd edition (Los Angeles, CA: Sage Publications, 1994), 105–254.

56. Ann Swidler, "Culture in Action: Symbols and Strategies," *American Sociological Review* 51, no. 2 (1986), 273.

57. Constitution of the Republic of Korea, chap. 2, art. 39: "(1) All citizens shall have the duty of national defense under the conditions as prescribed by the Act. (2) No citizen shall be treated unfavorably on account of the fulfillment of his obligation of military service."

58. *Daehansaram Daehaneuro*, issue 2007, 22.

59. *Daehansaram Daehaneuro*, issue 2007, 45.

60. *Daehansaram Daehaneuro*, issue 2007, 12–13.

61. *Daehansaram Daehaneuro*, issue 2010, 59.

62. *Daehansaram Daehaneuro*, issue 2012, 60.

63. *Daehansaram Daehaneuro*, issue 2007, 31–32.

64. Green is the color of the independent Taiwan flag and the official color of the pro-DPP faction.

65. Upon initiating martial rule on the island, KMT leader Chiang Kai-shek oversaw the period of "White Terror," where islander elites, along with some dissident members within the KMT, were systematically purged to eliminate opposition.

66. Arthur H. Miller et al., "Group Consciousness and Political Participation," *American Journal of Political Science* 25, no. 3 (1981), 494.

67. Michael S. Chase, "Defense Reform in Taiwan: Problems and Prospects," *Asian Survey* 45, no. 3 (2005), 367.

68. Author expert interview, November 15, 2013.

69. Author expert interview, November 18, 2013.

70. See Yao-Yuan Yeh et al., "Would Taiwan Fight China without U.S. Support?" *National Interest*, December 9, 2018. In a survey experiment, the authors find that the Taiwan public's willingness to fight in the event of a Chinese invasion, given US support, is 4.8 on a 10-point scale. But even without US support, in what would most certainly be a losing fight, the willingness to fight is still 3.9.

4. STRONG CIVIC DUTY IN THE NAME OF NATION IN SOUTH KOREA

1. The analysis in this chapter is adapted from work that has been previously published in Aram Hur, "Citizen Duty and the Ethical Power of Communities: Mixed-method Evidence from East Asia," *British Journal of Political Science* 50 no. 3 (2020), 1047–65.

2. Broockman, "Black Politicians," 522.

3. Immanuel Kant, *Critique of Practical Reason*, ed. Mary Gregor (Cambridge: Cambridge University Press, 1997), 73.

4. Kant, *Groundwork for the Metaphysics of Morals*, ed. Lara Denis (Ottawa: Broadview Press, 2005), 55–56.

5. Kant, *Groundwork*, 56.

6. Whether an individual is intrinsically motivated by a sense of obligation to her nation is a matter of intent and cannot be observed. I therefore proxy the nation's moral pull with strength of national identification, its measurable source. Psychological identification with a group as "mine" is what instills a sense of obligation to it.

7. Note that if national identification only mattered as another source of payoffs, such as through the pursuit of status or social praise, it would not produce such an interaction. All "inclinations" can be aggregated to a "sum total," to use Kant's words. In statistical terms, the cumulative effect of payoffs would be additive.

8. Aram Hur and Christopher Achen, "Coding Voter Turnout Responses in the Current Population Survey," *Public Opinion Quarterly* 77 no. 4 (2013), 985–93.

9. Blais and Achen, "Civic Duty and Voter Turnout," *Political Behavior* 41, no. 2 (2019), 479. The question wording has been adopted by several national election studies since it was piloted in the American National Election Study (ANES).

10. National pride is often distinguished from national identification in the literature. The former mixes "a love of country with political efforts" that imply a status comparison to other nations (see Huddy and Khatib, "American Patriotism," 64), and is often associated with chauvinist attitudes. The Korean survey question, however, does not ask about any "political efforts," and the Korean word for "pride" does not carry the connotation of superiority as the English word does.

11. Preference in the election outcome is a commonly cited incentive in turnout studies. See Campbell et al., *American Voter*, 89–119; Blais and Achen, "Civic Duty," 483; Riker and Ordeshook, "Calculus of Voting." Using a different payoff, such as interest in the election, does not change the substantive results in table 2.

12. John T. Scholz and Mark Lubell, "Trust and Taxpaying: Testing the Heuristic Approach to Collective Action," *American Journal of Political Science* 42, no. 2 (1998): 400.

13. See table 5.2 in Blais, *To Vote*, 98, where political interest is a powerful predictor of the duty to vote, and table 7.2 in David Campbell, *Why We Vote*, 160, where highest level of education—both of the parents and anticipated for the self—is the most powerful predictor after degree of political heterogeneity in the community. Duty to vote tends to increase quadratically with age in most surveys, so I also include age and age-squared in the model.

14. Negative interactions can be a spurious feature of the data, when the values of one variable are capped at a ceiling while those of the other continue to increase, for example. The logistic scale eliminates both ceiling and floor effects in this case.

15. The interaction coefficient will be directionally correct about the nature of the relationship but often fails to convey the full substantive significance of the interaction, which is best assessed visually. See Robert J. Franzese and Cindy D. Kam, *Modeling and Interpreting Interactive Hypotheses in Regression Analysis* (Ann Arbor: University of Michigan Press, 2007).

16. John Zaller, *The Nature and Origins of Mass Opinion* (Cambridge: Cambridge University Press, 1992).

17. The question wording for the duty to vote is identical across the survey and experimental studies, except that in the experiment I ask a follow-up about the strength of opinion.

18. See Alan S. Gerber and Donald P. Green, "The Effects of Canvassing, Telephone Calls, and Direct Mail on Voter Turnout: A Field Experiment," *American Political Science Review* 94, no. 3 (2000), 653–63, for a review of the treatment effects in the turnout literature. Recent studies find little support for the effectiveness of phone calls or mailers, and treatment effects for face-to-face canvassing typically range between 2 to 3 percentage

point increases in turnout. See Donald P. Green, Alan S. Gerber, and David W. Nickerson, "Getting Out the Vote in Local Elections: Results from Six Door-to-Door Canvassing Experiments," *Journal of Politics* 65, no. 4 (2003), 1083–96; Melissa R. Michelson, "Mobilizing the Latino Youth Vote: Some Experimental Results," *Social Science Quarterly* 87, no. 5 (2006), 1188–1206.

19. In Gerber and Green, "Effects of Canvassing," adjusting for the likelihood of being contacted, the authors estimate the effect of personal canvassing to be 8.7 percentage points. In Alan S. Gerber, Donald P. Green, and Christopher W. Larimer, "Social Pressure and Voter Turnout: Evidence from a Large-scale Field Experiment," *American Political Science Review* 102, no. 1 (2008), 33–48, the authors find that social pressure from the neighborhood list treatment increases turnout by 8.1 percentage points.

20. Gerber, Green, and Larimer, "Social Pressure," 38.

21. "Koreans Give Up Their Gold To Help Their Country," *BBC News*, January 14, 1998.

22. Frank Holmes, "How Gold Rode to the Rescue of South Korea," *Forbes*, September 27, 2016.

23. Quoted from William Pesek, "Greece's No-pain Bailout Fails Confucian Ethics," *Bloomberg*, May 9, 2010; Andreas Becker, "Koreans' Gold Donations—A Model for Greeks?" *Deutsche Welle*, February 4, 2015.

5. WEAK CIVIC DUTY AND FRAGMENTED NATION IN TAIWAN

1. The analysis in this chapter is adapted from work that has been previously published in Hur, "Citizen Duty."

2. I used propensity score weighting to generate the survey weights. I combined both online and face-to-face samples and estimated the propensity (=p) to be included in the online sample based on age category, education, gender, and father's ethnicity (Minnan, Hakka, and so on, not subjective national identification). Respondents in the online sample were then weighted by 1/p. After standardizing the weights to sum up to the total N of the online sample, respondents whose weights were larger than three times the median weight (=2.09) were replaced with that value to avoid overweighting extreme observations.

3. The identity battery follows the measurement strategy for national identities in Taiwan proposed in T.Y. Wang and I-Chou Liu, "Contending Identities in Taiwan: Implications for Cross-strait Relations," *Asian Survey* 44, no. 4 (2004), 568–90.

4. Chi Huang, "Dimensions of Taiwanese/Chinese Identity and National Identity in Taiwan: A Latent Class Analysis," *Journal of Asian and African Studies* 40, no. 1–2 (2005), 51–70.

5. A handful of respondents held logically incoherent identities from the perspective of Taiwan's nationalist history. For instance, they said that the territory of "my" Taiwan includes both the mainland and Taiwan but that Taiwanese culture is different from Chinese culture. Because it is difficult to deduce nation-state linkage for such individuals and generate clear theoretical predictions for them, I exclude them from the analysis (N=329).

6. In Tyler, *Why People Obey*, 174: "If there is a mechanism to assure that outcomes are distributed fairly, long-term membership in the group will be rewarding."

7. There is some correlation between the national-identity groups and perceived fairness of elections. While 24 percent of Taiwan nationalists see elections to be fair "most of the time," 42 percent of China nationalists do.

8. In South Korea, the duty to vote was measured dichotomously, so the national coefficient in table 2 is a logistic coefficient. When the model is fitted with OLS, the corresponding national coefficient is 0.37, or a 37 percent higher duty to vote. The comparison focuses on the substantive size of the coefficient, rather than a significance test across the models.

9. As the first collective calamity experienced after democratization, the 921 earthquake holds a special place in Taiwan's public consciousness. The 921 Earthquake Museum in Taichung is dedicated to victims of the disaster, and the earthquake often appears in popular culture, most recently as the backdrop to the movie *Turn Around*, released in 2017.

10. Crises tend to increase in-group cohesion, but scholars have also found that the boundaries of the in-group are malleable in experimental settings. For instance, in Charnysh, Lucas, and Singh, "Ties that Bind," the authors find that showing the Indian national flag increases prosocial donations to ethnic others in the context of a regional fire. The Taiwan experiment leverages that same kind of identity malleability in a democracy where multiple beliefs of "my" nation coexist.

6. STUNTED CIVIC DUTY IN REUNIFIED GERMANY

1. On the evolution of German national identity before and after World War II, see Jan-Werner Müller, *Another Country: German Intellectuals, Unification, and National Identity* (New Haven, CT: Yale University Press, 2000); Jürgen Habermas, *The New Conservatism: Cultural Criticism and the Historians' Debate*, ed. and trans. S.W. Nicholsen (Cambridge, MA: MIT Press, 1989).

2. By "East Germans," I refer conceptually to individuals who resided in the former East Germany prior to reunification. However, it is not always possible to identify individuals by their pre-reunification residence in official statistics or aggregate data. In such cases, I use the term interchangeably with "citizens in the new Länder," which could include some individuals who were socialized in former West Germany and relocated to the East. However, migration data show that interregional relocation following reunification was primarily from the East to the West, rather than vice versa, minimizing concerns about diluting estimates in the East. See Frank W. Heiland, "Trends in East-West German Migration from 1989 to 2002," *Demographic Research* 11 (2004), 173–94.

3. Former East Germany also held elections, but they were neither free nor fair, as they were heavily monitored by the Stasi.

4. For an overview of the political socialization literature on the intergenerational transmission of partisanship and participatory behaviors, see M. Kent Jennings and Richard G. Niemi, *Generations and Politics: A Panel Study of Young Adults and their Parents* (Princeton, NJ: Princeton University Press, 1981), 76–151; Philip E. Converse, "Of Time and Partisan Stability," *Comparative Political Studies* 2, no. 2 (1969), 139–71. In William Mishler and Richard Rose, "Generation, Age, and Time: The Dynamics of Political Learning during Russia's Transformation," *American Journal of Political Science* 51, no. 4 (2007), 822–34, the authors find that in contexts of regime liberalization, the youth generation adapts quickly to new institutional norms, despite the authoritarian socialization that is transmitted from the parent generation.

5. For representative studies that examine the democratic deficit thesis in East Germany, see Kendall L. Baker, Russell J. Dalton, and Kai Hildebrandt, *Germany Transformed: Political Culture and the New Politics* (Cambridge, MA: Harvard University Press, 1981); Thomas Kleinhenz, "A New Type of Nonvoter? Turnout Decline in German Elections, 1980–94," in *Stability and Change in German Elections: How Electorates Merge, Converge, or Collide*, ed. Christopher J. Anderson and Carsten Zelle (Westport, CT: Praeger, 1998); Rolf Becker, "Political Efficacy and Voter Turnout in East and West Germany," *German Politics* 13, no. 2 (2004), 317–40.

6. Hubert Tworzecki, "A Disaffected New Democracy? Identities, Institutions and Civic Engagement in Post-Communist Poland," *Communist and Post-Communist Studies* 41, no. 1 (2008), 47–62; Stephen White and Ian Mcallister, "Dimensions of Disengagement

in Post-Communist Russia," *Journal of Communist Studies and Transition Politics* 20, no. 1 (2004), 81–97.

7. Manfred Keuchler, "The Road to German Unity: Mass Sentiment in East and West Germany," *Public Opinion Quarterly* 56, no. 1 (1992), 62.

8. Hans Rattinger and Jurgen Kramer, "Economic Conditions and Voting Preferences in East and West Germany," in *Stability and Change in German Elections: How Electorates Merge, Converge, or Collide*, ed. Christopher J. Anderson and Carsten Zelle (Westport, CT: Praeger, 1998).

9. See Donna Bahry and Christine Lipsmeyer, "Economic Adversity and Public Mobilization in Russia," *Electoral Studies* 20, no. 3 (2001), 371–98; Tatiana Kostadinova, "Voter Turnout Dynamics in Post-Communist Europe," *European Journal of Political Research* 42, no. 6 (2003), 741–59; Alexander Pacek, Grigore Pop-Eleches, and Joshua A. Tucker, "Disenchanted or Discerning: Voter Turnout in Post-Communist Countries," *Journal of Politics* 71, no. 2 (2009), 473–91.

10. I use the following two questions from the *Politbarometer*:

> How do you evaluate your own economic situation? [Good, so-so, bad]
> How satisfied are you with democracy? [Rather satisfied, rather dissatisfied]

11. The GGSS asks respondents how strongly they agree or disagree with the following statement: "In a democracy, every citizen has the duty to vote in elections."

12. Quoted from Henry Krisch, "The Changing Politics of German National Identity," in *The Federal Republic of Germany at Fifty: At the End of a Century of Turmoil*, ed. Peter H. Merkl (New York: New York University Press, 1999), 37. See also Richard T. Gray and Sabine Wilke, *German Unification and Its Discontents* (Seattle: University of Washington Press, 1996) for a chronology of key speeches, public addresses, and official statements made by both sides surrounding German reunification, where a stark contrast is apparent between Western and Eastern conceptions of the German nation.

13. Marc Howard, "An East German Ethnicity? Understanding the New Division of Unified Germany," *German Politics and Society* 13, no. 4 (1995), 54–55.

14. Jennifer A. Yoder, *From East Germans to Germans? The New Postcommunist Elites* (Durham, NC: Duke University Press, 1999), 85–154.

15. Thomas A. Baylis, "East German Leadership After Unification: The Search for a Voice," in *The Federal Republic of Germany at Fifty: At the End of a Century of Turmoil*, ed. Peter H. Merkl (New York: New York University Press, 1999), 136.

16. Heinrich August Winkler et al., "Rebuilding of a Nation: The Germans before and after Unification," *Daedalus* 123, no. 1 (1994), 121.

17. Jürgen Kocka, "Crisis of Unification: How Germany Changes," *Daedalus* 123, no. 1 (1994), 186.

18. Kocka, "Crisis of Unification," 188.

19. Grigore Pop-Eleches and Joshua A. Tucker, *Communism's Shadow: Historical Legacies and Contemporary Political Attitudes* (Princeton, NJ: Princeton University Press, 2017).

20. Weights were standardized to sum up to the total N of the sample, and extreme weights—those larger than three times the median—were replaced with the median value (=2.59).

21. Ben Knight, "East Germans Still Victims of Cultural Colonialism by the West," *Deutsche Welle*, November 1, 2017.

22. United Nations High Commissioner for Refugees, "Global Trends: Forced Displacement in 2017."

23. Dagmar Breitenbach, "Where Racism and Xenophobia Are Manifest in Germany," *Deutsche Welle*, August 18, 2015.

24. Daniel Wighton, "Refugees in Eastern Germany '10 Times More Likely' To Be Hate Crime Victims: Report," *The Local*, February 27, 2019.

25. See Jens Alber, "Towards Explaining Anti-Foreign Violence in Germany," *CES Germany and Europe Working Papers*, no. 4.8 (1993); also see Brandon Tensley, "It's Been 25 Years Since German Reunification. Why Are Former East Germans Responsible for So Much Xenophobic Violence?" *Washington Post*, October 2, 2015.

26. Alan B. Krueger and Jörn-Steffen Pischke, "A Statistical Analysis of Crime against Foreigners in Unified Germany," *Journal of Human Resources* 32, no. 1 (1997), 183–84.

27. Friederike Heine, "Why Many Former East Germans Don't Vote," *Spiegel*, September 19, 2013.

7. NATIONALISM AND CIVIC DUTY ACROSS THE WORLD

1. The duty to vote question is asked in a handful of cross-national surveys, such as the World Values Survey (in specific waves), the European Social Survey, and the International Civic and Citizenship Education Study. See André Blais and Carol Galais, "Measuring the Civic Duty to Vote: A Proposal," *Electoral Studies* 41, no. 3 (2016), 60–69. It is also routinely asked in several national-election surveys, namely the American National Election Study, the British Election Study, the Japan Election Study, and the Taiwan Election and Democratization Study, among others.

2. The International Social Survey Program (ISSP) has an excellent and rotating national-identity module, for example, but does not concurrently ask questions on civic duty.

3. Carles Boix, Michael Miller, and Sebastian Rosato, "A Complete Data Set of Political Regimes, 1800–2007," *Comparative Political Studies* 46, no. 12 (2013), 1523–54.

4. For a discussion on the trade-offs between different democracy indexes, see Michael Coppedge et al., "Conceptualizing and Measuring Democracy: A New Approach," *Perspectives on Politics* 9, no. 2 (2011), 247–67.

5. In Eldad Davidov, "Measurement Equivalence of Nationalism and Constructive Patriotism in the ISSP: 34 Countries in a Comparative Perspective," *Political Analysis* 17, no. 1 (2009), 64–82, the author focuses on two nationalism measures in the ISSP: national chauvinism (i.e., is my country better than others?) and constructive patriotism (i.e., how proud I am about various aspects of my country). He finds that both measures have high conceptual comparability across countries. The national identification measure in the WVS is not specifically tested, but as the psychological prerequisite for both chauvinist or patriotic sentiments, I assume parallel conceptual comparability.

6. Davidov, "Measurement Equivalence," 79.

7. Rankings are from Friedrich Schneider, Andreas Buehn, and Claudio E. Montenegro, "New Estimates for the Shadow Economies All over the World," *International Economic Journal* 24, no. 4 (2010), 443–61. The study estimates the relative size of shadow economies for 162 countries from 1999 to 2007. While economists are divided on how to best estimate the absolute size of a shadow economy, they generally agree on the reliability of relative rankings.

8. Joel Slemrod, "Cheating Ourselves: The Economics of Tax Evasion," *Journal of Economic Perspectives* 21, no. 1 (2007), 34.

9. Military conscription status for countries is based on the CIA World Factbook's 2010 version.

10. Recent evidence suggests that the causal arrow also goes the other way, that is, members of ethnic groups who hold power in high political office are more likely to identify with the national identity espoused by the state. See Elliott Green, "Ethnicity, National Identity and the State: Evidence from Sub-Saharan Africa, *British Journal of Political Science* 50, no. 2 (2020), 757–79.

11. I use the EPR version 1.1 since the year coverage coincides with the WVS sixth wave.

12. The EPR codebook defines ethnicity as a "subjectively experienced sense of commonality based on a belief in common ancestry or shared culture." An ethnic group is minimally politically relevant if at least one significant political actor—typically a political party, politician, or candidate—makes claims on behalf of that group in the national political arena. A group is also politically relevant if it is identified and discriminated against by the central government.

13. The codebook notes that in coding "access to power" in the state, each country's de facto power constellation was taken into account based on expert surveys. For instance, in a country with a presidential system, membership in the senior cabinet was coded as high access, whereas in a country under military dictatorship, power in the military was coded as such.

14. See Andreas Wimmer, Lars-Erik Cederman, and Brian Min, "Ethnic Politics and Armed Conflict: A Configurational Analysis of a New Global Dataset," *American Sociological Review* 74, no. 2 (2009), 316–37 for details on the EPR dataset and an empirical application to ethnic war.

15. In a handful of cases, ethnic categories in the WVS were coarser than those in the EPR. For instance, whereas the WVS codes everyone in Japan as part of the "Asian–East Asia" ethnic group, the EPR distinguishes between the Japanese, Burakumins, Okinawans, Koreans, and Ainu. This discrepancy typically concerns minority groups that comprise less than 3 percent of the total citizen population of a country. In such cases, I imputed the linkage of the coarser group category onto the entire WVS sample for the analysis. Philippines and Pakistan are the two exceptions to this rule, where the more refined EPR ethnic categories account for 14 percent and 16 percent of their populations, respectively. Linkage data are also missing for Spain, Georgia, and Turkey, as the WVS sixth wave did not ask about ethnic identification in those countries. These countries are included in the full-sample analysis but excluded from the subgroup analysis that compares individuals in strong- versus weak-linkage contexts.

16. In multinational democracies, only identification with the "dominant" national category as defined by the state is measured.

17. See, for instance, in Blais, *To Vote*; David Campbell, *Why We Vote*; Brad Gomez, Thomas Hansford, and George Krause, "The Republicans Should Pray for Rain: Weather, Turnout, and Voting in U.S. Presidential Elections," *Journal of Politics* 69, no. 3 (2007): 649–63.

18. Levi, *Consent, Dissent*.

19. Vote eligibility starts at eighteen years in most democracies, according to the Institute for Democracy and Electoral Assistance. I cap age at seventy-five years to rule out physical (i.e., non–duty related) impediments to turnout. In democracies with compulsory voting, the voting obligation usually expires between ages sixty-five to seventy-five for that reason.

20. Subjective class is used due to well-known comparability issues of the income percentile question in the WVS. See Robert Andersen and Tina Fetner, "Economic Inequality and Intolerance: Attitudes toward Homosexuality in 35 Democracies," *American Journal of Political Science* 52, no. 4 (2008), 942–58. Following the recommendation in Michael Donnelly and Grigore Pop-Eleches, "Income Measures in Cross-national Surveys: Problems and Solutions," *Political Science Research and Methods* 6, no. 2 (2018), 355–63, I use the subjective class measure (upper, upper middle, lower middle, working, lower) instead to capture relative economic status within each country.

21. According to the CIA World Factbook, forty is the upper end of the eligible age range for military service in most democracies. I exclude women to maximize conceptual comparability of the duty-to-defend measure. Women certainly contribute to the state's defense needs during war time but mostly through means other than physical combat.

8. CIVIC CHALLENGES TO DEMOCRACY IN EAST ASIA

1. Billig, *Banal Nationalism*, 5.

2. Kai Kupferschmidt, "Vaccine Nationalism Threatens Global Plan to Distribute COVID-19 Shots Fairly," *Science*, July 28, 2020.

3. Yasemin N. Soysal, *Limits of Citizenship: Migrants and Postnational Membership in Europe*, (Chicago: University of Chicago Press, 1995), 159. See also David Jacobson, *Rights across Borders: Immigration and the Decline of Citizenship* (Baltimore: Johns Hopkins University Press, 1996).

4. Joshua Cohen and Martha C. Nussbaum, *For Love of Country?* (Boston, MA: Beacon Press, 1996), 4. The authors make the case for moral universalism and support a truly "global citizenship" as the normatively superior alternative to nation-bound citizenships. For more moderate variants of the cosmopolitan position, which advocate for universality over multiculturalism, see Brian Barry, *Culture and Equality: An Egalitarian Critique of Multiculturalism* (Cambridge, MA: Harvard University Press, 2002); Amartya Sen, *Identity and Violence: The Illusion of Destiny* (New York: W.W. Norton, 2006); Kwame Appiah, *Cosmopolitanism: Ethics in a World of Strangers* (London: W.W. Norton, 2006).

5. Hur and Yeo, "Democratic Ceilings."

6. Thomas Friedman, "The American Civil War, Part II," *New York Times*, October 2, 2018.

7. Stein Rokkan and Henry Valen, "The Mobilization of the Periphery: Data on Turnout, Party Membership and Candidate Recruitment in Norway," *Acta Sociologica* 6, no. 1 (1962), 111–52.

8. Ho-Jeong Lee, "Korea's Total Fertility Rate Falls Below 1," *Korea Joongang Daily*, February 28, 2019. According to Taiwan's National Development Council, the birth rate estimate for 2018 was 1.06.

9. Mitsuru Obe, "Asia's Worst Aging Fears Begin to Come True," *Nikkei Asian Review*, April 9, 2019.

10. Rick Gladstone, "As Birthrate Falls, South Korea's Population Declines, Posing Threat to Economy," *New York Times*, January 4, 2021.

11. See Elizabeth Hervey Stephen, *South Korea's Demographic Dividend: Echoes of the Past or Prologue to the Future?* (Washington, DC: Center for Strategic and International Studies, 2019). The high poverty rate among the elderly is due to South Korea's weak social welfare system, which has persisted due to the Confucian social contract of children taking care of parents, but has all but broken down with urbanization.

12. Ministry of Gender Equality and Family, Laws & Data, Statistics.

13. "Multicultural Children: Schools, Military Should Be Better Prepared To Cope with Demographic Changes," *Korea Herald*, November 12, 2019.

14. Katharine H.S. Moon, "South Korea's Demographic Changes and Their Political Impact," East Asia Policy Paper 6 (Center for East Asia Policy Studies, Brookings Institution, 2015), 1.

15. Hye-Kyung Lee, "International Marriage and the State in South Korea: Focusing on Governmental Policy," *Citizenship Studies* 12, no. 1 (2008), 107–24; James Palmer and Ga-Young Park, "South Koreans Learn to Love the Other," *Foreign Policy*, July 16, 2018.

16. See Hae Yeon Choo, *Decentering Citizenship: Gender, Labor, and Migrant Rights in South Korea* (Stanford, CA: Stanford University Press, 2016) for the limits of the South Korean government's integration efforts, as seen through the eyes of migrants.

17. Philip Iglauer, "South Korea's Foreign Bride Problem," *Diplomat*, January 29, 2015.

18. Erin Aeran Chung and Daisy Kim, "Citizenship and Marriage in a Globalizing World: Multicultural Families and Monocultural Nationality Laws in Korea and Japan," *Indiana Journal of Global Legal Studies* 19, no. 1 (2012), 195–219.

19. Nora Hui-jung Kim, "Multiculturalism and the Politics of Belonging: The Puzzle of Multiculturalism in South Korea," *Citizenship Studies* 16, no. 1 (2012), 103–17.

20. Rosa Minhyo Cho, "Waning Support for Ethnic Minorities in South Korea: Change in Public Mind from Cultural to Materialistic Concerns," *East Asia Institute*, July 22, 2020.

21. Choe Sang-Hun, "Just 2 of More Than 480 Yemenis Receive Refugee Status in South Korea," *New York Times,* December 14, 2018.

22. "Taiwan's New President Reflects Island's Changing Identity," *Time Magazine,* January 21, 2016.

23. Rob Schmitz, "'Born Independent,' Taiwan's Defiant New Generation Is Coming of Age," *NPR,* June 20, 2018.

24. See T.Y. Wang, "Changing Boundaries: The Development of the Taiwan Voters' Identity," in *The Taiwan Voter,* ed. Christopher H. Achen and T.Y. Wang (Ann Arbor: University of Michigan, 2017), 55–56, for a discussion of how the meaning of "Taiwanese" has changed over the five distinct generations on the island.

25. Yu-shan Wu, "From Identity to Economy: Shifting Politics in Taiwan," *Global Asia* 8, no. 1 (2013), 114–19.

26. T.Y. Wang, "Declining Taiwanese Identity?," *Asia Dialogue,* February 8, 2019.

27. Ming-sho Ho, "The Activist Legacy of Taiwan's Sunflower Movement," *Carnegie Endowment for International Peace,* August 2, 2018.

28. Dominique Reichenbach, "The Rise and Rapid Fall of Han Kuo-yu," *Diplomat,* March 18, 2020.

29. Kevin Luo and Fang-Yu Chen, "Four Key Takeaways from Taiwan's Recent Election Surprises," *Washington Post,* December 17, 2018.

30. Wimmer, *Nation Building.*

31. Wimmer, *Nation Building,* 265.

32. Vasiliki Fouka, "Backlash: The Unintended Effects of Language Prohibition in U.S. Schools after World War I," *Review of Economic Studies* 87, no. 1 (2020), 204–39.

33. Robert Putnam, *Bowling Alone: The Collapse and Revival of American Community* (New York: Simon & Schuster, 2000).

34. Lucy Williamson, "France's Macron Brings Back National Service," *BBC News,* June 27, 2018.

35. Dong-Hoon Seol and John D. Skrenty, "Ethnic Return Migration and Hierarchical Nationhood: Korean Chinese Foreign Workers in South Korea," *Ethnicities* 9, no. 2 (2009), 147–74.

36. An interview with Wang Kena, a naturalized migrant wife who recently ran for a city council seat in Suwon, South Korea, highlights some of these issues, such as the outsider stigma attached to the label of a "multicultural" family and the need for more associational opportunities outside the multicultural centers. See Jo He-rim, "Migrant Families Should Contribute to Korean Society for Equal Share," *Korea Herald,* May 14, 2018.

37. See Chung and Kim, "Citizenship and Marriage," for an extended discussion on South Korea's "targeted multiculturalism." The inclusive approach toward marriage migrants is labeled as multicultural, but "the status of marriage migrants themselves as potential citizens is often contingent on the female migrant's capacity to fulfill her assigned roles in the family as wife, mother, and daughter-in-law, thereby solidifying the links between marriage, family, and national membership" (218).

38. Timothy Rich and Madelynn Einhorn, "Taiwan's Immigration Policy: Support, Concerns, and Challenges," *Taiwan Insight,* January 14, 2020.

39. Timothy Martin and Marcus Walker, "East vs. West: Coronavirus Fight Tests Divergent Strategies," *Wall Street Journal,* March 13, 2020; Ralph Jennings, "How Cultural

Differences Help Asian Countries Beat COVID-19, While U.S. Struggles," *Voice of America*, July 22, 2020.

40. Kemal Kirişci and Amanda Sloat, "The Rise and Fall of Liberal Democracy in Turkey: Implications for the West," *Brookings Institution Policy Brief,* February 2019; Max Fisher and Amanda Taub, "How Does Populism Turn Authoritarian? Venezuela Is a Case in Point," *New York Times*, April 1, 2017.

Bibliography

Achen, Christopher H., and T. Y. Wang, eds. *The Taiwan Voter*. Ann Arbor: Michigan University Press, 2017.

Alber, Jens. "Towards Explaining Anti-Foreign Violence in Germany." *CES Germany and Europe Working Papers*, no. 04.8 (1993).

Allen, Chizuko T. "Northeast Asia Centered around Korea: Ch'oe Namsŏn's View of History." *Journal of Asian Studies* 49, no. 4 (1990): 787–806.

Alm, James, and Benno Torgler. "Culture Differences and Tax Morale in the United States and Europe." *Journal of Economic Psychology* 27, no. 2 (2006): 224–46.

Almond, Gabriel A., and Sidney Verba. *The Civic Culture: Political Attitudes in Five Western Democracies*. Princeton, NJ: Princeton University Press, 1963.

Andersen, Robert, and Tina Fetner. "Economic Inequality and Intolerance: Attitudes toward Homosexuality in 35 Democracies." *American Journal of Political Science* 52, no. 4 (2008): 942–58.

Anderson, Benedict. *Imagined Communities: Reflections on the Origin and Spread of Nationalism*. London: Verso, 1983.

Appiah, Kwame. *Cosmopolitanism: Ethics in a World of Strangers*. London: W.W. Norton, 2006.

Bahry, Donna, and Christine Lipsmeyer. "Economic Adversity and Public Mobilization in Russia." *Electoral Studies* 20, no. 3 (2001): 371–98.

Baker, Kendall L., Russell J. Dalton, and Kai Hildebrandt. *Germany Transformed: Political Culture and the New Politics*. Cambridge, MA: Harvard University Press, 1981.

Barry, Brian. *Culture and Equality: An Egalitarian Critique of Multiculturalism*. Cambridge, MA: Harvard University Press, 2002.

Baylis, Thomas A. "East German Leadership after Unification: The Search for a Voice." In *The Federal Republic of Germany at Fifty: At the End of a Century of Turmoil*, edited by Peter H. Merkl, 135–46. New York: New York University Press, 1999.

Becker, Andreas. "Koreans' Gold Donations—A Model for Greeks?" *Deutsche Welle*, February 4, 2015.

Becker, Rolf. "Political Efficacy and Voter Turnout in East and West Germany." *German Politics* 13, no. 2 (2004): 317–40.

Belson, Ken, and Norimitsu Onishi. "In Deference to Crisis, a New Obsession Sweeps Japan: Self-Restraint." *New York Times*, March 27, 2011.

Bermeo, Nancy. "On Democratic Backsliding." *Journal of Democracy* 27, no. 1 (2016): 5–19.

Billig, Michael. *Banal Nationalism*. London: Sage Publications, 1995.

Bing, Su. *Taiwan's 400 Year History*. Washington, DC: Taiwanese Cultural Grassroots Association, 1986.

Blais, André. *To Vote or Not to Vote? The Merits and Limits of Rational Choice Theory*. Pittsburgh, PA: University of Pittsburgh Press, 2000.

Blais, André, and Christopher H. Achen. "Civic Duty and Voter Turnout." *Political Behavior* 41, no. 2 (2019): 473–97.

Blais, André, and Carol Galais. "Measuring the Civic Duty to Vote: A Proposal." *Electoral Studies* 41, no. 3 (2016): 60–69.

Bleiker, Roland. "Identity and Security in Korea." *Pacific Review* 14, no. 1 (2001): 121–48.

Boix, Carles, Michael Miller, and Sebastian Rosato. "A Complete Data Set of Political Regimes, 1800–2007." *Comparative Political Studies* 46, no. 12 (2013): 1523–54.

Bonikowski, Bart. "Nationalism in Settled Times." *Annual Review of Sociology* 42 (2016): 427–49.

Bouchard, Gérard. "The Small Nation with a Big Dream: Québec National Myths." In *National Myths: Constructed Pasts, Contested Presents,* edited by Gérard Bouchard. London: Routledge, 2013.

———. *Social Myths and Collective Imaginaries.* Translated by Howard Scott. Toronto: University of Toronto Press, 2017.

Braithwaite, Valerie, and Margaret Levi, eds. *Trust and Governance.* New York: Russell Sage Foundation, 1998.

Brazinsky, Gregg A. "South Korea Is Winning the Fight Against COVID-19. The U.S. Is Failing." *Washington Post,* April 10, 2020.

Breitenbach, Dagmar. "Where Racism and Xenophobia Are Manifest in Germany." *Deutsche Welle,* August 18, 2015.

Broockman, David. "Black Politicians Are More Intrinsically Motivated to Advance Blacks' Interests: A Field Experiment Manipulating Political Incentives." *American Journal of Political Science* 57, no. 3 (2013): 521–36.

Brubaker, Rogers. "In the Name of the Nation: Reflections on Nationalism and Patriotism." *Citizenship Studies* 8, no. 2 (2004): 115–27.

———. "The Manichean Myth: Rethinking the Distinction between <Civic> and <Ethnic> Nationalism." In *Nation and National Identity: The European Experience in Perspective,* edited by Hanspeter Kriesl, Klaus Armingeon, Hannels Slegrist, and Andreas Wimmer, 55–72. Zurich: Rüegger, 1999.

———. *Nationalism Reframed: Nationhood and the National Question in the New Europe.* Cambridge: Cambridge University Press, 1996.

Campbell, Angus, Philip E. Converse, Warren E. Miller, and Donald E. Stokes. *The American Voter.* Chicago: University of Chicago Press, 1960.

Campbell, Charlie. "Taiwan's New President Reflects Island's Changing Identity." *Time Magazine,* January 21, 2016.

Campbell, David E. *Why We Vote: How Schools and Communities Shape Our Civic Life.* Princeton, NJ: Princeton University Press, 2006.

Campbell, Emma. *South Korea's New Nationalism: The End of 'One Korea'?* Boulder, CO: First Forum Press, 2016.

Cederman, Lars-Erik. "Blood for Soil: The Fatal Temptations of Ethnic Politics." *Foreign Affairs* 98 (2019): 61–68.

Chang, Paul Y. *Protest Dialectics: State Repression and South Korea's Democracy Movement, 1970–1979.* Stanford, CA: Stanford University Press, 2015.

Charnysh, Volha, Christopher Lucas, and Prerna Singh. "The Ties That Bind: National Identity Salience and Pro-Social Behavior toward the Ethnic Other." *Comparative Political Studies* 48, no. 3 (2015): 267–300.

Chase, Michael S. "Defense Reform in Taiwan: Problems and Prospects." *Asian Survey* 45, no. 3 (2005): 362–82.

Cho, Rosa Minhyo. "Waning Support for Ethnic Minorities in South Korea: Change in Public Mind from Cultural to Materialistic Concerns." *East Asia Institute,* July 22, 2020.

Choe, Sang-Hun. "Just 2 of More Than 480 Yemenis Receive Refugee Status in South Korea." *New York Times*, December 14, 2018.

Choo, Hae Yeon. *Decentering Citizenship: Gender, Labor, and Migrant Rights in South Korea*. Stanford, CA: Stanford University Press, 2016.

Chu, Yun-han, Larry Diamond, and Kharis Templeman, eds. *Taiwan's Democracy Challenged: The Chen Shui-bian Years*. Boulder, CO: Lynne Rienner Publishing, 2016.

Chu, Yun-han, and Jih-wen Lin. "Political Development in 20th Century Taiwan." *China Quarterly* 165 (2001): 102–29.

Chun, Allen. "From Nationalism to Nationalizing: Cultural Imagination and State Formation in Postwar Taiwan." *Australian Journal of Chinese Affairs* 31 (January 1994): 49–69.

Chung, Erin Aeran, and Daisy Kim. "Citizenship and Marriage in a Globalizing World: Multicultural Families and Monocultural Nationality Laws in Korea and Japan." *Indiana Journal of Global Legal Studies* 19, no. 1 (2012): 195–219.

Cohen, Joshua, and Martha C. Nussbaum. *For Love of Country?* Boston: Beacon Press, 1996.

Cole, J. Michael. "Forget the PLA, Taiwan's Military Threatens Itself." *Diplomat*, August 2, 2013.

Connor, Walker. *Ethnonationalism: The Quest for Understanding*. Princeton, NJ: Princeton University Press, 1994.

———. "Nation-Building or Nation-Destroying?" *World Politics* 24, no. 3 (1972): 335–36.

Converse, Philip E. "Of Time and Partisan Stability." *Comparative Political Studies* 2, no. 2 (1969): 139–71.

Coppedge, Michael, John Gerring, David Altman, Michael Bernhard, Steven Fish, Allen Hicken, Matthew Kroenig, Staffan I. Lindberg, Kelly McMann, Pamela Paxton, Holli A. Semetko, Svend-Erik Skaaning, Jeffrey Staton, and Jan Teorell. "Conceptualizing and Measuring Democracy: A New Approach." *Perspectives on Politics* 9, no. 2 (2011): 247–67.

Corcuff, Stéphane. "Taiwan's 'Mainlanders,' New Taiwanese?" In *Memories of the Future: National Identity Issues and the Search for a New Taiwan*, edited by Stéphane Corcuff, 163–95. Armonk, NY: M. E. Sharpe, 2002.

Cumings, Bruce. "The Legacy of Japanese Colonialism in Korea." In *The Japanese Colonial Empire*, edited by Ramon Myers and Mark Peattie. Princeton, NJ: Princeton University Press, 1984.

Dalton, Russell J., and Christian Welzel. *The Civic Culture Transformed: From Allegiant to Assertive Citizens*. Cambridge: Cambridge University Press, 2014.

Davidov, Eldad. "Measurement Equivalence of Nationalism and Constructive Patriotism in the ISSP: 34 Countries in a Comparative Perspective." *Political Analysis* 17, no. 1 (2009): 64–82.

De Figueiredo, Rui J. P., Jr., and Zachary Elkins. "Are Patriots Bigots? An Inquiry into the Vices of In-Group Pride." *American Journal of Political Science* 47, no. 1 (2003): 171–88.

Diamond, Larry. "Facing Up to the Democratic Recession." *Journal of Democracy* 26, no. 1 (2015): 141–55.

Diamond, Larry, and Gi-Wook Shin. *New Challenges for Maturing Democracies in Korea and Taiwan*. Stanford, CA: Stanford University Press, 2014.

Donnelly, Michael, and Grigore Pop-Eleches. "Income Measures in Cross-national Surveys: Problems and Solutions." *Political Science Research and Methods* 6, no. 2 (2018): 355–63.

Dunn, John. *Western Political Theory in the Face of the Future.* 1979. Reprint, Cambridge: Cambridge University Press, 1993.

Easton, David. "A Re-assessment of the Concept of Political Support." *British Journal of Politics Science* 5, no. 4 (1975): 435–57.

Edmondson, Robert. "The February 28 Incident and National Identity." In *Memories of the Future: National Identity Issues and the Search for a New Taiwan,* edited by Stéphane Corcuff, 25–46. Armonk, NY: M. E. Sharpe, 2002.

Em, Henry H. "Minjok as a Modern and Democratic Construct: Sin Ch'aeho's Histriography." In *Colonial Modernity in Korea,* edited by Gi-Wook Shin and Michael Edson Robinson, 336–61. Cambridge, MA: Harvard University Press, 1999.

———. "Nationalism, Post-Nationalism, and Shin Ch'ae-ho." *Korea Journal* 39, no. 2 (1999): 283–317.

Fisher, Max. "A Revealing Map of the World's Most and Least Ethnically Diverse Countries." *Washington Post,* May 16, 2013.

Fisher, Max, and Amanda Taub. "How Does Populism Turn Authoritarian? Venezuela Is a Case in Point." *New York Times,* April 1, 2017.

Fouka, Vasiliki. "Backlash: The Unintended Effects of Language Prohibition in U.S. Schools after World War I." *Review of Economic Studies* 87, no. 1 (2020): 204–39.

Franzese, Robert J., and Cindy D. Kam. *Modeling and Interpreting Interactive Hypotheses in Regression Analysis.* Ann Arbor: University of Michigan Press, 2007.

Friedman, Thomas L. "The American Civil War, Part II." *New York Times,* October 2, 2018.

Fukuyama, Francis. "Confucianism and Democracy." *Journal of Democracy* 6, no. 2 (1995): 20–33.

Geertz, Clifford. "The Integrative Revolution: Primordial Sentiments and Politics in New States." In *Old Societies and New States: The Quest for Modernity in Asia and Africa,* edited by Clifford Geertz, 117–60. New York: Free Press, 1963.

———. "Thick Description: Toward an Interpretive Theory of Culture." In *The Interpretation of Cultures.* New York: Basic Books, 1973.

Gellner, Ernest. *Nations and Nationalism.* Ithaca, NY: Cornell University Press, 1983.

Gerber, Alan S., and Donald P. Green. "The Effects of Canvassing, Telephone Calls, and Direct Mail on Voter Turnout: A Field Experiment." *American Political Science Review* 94, no. 3 (2000): 653–63.

Gerber, Alan S., Donald P. Green, and Christopher W. Larimer. "Social Pressure and Voter Turnout: Evidence from a Large-scale Field Experiment." *American Political Science Review* 102, no. 1 (2008): 33–48.

Gladstone, Rick. "As Birthrate Falls, South Korea's Population Declines, Posing Threat to Economy." *New York Times,* January 4, 2021.

Gomez, Brad, Thomas Hansford, and George Krause. "The Republicans Should Pray for Rain: Weather, Turnout, and Voting in U.S. Presidential Elections." *Journal of Politics* 69, no. 3 (2007): 649–63.

Gone, Joseph P., Peggy J. Miller, and Julian Rappaport. "Conceptual Self as Normatively Oriented: The Suitability of Past Personal Narrative for the Study of Cultural Identity." *Culture and Psychology* 5, no. 4 (1999): 371–98.

Goodin, Robert E. "What Is So Special about Our Fellow Countrymen?" *Ethics* 98, no. 4 (1988): 663–86.

Graham, Matthew, and Milan Svolik. "Democracy in America? Partisanship, Polarization, and the Robustness of Support for Democracy in the United States." *American Political Science Review* 114, no. 2 (2020): 392–409.

Gray, Richard T., and Sabine Wilke. *German Unification and Its Discontents*. Seattle: University of Washington Press, 1996.

Green, Donald P., Alan S. Gerber, and David W. Nickerson. "Getting Out the Vote in Local Elections: Results from Six Door-to-Door Canvassing Experiments." *Journal of Politics* 65, no. 4 (2003): 1083–96.

Green, Elliott. "Ethnicity, National Identity and the State: Evidence from Sub-Saharan Africa." *British Journal of Political Science* 50, no. 2 (2020): 757–79.

Greitens, Sheena Chestnut. *Dictators and Their Secret Police: Coercive Institutions and State Violence*. New York: Cambridge University Press, 2016.

Habermas, Jürgen. *The New Conservatism: Cultural Criticism and the Historians' Debate*. Edited and translated by S.W. Nicholsen. Cambridge, MA, MIT Press, 1989.

Habyarimana, James, Macartan Humphreys, Daniel N. Posner, and Jeremy M. Weinstein, "Why Does Ethnic Diversity Undermine Public Goods Provision?" *American Political Science Review* 101, no. 4 (2007): 709–25.

Halbfinger, David, Wendy Ruderman, and Corey Kilgannon. "Displaced by Hurricane, but Returning Home, Briefly, to Vote." *New York Times*, November 6, 2012.

Hall, Peter, and Michèle Lamont, eds. *Successful Societies: How Institutions and Culture Affect Health*. Cambridge: Cambridge University Press, 2009.

Hechter, Michael. *Containing Nationalism*. Oxford: Oxford University Press, 2000.

Heiland, Frank W. "Trends in East-West German Migration from 1989 to 2002." *Demographic Research* 11 (2004): 173–94.

Heine, Friederike. "Why Many Former East Germans Don't Vote." *Spiegel*, September 19, 2013.

Hirschman, Albert. *Exit, Voice, and Loyalty: Responses to Decline in Firms, Organizations, and States*. Cambridge, MA: Harvard University Press, 1970.

Ho, Ming-sho. "The Activist Legacy of Taiwan's Sunflower Movement." *Carnegie Endowment for International Peace*, August 2, 2018.

Hogg, Michael A., and Dominic Abrams. *Social Identifications: A Social Psychology of Intergroup Relationships and Group Processes*. New York: Routledge, 1988.

Holbein, John B., and D. Sunshine Hillygus. *Making Young Voters: Converting Civic Attitudes into Civic Action*. New York: Cambridge University Press, 2020.

Holmes, Frank. "How Gold Rode to the Rescue of South Korea." *Forbes*, September 27, 2016.

Howard, Marc. "An East German Ethnicity? Understanding the New Division of Unified Germany." *German Politics and Society* 13, no. 4 (1995): 54–55.

Hsieh, John Fuh-sheng. "Ethnicity, National Identity, and Domestic Politics in Taiwan." *Journal of Asian and African Studies* 40, no. 1–2 (2005): 13–28.

Huang, Chi. "Dimensions of Taiwanese/Chinese Identity and National Identity in Taiwan: A Latent Class Analysis." *Journal of Asian and African Studies* 40, no. 1–2 (2005): 51–70.

Huddy, Leonie, and Nadia Khatib. "American Patriotism, National Identity, and Political Involvement." *American Journal of Political Science* 51, no. 1 (2007): 63–77.

Huntington, Samuel. *The Third Wave: Democratization in the Late Twentieth Century*. Norman: University of Oklahoma Press, 1991.

Hur, Aram. "Citizen Duty and the Ethical Power of Communities: Mixed-method Evidence from East Asia," *British Journal of Political Science* 50 no. 3 (2020): 1047–65.

———. "Is There an Intrinsic Duty to Vote? Comparative Evidence from East and West Germans." *Electoral Studies* 45 (2017): 55–62.

Hur, Aram, and Christopher Achen. "Coding Voter Turnout Responses in the Current Population Survey." *Public Opinion Quarterly* 77, no. 4 (2013): 985–93.

Hur, Aram, and Andrew Yeo. "Democratic Ceilings in East Asia: The Long Shadow of Nationalist Polarization." American Political Science Association, 2020.

Iglauer, Philip. "South Korea's Foreign Bride Problem." *Diplomat,* January 29, 2015.

Inglehart, Ronald, and Christian Welzel. *Modernization, Cultural Change, and Democracy: The Human Development Sequence.* Cambridge: Cambridge University Press, 2005.

Jacobson, David. *Rights across Borders: Immigration and the Decline of Citizenship.* Baltimore: Johns Hopkins University Press, 1996.

Jager, Sheila Miyoshi. *Narratives of Nation Building in Korea.* New York: M. E. Sharpe, 2003.

Jennings, M. Kent, and Richard G. Niemi. *Generations and Politics: A Panel Study of Young Adults and Their Parents.* Princeton, NJ: Princeton University Press, 1981.

Jennings, Ralph. "How Cultural Differences Help Asian Countries Beat COVID-19, While U.S. Struggles." *Voice of America,* July 22, 2020.

Jo, He-rim. "Migrant Families Should Contribute to Korean Society for Equal Share." *Korea Herald,* May 14, 2018.

Kang, David C. *China Rising: Peace, Power, and Order in East Asia.* New York: Columbia University Press, 2007.

Kant, Immanuel. *Critique of Practical Reason.* 1788. Reprint edited by Mary Gregor. Cambridge: Cambridge University Press, 1997.

———. *Groundwork for the Metaphysics of Morals.* 1785. Reprint edited by Lara Denis. Ottawa: Broadview Press, 2005.

Keuchler, Manfred. "The Road to German Unity: Mass Sentiment in East and West Germany." *Public Opinion Quarterly* 56, no. 1 (1992): 53–76.

Kim, Charles R. *Youth for Nation: Culture and Protest in Cold War South Korea.* Honolulu: University of Hawaii, 2017.

Kim, Jiyoon, Karl Friedhoff, Kang Chungku, and Lee Euicheol. "South Korean Attitudes toward North Korea and Reunification." *Asan Institute for Policy Studies,* February 2015.

Kim, Nora Hui-jung. "Multiculturalism and the Politics of Belonging: The Puzzle of Multiculturalism in South Korea." *Citizenship Studies* 16, no. 1 (2012): 103–17.

King, Charles. *Extreme Politics: Nationalism, Violence, and the End of Eastern Europe.* Oxford: Oxford University Press, 2010.

Kingsley, Patrick. "How Viktor Orban Bends Hungarian Society to His Will." *New York Times,* March 27, 2018.

Kirişci, Kemal, and Amanda Sloat. "The Rise and Fall of Liberal Democracy in Turkey: Implications for the West." *Brookings Institution Policy Brief,* February 2019.

Kleinhenz, Thomas. "A New Type of Nonvoter? Turnout Decline in German Elections, 1980–94." In *Stability and Change in German Elections: How Electorates Merge, Converge, or Collide,* edited by Christopher J. Anderson and Carsten Zelle, 173–98. Westport, CT: Praeger, 1998.

Knight, Ben. "East Germans Still Victims of Cultural Colonialism by the West." *Deutsche Welle,* November 1, 2017.

Kocka, Jürgen. "Crisis of Unification: How Germany Changes." *Daedalus* 123, no. 1 (1994): 173–92.

Kohn, Hans. *The Idea of Nationalism: A Study of the Origins and Background.* New York: Macmillan, 1944.

Kostadinova, Tatiana. "Voter Turnout Dynamics in Post-Communist Europe." *European Journal of Political Research* 42, no. 6 (2003): 741–59.

Krisch, Henry. "The Changing Politics of German National Identity." In *The Federal Republic of Germany at Fifty: At the End of a Century of Turmoil*, edited by Peter H. Merkl, 33–42. New York: New York University Press, 1999.

Krueger, Alan B., and Jörn-Steffen Pischke. "A Statistical Analysis of Crime against Foreigners in Unified Germany." *Journal of Human Resources* 32, no. 1 (1997): 182–209.

Kupferschmidt, Kai. "Vaccine Nationalism Threatens Global Plan to Distribute COVID-19 Shots Fairly." *Science*, July 28, 2020.

Laitin, David D. *Identity in Formation: The Russian-speaking Populations in the Near Abroad*. Ithaca, NY: Cornell University Press, 1998.

———. *Nations, States, and Violence*. Oxford: Oxford University Press, 1995.

Lee, Ho-Jeong. "Korea's Total Fertility Rate Falls Below 1." *Korea Joongang Daily*, February 28, 2019.

Lee, Hye-Kyung. "International Marriage and the State in South Korea: Focusing on Governmental Policy." *Citizenship Studies* 12, no. 1 (2008): 107–24.

Lee, Namhee. *The Making of Minjung: Democracy and the Politics of Representation in South Korea*. Ithaca, NY: Cornell University Press, 2007.

Lee, Teng-hui. "Understanding Taiwan: Bridging the Perception Gap." *Foreign Affairs* 78 (1999): 9–14.

Lepore, Jill. "A New Americanism: Why a Nation Needs a National Story." *Foreign Affairs* 98 (2019): 10–19.

Levi, Margaret. *Consent, Dissent, and Patriotism*. Cambridge: Cambridge University Press, 1997.

———. *Of Rule and Revenue*. Berkeley: University of California Press, 1988.

Levitsky, Steven, and Daniel Ziblatt. *How Democracies Die*. New York: Crown, 2018.

Lieberman, Evan. *Race and Regionalism in the Politics of Taxation in Brazil and South Africa*. New York: Cambridge University Press, 2003.

Luo, Kevi, and Fang-Yu Chen. "Four Key Takeaways from Taiwan's Recent Election Surprises." *Washington Post*, December 17, 2018.

Martin, Timothy, and Marcus Walker. "East vs. West: Coronavirus Fight Tests Divergent Strategies." *Wall Street Journal*, March 13, 2020.

McClendon, Gwyneth. *Envy in Politics*. Princeton, NJ: Princeton University Press, 2018.

Mendel, Douglas. *Politics of Formosan Nationalism*. Berkeley: University of California Press, 1970.

Michelson, Melissa R. "Mobilizing the Latino Youth Vote: Some Experimental Results." *Social Science Quarterly* 87, no. 5 (2006): 1188–1206.

Miguel, Edward. "Tribe or Nation? Nation Building and Public Goods in Kenya and Tanzania." *World Politics* 56, no. 3 (2004): 327–62.

Miles, Matthew B., A. Michael Huberman, and Johnny Saldaña. *Qualitative Data Analysis: A Methods Sourcebook*, 3rd ed. Los Angeles: Sage Publications, 1994.

Miller, Arthur H., Patrician Gurin, Gerald Gurin, and Oksana Malanchuk. "Group Consciousness and Political Participation." *American Journal of Political Science* 25, no. 3 (1981): 494–511.

Miller, Benjamin. *States, Nations, and the Great Powers: The Sources of Regional War and Peace*. Cambridge: Cambridge University Press, 2007.

Mishler, William, and Richard Rose. "Generation, Age, and Time: The Dynamics of Political Learning during Russia's Transformation." *American Journal of Political Science* 51, no. 4 (2007): 822–34.

Moody, Peter R. *Political Change on Taiwan: A Study of Ruling Party Adaptability*. New York: Praeger, 1992.

Moon, Katharine H. S. "South Korea's Demographic Changes and Their Political Impact." *East Asia Policy Paper* 6, no. 10 (Center for East Asia Policy Studies, Brookings Institution, 2015): 1–7.

Müller, Jan-Werner. *Another Country: German Intellectuals, Unification, and National Identity*. New Haven, CT: Yale University Press, 2000.

Mummendey, Amelie, Andreas Klink, and Rupert Brown. "Nationalism and Patriotism: National Identification and Out-group Rejection." *British Journal of Social Psychology* 40, no. 2 (2001): 159–72.

Mylonas, Harris, and Maya Tudor. "Nationalism: What We Know and What We Still Need to Know." *Annual Review of Political Science* 24 (2021): 109–32.

Obe, Mitsuru. "Asia's Worst Aging Fears Begin to Come True." *Nikkei Asian Review*, April 9, 2019.

Pacek, Alexander, Grigore Pop-Eleches, and Joshua A. Tucker. "Disenchanted or Discerning: Voter Turnout in Post-Communist Countries." *Journal of Politics* 71, no. 2 (2009): 473–91.

Palmer, James, and Ga-Young Park. "South Koreans Learn to Love the Other." *Foreign Policy*, July 16, 2018.

Park, Sunyoung. "Introduction." In *Revisiting Minjung: New Perspectives on the Cultural History of 1980s South Korea*. Ann Arbor: University of Michigan Press, 2019.

Patterson, Molly, and Kristen Renwick Monroe. "Narrative in Political Science." *Annual Review of Political Science* 1, no. 1 (1998): 315–31.

Pesek, William. "Greece's No-pain Bailout Fails Confucian Ethics." *Bloomberg*, May 9, 2010.

Pharr, Susan. *Political Women in Japan: The Search for a Place in Political Life*. Berkeley: University of California Press, 1981.

Piccone, Ted. "Latin America's Struggle with Democratic Backsliding." *Brookings Foreign Policy Report*, 2019.

Pop-Eleches, Grigore, and Joshua A. Tucker. *Communism's Shadow: Historical Legacies and Contemporary Political Attitudes*. Princeton, NJ: Princeton University Press, 2017.

Posner, Daniel N. "The Political Salience of Cultural Difference: Why Chewas and Tumbukas Are Allies in Zambia and Adversaries in Malawi." *American Political Science Review* 98, no. 4 (2004): 529–45.

Putnam, Robert. *Bowling Alone: The Collapse and Revival of American Community*. New York: Simon & Schuster, 2000.

Pye, Lucian. *Asian Power and Politics: The Cultural Dimensions of Authority*. Cambridge, MA: Harvard University Press, 1985.

Rattinger, Hans, and Jurgen Kramer. "Economic Conditions and Voting Preferences in East and West Germany." In *Stability and Change in German Elections: How Electorates Merge, Converge, or Collide*, edited by Christopher J. Anderson and Carsten Zelle, 99–121. Westport, CT: Praeger, 1998.

Reichenbach, Dominique. "The Rise and Rapid Fall of Han Kuo-yu." *Diplomat*, March 18, 2020.

Renan, Ernst. "Qu'est-ce qu'une nation?" 1882. In *Nation and Narration*, edited by Homi K. Bhaba. New York: Routledge, 1990.

Reuter, Ora John. "Civic Duty and Voting under Autocracy." *Journal of Politics* 83, no. 4 (2021). https://doi.org/10.1086/711718.

Rich, Timothy, and Madelynn Einhorn. "Taiwan's Immigration Policy: Support, Concerns, and Challenges." *Taiwan Insight*, January 14, 2020.

Rigger, Shelley. *From Opposition to Power: Taiwan's Democratic Progressive Party.* Boulder, CO: Lynne Reiner Publishers, 2001.

Riker, William H., and Peter C. Ordeshook. "A Theory of the Calculus of Voting." *American Political Science Review* 62, no. 1 (1968): 25–42.

Rizal, José. *Noli Me Tángere.* 1886. Translated by Harold Augenbraum. New York: Penguin, 2006.

Robinson, Michael Edson. *Cultural Nationalism in Colonial Korea, 1920–1925.* Seattle: University of Washington Press, 1988.

Rokkan, Stein, and Henry Valen. "The Mobilization of the Periphery: Data on Turnout, Party Membership and Candidate Recruitment in Norway." *Acta Sociologica* 6, no. 1 (1962): 111–52.

Sandel, Michael. *Liberalism and the Limits of Justice.* Cambridge: Cambridge University Press, 1998.

Schmitz, Rob. "'Born Independent,' Taiwan's Defiant New Generation Is Coming of Age." *NPR*, June 20, 2018.

Schneider, Friedrich, Andreas Buehn, and Claudio E. Montenegro. "New Estimates for the Shadow Economies All over the World." *International Economic Journal* 24, no. 4 (2010): 443–61.

Scholz, John T., and Mark Lubell. "Trust and Taxpaying: Testing the Heuristic Approach to Collective Action." *American Journal of Political Science* 42, no. 2 (1998): 398–417.

Scholz, John T., and Neil Pinney. "Duty, Fear, and Tax Compliance: The Heuristic Basis of Citizenship." *American Journal of Political* Science 39, no. 2 (1995): 490–512.

Sen, Amartya. *Identity and Violence: The Illusion of Destiny.* New York: W.W. Norton, 2006.

Seol, Dong-Hoon, and John D. Skrenty. "Ethnic Return Migration and Hierarchical Nationhood: Korean Chinese Foreign Workers in South Korea." *Ethnicities* 9, no. 2 (2009): 147–74.

Shayo, Moses. "A Model of Social Identity with an Application to Political Economy: Nation, Class, and Redistribution." *American Political Science Review* 103, no. 2 (2009): 147–74.

Shih, Hsiu-chuan, and Yan-chih Mo. "Military Raises Wages to Lure Recruits." *Taipei Times*, December 27, 2013.

Shils, Edward. "Primordial, Personal, Sacred, and Civil Ties: Some Particular Observations on the Relationships of Sociological Research and Theory." *British Journal of Sociology* 8, no. 2 (1957): 130–45.

Shin, Gi-Wook. *Ethnic Nationalism in Korea: Genealogy, Politics, and Legacy.* Stanford, CA: Stanford University Press, 2006.

Shin, Gi-Wook, James Freda, and Gihong Yi. "The Politics of Ethnic Nationalism in Divided Korea." *Nations and Nationalism* 5, no. 4 (1999): 465–84.

Singh, Prerna. *How Solidarity Works for Welfare: Subnationalism and Social Development in India.* Cambridge: Cambridge University Press, 2015.

Skocpol, Theda, and Eric Schickler. "A Conversation with Theda Skocpol." *Annual Review of Political Science* 22 (2019): 1–16.

Slater, Dan, and Joseph Wong, "The Strength to Concede: Ruling Parties and Democratization in Developmental Asia." *Perspectives on Politics* 11 no. 3 (2013): 717–33.

Slater, Dan, and Daniel Ziblatt. "The Enduring Indispensability of the Controlled Comparison." *Comparative Political Studies* 46, no.10 (2013): 1301–27.

Slemrod, Joel. "Cheating Ourselves: The Economics of Tax Evasion." *Journal of Economic Perspectives* 21, no. 1 (2007): 25–48.

Smith, Rogers. "Citizenship and the Politics of People-Building." *Citizenship Studies* 5, no. 1 (2001): 73–96.

Snyder, Jack. *From Voting to Violence: Democratization and Nationalist Conflict*. New York: W. W. Norton, 2000.

Soysal, Yasemin N. *Limits of Citizenship: Migrants and Postnational Membership in Europe*. Chicago: University of Chicago Press, 1995.

Stephen, Elizabeth Hervey. *South Korea's Demographic Dividend: Echoes of the Past or Prologue to the Future?* Washington, DC: Center for Strategic and International Studies, 2019.

Stilz, Anna. *Liberal Loyalty: Freedom, Obligation, and the State*. Princeton, NJ: Princeton University Press, 2009.

Stoker, Laura. "Interests and Ethics in Politics." *American Political Science Review* 86, no. 2 (1992): 369–80.

Swidler, Ann. "Culture in Action: Symbols and Strategies." *American Sociological Review* 51, no. 2 (1986): 273–86.

Tajfel, Henri, and John C. Turner. "The Social Identity Theory of Intergroup Behavior." In *Psychology of Intergroup Relations*, edited by S. Worchel and L. W. Austin. Chicago: Nelson-Hall, 1986.

Tamir, Yael. "Not So Civic: Is There a Difference between Ethnic and Civic Nationalism?" *Annual Review of Political Science* 22 (2019): 419–34.

Taylor, Charles. *Sources of the Self: The Making of the Modern Identity*. Cambridge, MA: Harvard University Press, 1989.

Templeman, Kharis. "After Hegemony: State Capacity, the Quality of Democracy, and the Legacies of the Party-State in Democratic Taiwan." In *Stateness and the Quality of Democracy in East Asia*, edited by Aurel Croissant and Olli Hellman, 71–102. Cambridge: Cambridge University Press, 2020.

Tensley, Brandon. "It's Been 25 Years Since German Reunification. Why Are Former East Germans Responsible for So Much Xenophobic Violence?" *Washington Post*, October 2, 2015.

Thim, Michael. "No Pain, No Gain: Successful AVF Transition Requires Greater Commitment from Government." *Strategic Vision for Taiwan Security* 3, no.18 (2014): 22–27.

Thompson, Derek. "What's behind South Korea's COVID-19 Exceptionalism?" *Atlantic*, May 6, 2020.

Tilly, Charles. "States and Nationalism in Europe, 1492–1992." *Theory and Society* 23, no. 1 (1994): 131–46.

Tocqueville, Alexis de. *Democracy in America*. 1835. Translated by Gerald Bevan. New York: Penguin Books, 2003.

Tudor, Maya, and Dan Slater. "The Content of Democracy: Nationalist Parties and Inclusive Ideologies in India and Indonesia." In *Parties, Movements, and Democracy in the Developing World*, edited by Nancy Bermeo and Deborah J. Yashar. Cambridge: Cambridge University Press, 2016.

———. "Nationalism, Authoritarianism, and Democracy: Historical Lessons from South and Southeast Asia." *Perspectives on Politics* (2020): 1–17. https://doi.org/10.1017/S153759272000078X.

Tworzecki, Hubert. "A Disaffected New Democracy? Identities, Institutions and Civic Engagement in Post-Communist Poland." *Communist and Post-Communist Studies* 41, no. 1 (2008): 47–62.

Tyler, Tom. *Why People Obey the Law*. Princeton, NJ: Princeton University Press, 2006.

Verdery, Katherine. "Whither 'Nation' and 'Nationalism'?" *Daedalus* 122, no. 3 (1993): 37–46.

Wachman, Alan. "Competing Identities in Taiwan." In *The Other Taiwan: 1945 to the Present*, edited by Murray Rubinstein, 17–80. Armonk, NY: M. E. Sharpe, 1994.

Walzer, Michael. "The Communitarian Critique of Liberalism." *Political Theory* 18, no. 1 (1990): 6–23.

Wang, T. Y. "Changing Boundaries: The Development of the Taiwan Voters' Identity." In *The Taiwan Voter*, edited by Christopher H. Achen and T. Y. Wang, 45–70. Ann Arbor: University of Michigan, 2017.

———. "Declining Taiwanese Identity?" *Asia Dialogue*, February 8, 2019.

Wang, T. Y., and I-Chou Liu. "Contending Identities in Taiwan: Implications for Cross-strait Relations." *Asian Survey* 44, no. 4 (2004): 568–90.

Weber, Max. "The Chinese Literati." In *From Max Weber: Essays in Sociology*, edited by H. H. Gerth and C. Wright Mills, 416–44. Abingdon, UK: Routledge, 1948.

———. *The Theory of Social and Economic Organization*. 1947. Reprint, edited by Talcott Parsons. New York: Free Press, 1964.

Weiss, Jessica Chen. "A World Safe for Autocracy? China's Rise and the Future of Global Politics." *Foreign Affairs* 98 (2019): 92–108.

White, Stephen, and Ian Mcallister. "Dimensions of Disengagement in Post-Communist Russia." *Journal of Communist Studies and Transition Politics* 20, no. 1 (2004): 81–97.

Wighton, Daniel. "Refugees in Eastern Germany '10 Times More Likely' To Be Hate Crime Victims: Report." *Local*, February 27, 2019.

Williamson, Lucy. "France's Macron Brings Back National Service." *BBC News*, June 27, 2018.

Wilson, Richard W. *Learning To Be Chinese: The Political Socialization of Children in Taiwan*. Cambridge, MA: MIT Press, 1970.

Wimmer, Andreas. *Nation Building: Why Some Countries Come Together While Others Fall Apart*. Princeton, NJ: Princeton University Press, 2018.

———. "Why Nationalism Works, and Why It Isn't Going Away." *Foreign Affairs* 98, no. 2 (2019): 27–34.

Wimmer, Andreas, Lars-Erik Cederman, and Brian Min. "Ethnic Politics and Armed Conflict: A Configurational Analysis of a New Global Dataset." *American Sociological Review* 74, no. 2 (2009): 316–37.

Winkler, Heinrich August, C. Michelle Murphy, Cornelius Partsch, and Susan List. "Rebuilding of a Nation: The Germans before and after Unification." *Daedalus* 123, no. 1 (1994): 107–27.

Wong, Cara J. *Boundaries of Obligation: Geographic, Racial, and National Communities*. New York: Cambridge University Press, 2010.

Wright, Robin. "Is America Headed for a New Kind of Civil War?" *New Yorker*, August 14, 2017.

Wu, Yu-shan. "From Identity to Economy: Shifting Politics in Taiwan." *Global Asia* 8, no. 1 (2013): 114–19.

Wuthnow, Robert. *American Mythos: Why Our Best Efforts To Be a Better Nation Fall Short*. Princeton, NJ: Princeton University Press, 2006.

Yack, Bernard. *Nationalism and the Moral Psychology of Community*. Chicago: University of Chicago Press, 2012.

Yeh, Yao-Yuan, Austin Wang, Charles K. S. Wu, and Fang-Yu Chen. "Would Taiwan Fight China without U.S. Support?" *National Interest*, December 9, 2018.

Yoder, Jennifer A. *From East Germans to Germans? The New Postcommunist Elites*. Durham, NC: Duke University Press, 1999.

Yoon, In-jin. "Migration and the Korean Diaspora: A Comparative Description of Five Cases." *Journal of Ethnic and Migration Studies* 38, no. 3 (2012): 413–35.

Zakaria, Fareed. "Culture Is Destiny: A Conversation with Lee Kuan Yew." *Foreign Affairs* 73, no. 2 (1994): 109–26.

Zaller, John. *The Nature and Origins of Mass Opinion.* Cambridge: Cambridge University Press, 1992.

Index

Achen, Christopher, 64
All-Volunteer Force (AVF) military (Taiwan), 35, 48–49, 54–58, 158n41
Alternative für Deutschland (AfD), 99, 114
altruism, and survey experiment on civic duty and crisis in Taiwan, 90–91
Anderson, Benedict, 8, 18, 22
anti-immigrant violence, 113–15
anti-Yemeni refugee protests, 142
Asian financial crisis (1997), 3–4, 74, 132, 148–49
assimilation, 141, 146–148
authoritarian states, 26–27, 135–37

Berlin Wall, fall of, 97, 103
Billig, Michael, 18
birthrates, declining, 139–41
Blais, André, 64
Bouchard, Gérard, 21, 153n28
Brandt, Willy, 97, 113
Broockman, David, 29, 61
Brubaker, Rogers, 20, 22, 23, 25

case selection, 29
Charnysh, Volha, 162n10
Chen, Chingpu, 58
Chen Shui-bian, 43, 44, 143, 158n41
Chiang Ching-kuo, 43
Chiang Kai-shek, 41, 54, 55f, 159n65
China
  and nationalist history of Taiwan, 41–45, 93
  nation-state linkage in, 24
  and Taiwanese military recruitment, 54, 56–57
  and Taiwanese national identification, 80, 144
  taxation for improvement of air pollution in, 86–87
China nationalists, 45, 78–79, 80, 81t, 82, 83t, 84–87, 90–92
citizenship
  access to, 147–48
  contractual approaches to, 16, 66, 153n2
  counter-state, 54–56
  democratic, 31, 69, 136

state-supportive, 37, 59, 147
civic duty
  anti-civic duty, 25, 109, 142
  defined, 4
  and democracy, 4–6, 135
  East Asia as lens for studying, 6–7
  identity-based (thick) and incentive-based (thin), 12, 27, 61–62, 135
  Korean gold drives as matter of, 3–4, 15
  as nationalist phenomenon, 7–9, 15–16, 26–28, 136
  national theory of, 24–27, 115, 117, 120, 126
  as political loyalty, 16
  as renewable and reparable, 10, 150
civil servants, 44, 57, 70, 85
collective imaginaries, 22, 155n25. See also national stories
colonialism, 28–29
  in South Korea, 37–38
  in Taiwan, 41–42
Communism, and stunted civic duty in Germany, 110–13
communitarianism, 17, 153–54n6. See also special community
comparability issues, 118–120, 165n20
  conceptual comparability, 119, 164n5, 165n21
  compliance context, 119–120
  scalar comparability, 119, 126
compliance, 4, 66, 119, 151n6
Confucianism, 6, 49, 66, 74, 140, 149
Connor, Walker, 24, 155n28
constitutive narrative of nation, 21
corruption, in Taiwanese military, 49
cosmopolitanism, 136, 166n4
COVID-19 pandemic, 7, 135, 149
crises
  and in-group cohesion, 162n10
  and national stories, 22
  survey experiment on civic duty and, in Taiwan, 88–93, 162n9
Cross-Strait Services Trade Agreement (CSSTA), 144

Studies of the Weatherhead East Asian Institute, Columbia University

Selected Titles

(Complete list at: weai.columbia.edu/content/publications)

Policing China: Street-Level Cops in the Shafow of Protest, by Suzanne Scoggins. Cornell University Press, 2021.

Mobilizing Japanese Youth: The Cold War and the Making of the Sixties Generation, by Christopher Gerteis. Cornell University Press, 2021.

Middlemen of Modernity: Local Elites and Agricultural Development in Modern Japan, by Christopher Craig. University of Hawai'i Press, 2021.

Isolating the Enemy: Diplomatic Strategy in China and the United States, 1953–1956, by Tao Wang. Columbia University Press, 2021.

A Medicated Empire: The Pharmaceutical Industry and Modern Japan, by Timothy M. Yang. Cornell University Press, 2021.

Dwelling in the World: Family, House, and Home in Tianjin, China, 1860–1960, by Elizabeth LaCouture. Columbia University Press, 2021.

Disunion: Anticommunist Nationalism and the Making of the Republic of Vietnam, by Nu-Anh Tran. University of Hawai'i Press, 2021.

Made in Hong Kong: Transpacific Networks and a New History of Globalization, by Peter Hamilton. Columbia University Press, 2021.

China's influence and the Center-periphery Tug of War in Hong Kong, Taiwan and Indo-Pacific, by Brian C.H. Fong, Wu Jieh-min, and Andrew J. Nathan. Routledge, 2020.

The Power of the Brush: Epistolary Practices in Chosŏn Korea, by Hwisang Cho. University of Washington Press, 2020.

On Our Own Strength: The Self-Reliant Literary Group and Cosmopolitan Nationalism in Late Colonial Vietnam, by Martina Thucnhi Nguyen. University of Hawai'i Press, 2020.

A Third Way: The Origins of China's Current Economic Development Strategy, by Lawrence Chris Reardon. Harvard University Asia Center, 2020.

Disruptions of Daily Life: Japanese Literary Modernism in the World, by Arthur M. Mitchell. Cornell University Press, 2020.

Recovering Histories: Life and Labor after Heroin in Reform-Era China, by Nicholas Bartlett. University of California Press, 2020.

Figures of the World: The Naturalist Novel and Transnational Form, by Christopher Laing Hill. Northwestern University Press, 2020.

Arbiters of Patriotism: Right Wing Scholars in Imperial Japan, by John Person. University of Hawai'i Press, 2020.

The Chinese Revolution on the Tibetan Frontier, by Benno Weiner. Cornell University Press, 2020.

Making It Count: Statistics and Statecraft in the Early People's Republic of China, by Arunabh Ghosh. Princeton University Press, 2020.

Tea War: A History of Capitalism in China and India, by Andrew B. Liu. Yale University Press, 2020.

Revolution Goes East: Imperial Japan and Soviet Communism, by Tatiana Linkhoeva. Cornell University Press, 2020.

Vernacular Industrialism in China: Local Innovation and Translated Technologies in the Making of a Cosmetics Empire, 1900–1940, by Eugenia Lean. Columbia University Press, 2020.

Fighting for Virtue: Justice and Politics in Thailand, by Duncan McCargo. Cornell University Press, 2020.

Beyond the Steppe Frontier: A History of the Sino-Russian Border, by Sören Urbansky. Princeton University Press, 2020.

CPSIA information can be obtained
at www.ICGtesting.com
Printed in the USA
LVHW101203141122
732933LV00005B/303

9 781501 766213